GROUNDED

Frank Lorenzo
and the Destruction
of Eastern Airlines

AARON BERNSTEIN

SIMON AND SCHUSTER
New York   London   Toronto   Sydney   Tokyo   Singapore

Simon and Schuster
Simon & Schuster Building
Rockefeller Center
1230 Avenue of the Americas
New York, New York 10020

Designed by Deirdre C. Amthor

Manufactured in the United States of America

10 9 8 7 6 5 4 3 2 1

Library of Congress Cataloging in Publication Data

Bernstein, Aaron, date.
    Grounded : Frank Lorenzo and the destruction of Eastern Airlines /
Aaron Bernstein.
        p.   cm.
    Includes bibliographical references and index.
    1. Eastern Air Lines, inc.   2. Lorenzo, Frank.   3. Strikes and
lockouts—Airlines—United States.   I. Title.
HE9803.E2B47   1990
387.7'06'573—dc20   90-36862
                                                             CIP

ISBN 0-671-69538-X

Contents

INTRODUCTION

In 1986, when Frank Lorenzo took over Eastern Airlines, the country's third largest carrier was in decline: its route structure was inherently weak, its costs were sky high, and its stiff-necked labor unions fought with each other almost as much as they fought with management.

To many in corporate America, Lorenzo seemed just the man to whip Eastern back into shape. Lorenzo, with the help of Michael Milken and Drexel Burnham Lambert's junk bond machine, had built his tiny Texas Air Corporation into an empire. Indeed, with the addition of Eastern to Continental, Frontier, and People Express airlines, Lorenzo controlled the largest airline in the country, flying more than a fifth of the nation's air passengers on his planes.

Moreover, Lorenzo represented the get-tough approach to management that Ronald Reagan had revived when the President fired striking air traffic controllers in 1981. While some U.S. companies had started to experiment with the Japanese-inspired labor–management cooperation techniques as a way of restoring America to global competitiveness, Lorenzo went in the opposite direction. In 1983, his uncompromising style had brought about an apparently miraculous turnaround at

Continental and set him up as a shining example of a business leader willing to fight labor to create a lean and successful company. Wall Street celebrated the renewal of a dying breed of tough managers.

But, like Drexel Burnham and the junk-bond takeover binge of the 1980s, Lorenzo's effort blew up in his face. Although his brilliant financial manipulations enabled him to build an empire out of nothing, Lorenzo was unable to run an airline on a daily basis. Instead of fixing the operational problems of the airlines he bought, Lorenzo let them flounder as he focused on making new deals.

Lorenzo also failed because he alienated the people who worked for him. Lorenzo's giant debt load led him to turn to labor as a way of reducing overhead. His efforts to get more for less by intimidating employees into working harder and taking unprecedented wage and benefit cuts proved to be a disaster, particularly in a highly service-oriented business like air travel. At Continental, once known for its quality service, Lorenzo has created an airline with embittered workers who dislike their jobs almost as much as passengers dislike flying on their planes.

When Lorenzo applied similar tactics at Eastern, he soon found that he had stepped into a hornets' nest. Instead of trying to make peace with the carrier's employees, who had feuded for years with each other and with Frank Borman, Eastern's previous chairman, Lorenzo struck out harder and harder, until finally Eastern's workers were willing to sacrifice their jobs to get rid of him.

Frank Lorenzo exemplifies the failure of the traditional antagonistic methods of dealing with employees. He never understood that an airline's success depends on motivated workers providing quality service. The story of Lorenzo's struggle to bend Eastern employees to his will is a case study in why the confrontational approach is destined to fail. It is also a tale that explores the darker effects of the junk bond takeover era of the past decade. Lorenzo brought a corporate raider's ruthlessness to bear on the running of a company. His determination to get his way with employees led him to dismember the very company he wanted to build. Lorenzo fought a no-holds-barred war against labor that ended with the destruction of both sides: tens of thousands of employees lost their jobs, and the United States lost one of its oldest major airlines.

CHAPTER ONE
Tough Guy

Francisco Anthony Lorenzo came into the airline business from a middle-class family in Queens, New York. Born in 1940, the third son of Spanish immigrants who ran a New York beauty parlor, Lorenzo grew up next to the runways of La Guardia Airport. He put himself through Columbia University and then got a master's in business administration from Harvard University. After a stint in the army, he worked as a financial analyst at TWA and then Eastern Airlines. In 1966, at 26, Lorenzo joined forces with Robert J. Carney, a buddy from Harvard, to start an airline consulting firm called Lorenzo, Carney & Co.

The two men tried their hand at aircraft leasing without much success. In 1969, they each put up $25,000 to start a new company, Jet Capital Corporation. In the heady stock-market atmosphere of that time they raised $1.4 million in a public stock offering.

In 1971, Chase Manhattan Bank asked the two to figure out how to save a small, failing airline called Texas International Airlines, Incorporated (TXI). The Houston-based carrier, which had just changed its name from Trans Texas Airlines, flew primarily within Texas and the Southwest. Its claim to

11

be an international airline rested on a weekly run to Veracruz and Tampico, Mexico. Locals referred to the carrier as Tree Tops Airlines.

TXI paid Lorenzo and Carney $15,000 a month to study its problems. A year later, Lorenzo came up with a plan that would set the pattern for his future financial dealings. He proposed that his company, Jet Capital, take over TXI, and he persuaded Chase and the other creditors—including majority stockholder Carl R. Pohlad, a Minneapolis businessman who later bought the Minnesota Twins baseball team—to defer their claims.

Lorenzo's $35 million recapitalization plan gave him his first real foothold in the airline industry. Jet Capital put in $1.15 million. Another $350,000 came from National Aviation Corporation, where Donald C. Burr, another graduate of Harvard Business School whom Lorenzo and Carney had met at an industry gathering, worked. The rest came from the debt that the creditors extended or reissued. In exchange for Jet Capital's tiny contribution, Lorenzo received 26 percent of TXI's stock and 59 percent of the voting rights, giving him control even though he didn't own a majority share. Lorenzo made himself president and chief executive and Carney and Burr joined the company as top officers.

Once he had control of TXI, Lorenzo began to develop a series of unorthodox managerial tactics. Since his reorganization had left the airline with almost no capital to rebuild, he turned to the employees' wages and benefits. When the sale became official in 1972, he cut back the work force; then, in mid-1974, he demanded that the Airline Employees Association, which represented ticket agents and other ground personnel, do 20 percent to 30 percent of their work on a part-time basis. In December, the union struck, and five days later, after Lorenzo began hiring replacement workers, TXI's other unions walked off the job in sympathy.

The strike grounded TXI for four months. Lorenzo survived with the help of the Mutual Aid Pact, an arrangement among the major airlines under which carriers were assessed set amounts to be paid any member shut down by a strike; assessments were based on estimates of the added revenue the other airlines received from flying passengers of the strike-bound carrier. TXI received more than $10 million in Mutual Aid Pact funds—angering the other airlines, who thought they were being taken advantage of, and earning more than it would have had it been flying those four months. In April 1975, TXI's unions capitulated.

Not long after the strike ended, Lorenzo put his final strategy into place. He applied to the government for permission to cut some fares in half; "peanut fares," he called them. The idea was as bold as his TXI takeover scheme. At that time the federal government regulated the airline industry, controlling ticket prices and routes stringently. The major airlines were allowed to raise fares to offset cost increases. Regulation provided a stable and predictable travel system, but at prices that mainly businesspeople could afford. Regulation also blocked smaller players, like Lorenzo, from taking market share from established airlines. Nevertheless, after much debate, in early 1977 the Civil Aeronautics Board granted TXI a one-year trial period at the lower fare rate. A few weeks later, American Airlines won permission to sell "Super Saver" fares on some flights, and other major carriers began to follow suit.

Lorenzo began to buck the system in other ways. In a bid for the major carrier National Airlines in 1978, Lorenzo became the first airline executive to attempt a hostile takeover. Even though giant Pan Am wound up buying National, Lorenzo earned $40 million in profit when he sold the National stock TXI had accumulated. In the late 1970s, he also made several attempts to take over TWA.

Then, in November 1978, Congress deregulated the airlines. Although Lorenzo, along with most other airline executives, was opposed, the now-freed industry proved an ideal environment for him. In 1980, the election of Ronald Reagan ushered in an era of laissez-faire politics and gloves-off competition. Lorenzo was among the first to jump at the opportunities. In 1980, he founded New York Air, the first major nonunion airline in the United States, a low-fare air carrier aimed at stealing business from Eastern Airlines' lucrative shuttle markets in the Boston-to-Washington corridor. He created a shell holding company, Texas Air Corporation, which became the parent of both TXI and New York Air.

Now Lorenzo was resented by the airline unions. They hadn't paid much attention to his actions at TXI, but New York Air operated in a highly visible market and top union leaders saw the new company destroying union jobs. They recognized that Lorenzo was introducing an antiunion attitude into an industry where organized labor had long been dominant.

Next, Lorenzo launched the fiercest takeover struggle of his career. Even before his runs at National and TWA, TXI had secretly begun buying stock in Continental Airlines, a financially troubled national carrier with high-quality service and loyal, dedicated employees. Continental was plagued by high costs, poor marketing, and a weak economy at its big Houston hub. When Lorenzo announced his intentions in 1980, the company was vulnerable; its stock was worth less than the value of its planes.

Continental resisted and the struggle lasted for more than a year. Lorenzo wrote California officials that he would not move Continental's headquarters from Los Angeles, that he had no intention of firing anyone, that he wouldn't sell planes to raise money. On August 9, 1981, Alvin L. Feldman, Continental's chief executive, conceded defeat and shot himself through the head in his office at Los Angeles airport.

After less than 10 years in the airline business, Lorenzo, who started with no money of his own, controlled a national airline. He set up a financial structure similar to the one he had established at TXI. Jet Capital, of which he owned 50 percent, became the parent holding company for Continental and Texas Air. Though Jet Capital would eventually own only 3 percent of Texas Air stock, the company retained control through a special class of voting stock. Texas Air, in turn, served as the holding company for New York Air and for Continental, which was merged with TXI.

The result was a pyramid of companies with Lorenzo at the top. When Don Burr left to start People Express and Carney removed himself from day-to-day management, Lorenzo was left with complete control over a public corporation. He had the sort of power ordinarily enjoyed only by the owner of a private company.

Almost immediately, Lorenzo went after Continental's unions. He offered the International Association of Machinists and Aerospace Workers (IAM) a 19-percent raise if they would allow management to subcontract repair work to outside machine shops. The IAM, knowing that Lorenzo could fire nearly half its members and pay other companies to do their work, refused. In August 1983, the machinists walked off the job and Lorenzo began hiring replacement workers at $10 an hour instead of the $16 the unions had been getting. Next, he demanded that the Air Line Pilots Association (ALPA) accept 27-percent concessions and longer flying hours. The pilots refused.

While the pilots threatened to walk out with the machinists, Lorenzo hired Harvey Miller, a prominent bankruptcy lawyer from the New York law firm of Weil Gotshal & Manges. Miller suggested that Continental circumvent its unions by declaring bankruptcy. In addition to allowing Continental to suspend debt payments, Miller suggested bankruptcy under Chapter 11 of the U.S. Bankruptcy Code could allow Lorenzo to tear up Continental's labor contracts.

No major company had ever attempted anything like it. What's more, Continental, which had some $60 million in cash and was still able to make its debt payments, didn't seem to be bankrupt. Nevertheless, on September 24, Lorenzo declared bankruptcy, abrogated the union contracts, and told his employees that they could work twice as many hours at half the pay. A pilot making $89,000 a year would see his salary drop to $43,000. Within a week, the outraged pilots were on the picket line with the machinists.

Once again, Lorenzo had grounded his company in an all-or-nothing gamble to force labor to its knees, and this time there was no help from other airlines: the Mutual Aid Pact had been abolished when deregulation passed in 1978. By the strike's fourth day, Continental wasn't even running a quarter of its flights. By the fifth day, the company had gone through nearly $9 million. Since the bankruptcy filing had placed restrictions on more than half of the company's $60 million, Lorenzo could hold out for a few weeks at most.

Lorenzo, however, got a break. Caught off guard and demoralized by the bankruptcy, union members began to lose their nerve, and started drifting back to work. Wi.hin weeks, half the machinists had crossed their own picket lines. After several months, one-third of the pilots had returned.

Continental's bankruptcy shocked the airline industry. (Indeed, Congress would change the law in 1984 to close the loophole Lorenzo had exploited.) Low-cost start-up carriers like Muse Air and People Express were causing havoc for the major airlines. Though the clubby, genteel management at the big carriers had responded by asking their employees for 5- to 10-percent cuts, they never had engaged in all-out war like Lorenzo. Continental, the country's eighth-largest airline, with 12,000 employees, had chopped wages in half, lowering its labor expenses from 35 percent to 22 percent of total costs. Lorenzo drove home his point by offering giveaway $49 fares to anywhere Continental flew.

Lorenzo's move triggered a wave of labor strife throughout the industry. To compete with Continental, every other airline began to ask employees for drastic concessions.

Lorenzo quickly saw that he had the opportunity to get rid of Continental's unions. As the airline began to rebuild its flight schedule, the machinists searched for a middle ground. Lorenzo refused to compromise. Federal law required him to negotiate, but it couldn't force him to reach an agreement.

As the strike foundered, the pilots dumped their hard-line chief negotiator. By Christmas 1983, they had agreed to all of management's demands. However, Lorenzo refused to give them their jobs back, insisting that he owed more loyalty to the replacement pilots hired to break the strike. Airline employees—particularly the pilots, who were well paid and largely Republican—weren't accustomed to this sort of treatment. As it became clear that many might never fly for Continental again, some became desperate. A bloody, rotting elk head was thrown through the window of the home of one pilot who had returned to work. Strikers spat and yelled at their former colleagues and at the replacement pilots. In San Antonio, Texas, police apprehended two striking pilots carrying pipe bombs and a map with directions to the homes of strikebreakers.

The Continental strike was a watershed for airline unions. For years afterward, pilots at other airlines scorned Continental strikebreakers, often refusing even to acknowledge someone in a Continental uniform. Although Lorenzo denied that he had intended to break the unions, Continental had hired so many new pilots that only about a third were union members. In 1985, two years after the walkout, Continental's pilots decertified the union.

Lorenzo soon began to treat his new employees as he had the old ones. In some respects, his goal of putting together the biggest airline in the country impelled him to this end. He also was encouraged by Wall Street. America's money men couldn't get enough of the tough boss who by late 1985 had pulled through a bankruptcy and a strike and emerged the winner. Despite the $60 million in fees that made the Continental bankruptcy one of the costliest in history, and even though Continental turned a profit only because the bankruptcy allowed it to forgo interest payments to creditors, Texas Air's stock price shot through the roof. Michael R. Milken, Drexel Burnham Lambert's financial wizard, helped Lorenzo raise more than $1 billion. With this assistance, Lorenzo snapped up Frontier, People Express, and other foundering carriers, and folded them into Continental.

By 1986 Lorenzo's formula of success through growth had tripled Continental's size. It also caused chaos as the company struggled to integrate its diverse components. Increasingly aware that neither Lorenzo's financial wizardry nor his negotiating tactics did much good in daily operations, Wall Street pressured the Texas Air boss to let professional managers run the show. But Lorenzo could never let go. He became the

George Steinbrenner of the financial world: in the six years following the bankruptcy, Lorenzo went through one Continental president a year.

Most couldn't fit in with his one-man band. For years, Texas Air consisted of about three dozen people. At Continental, Lorenzo slashed the number of vice presidents from 54 to 19. He also went to great lengths to keep his top advisors divided. The labor-relations vice president coordinated labor strategy directly with Lorenzo. The finance vice president did the same with financial strategy. Neither knew the details of what the other was doing.

The ensuing managerial chaos compounded Lorenzo's problems. The pressure on Continental's employees grew with the company's debt payments. Continental came to have the worst morale of any airline. To keep a lid on growing employee restiveness, management by intimidation became the rule of the day. To complicate matters, an improved job market for airline workers in 1987 gave Continental employees the opportunity to go elsewhere. They left first in a slow trickle and soon in a steady stream.

This was a dramatic statement, particularly for the pilots. The way pilots are paid creates overwhelming disincentives against leaving one airline for another. The major airlines start pilots at a relatively low salary—in 1987, a typical rate was about $20,000. But after two years, pilots' wages rise with seniority and the size of the planes they fly. In 1987, the average captain with a decade of seniority was earning $108,000 a year. ALPA's rules stipulate that a pilot who goes to a new airline starts at the bottom of the seniority list. To leave for another job, a pilot has to be angry enough to take a huge pay cut and begin again the long climb to the top.

Lorenzo made sure that Continental's salaries for new pilots remained high enough to attract the pilots from small regional airlines and corporate aircraft who wanted a chance to break into the majors. But after a pilot's first two years, Continental's pay rose very slowly. After 10 years, a pilot working for Lorenzo would earn only $52,000, half of what he'd earn in the same job at United or American.

When the media began reporting on Continental's problems, Texas Air's stock began to drop. Lorenzo responded with what had become his standard line: The unions didn't want to come to grips with the reality of deregulation; the marketplace had changed and high wages were obsolete; the noise about morale problems was nothing more than a union and media smear. In the late spring of 1987, Continental sent a memo to employees asking them to go on the offensive against the critics who were "Continental-bashing." It said: "Unless we do something about all of this," the future of the airline and its employees "could be gravely threatened."

Shortly thereafter, Lorenzo set out to demonstrate that most of his employees liked working for him. Continental hired the Hay Group, a national management consulting firm, to survey employee attitudes. Hay sent out detailed questionnaires to all 32,000 Continental employees. It got 16,000 back, a very high response rate. Almost 80 percent said they liked the kind of work they did. But only 16 percent liked Continental. Four percent said that they thought their pay was competitive with other airlines. Less than a third thought Continental had a fair system for evaluating employee performance. Only 14 percent thought company officers did anything about their problems and suggestions. Hay officials told some pilots privately that Continental had the worst morale of any company they had ever surveyed.

There is some truth to the union's claim of Lorenzo's avarice. He made $977,000 in salary and bonuses in 1988, and tens of millions of dollars more by well-timed transactions involving his companies. In 1986 and early 1987, for example, Texas Air's stock shot up to an all-time high of just over $50 a share. Did Lorenzo hold onto his stock to show his faith in the company he was building? Hardly. He cashed out at the top.

In March 1987, when Texas Air was raising cash by issuing new shares to be sold to the public, Lorenzo sold 40,000 of his shares to his own company. In all, he dumped nearly 200,000 shares between October 1986 and September 1987, raking in more than $7 million. By September 1987 he would own less than 200 shares in his own company, though he still controlled it through Jet Capital. By then, Texas Air's stock was on the way downhill. By the end of 1987 it had collapsed to less than $20 per share.

But Lorenzo has seemed to be driven less by money than by a burning desire to run the biggest and strongest airline in the country. That's what lay behind his efforts to cut down labor costs and his impulse to buy up every airline in sight. It drove him to wrench Continental away from its managers and to take People Express off the hands of his former partner, Don Burr. And it drove him to go after the nation's third-largest airline. In 1986, Frank Lorenzo, the bane of the industry and of the industry's unions, went after Eastern Airlines.

CHAPTER TWO
Eastern's Life Before Lorenzo

For much of his tenure as president of Eastern Airlines, Frank Borman embodied the image of a leader of one of the nation's largest airlines. In television commercials for the company in the early 1980s, his strong jaw and confident voice portrayed just the right mix of authority and concern. Passengers could see that they were in the hands of a person capable of guiding an airline whose motto was "The Wings of Man."

When Borman came to Eastern, many of the airline's employees felt the same way. An air force colonel and test pilot who joined the National Aeronautics and Space Administration (NASA) in its early days, he became one of the country's most famous astronauts in the salad days of the space program. In 1969, Borman left NASA for an executive job at Eastern and became its president six years later. Starstruck employees, who had been accustomed to the charisma of Captain Eddie Rickenbacker, the World War I flying ace who led Eastern from the 1930s to the early 1960s, were thrilled to have a world-famous astronaut at the helm. They treated Borman with something like awe, stopping him in the halls to ask for autographs. Pilots especially saw Borman as someone who personified all the glory of their calling.

Unfortunately, Borman's military background and impatient nature served him poorly in this civilian executive position. Initially, employees called him Colonel Borman as an endearing reminder of his august background; it soon became a symbol of his autocratic style.

Eastern was plagued by incessant labor turmoil long before Borman signed on. The problem extended to the carrier's early days in the 1930s. Eastern, along with United, American, and TWA, was one of the four original trunk carriers that provided the bulk of the country's air service. But while the other three airlines were truly national in scope, Eastern, as the name implies, was a regional carrier. Captain Eddie developed routes along the Eastern seaboard, especially from Florida to the populous cities of the Northeast. Unlike most other executives at the major airlines, Rickenbacker didn't care about coddling customers with good service. And he hated spending money on new planes: when the jet plane first appeared, Rickenbacker feared that their engines would be underpowered and decided he could get by with the old propeller-driven ones. Captain Eddie's militaristic management style—he often referred to his employees as "privates"—generated a steady succession of strikes by Eastern's stiff-necked unions. Nonetheless, the airline prospered as air travel grew and the tourist business in sunny Florida grew even faster.

From the early 1960s to 1975, Rickenbacker's five successors at Eastern felt obliged to buy new planes and improve service. As Borman assumed the helm, the bills were coming due. As profits dropped, he slashed overhead and moved the company's headquarters from Rockefeller Center in Manhattan to Building 16, Eastern's towering premises on the outskirts of Miami Airport. But as Eastern continued to stumble, Borman concluded that the best way to breathe life into the airline was to continue replacing its aging fleet with new planes.

In 1975, when Borman became president, Eastern was $1 billion in debt. A few years later, Borman ordered $1.4 billion worth of spiffy, European-made Airbus A-300s and highly fuel-efficient Boeing 757s. Over the next decade, he bought 142 new planes. The result was that Eastern's costs far outstripped its revenues. In 1977, Eastern's long-term debt shot up by 50 percent, by 122 percent in 1979, 200 percent in 1981, and a staggering 328 percent in 1983.

The real crunch came after deregulation in 1978. Eastern's business got an initial boost when deregulation flooded the skies with budget-conscious leisure travelers. But the new low-cost start-up airlines targeted these new flyers and lured them with lower fares than Eastern could afford. Soon Rickenbacker's Florida routes looked like the dumbest idea in the world: Eastern's flights catered to vacationers and retirees who could put off their trip if they didn't like the price.

Other major carriers fought the new competition with better service and sophisticated reservation systems, while Eastern was forced to match each new fare or risk losing the fickle wintertime tourist. Borman continued to buy fuel-efficient planes, even as the advantage they offered was being stripped away by the plummeting price of oil. He did little to address the fundamental problem of Eastern's route structure. Eastern twice flew to the brink of bankruptcy in the mid-1980s.

The company's economic woes set the stage for endless civil wars with employees. Labor brawls struck Eastern with the regularity of tropical storms in Florida. The debt Borman piled up cut two ways. It forced him to return repeatedly to his employees for concessions, and it hamstrung the company. Borman would issue dire threats that brought the unions to the very edge of a strike. Then he'd look at the balance sheet and realize that if they walked off the job, the company wouldn't be able to make the payments on its monumental loans. Facing bankruptcy, he would have no choice but to back off.

Borman's most consistent clashes came with the machinists. Eastern's machinists were more militant than the pilots, who continued to identify with Borman the test pilot and astronaut. In addition, in 1980 Eastern's machinists union elected as its president a tough and outspoken man named Charlie Bryan.

Borman and Bryan quickly developed an intense personal

rivalry that drove each to ludicrous lengths. A telling episode took place not long after Bryan took office. At that time, most airlines used three people to move a plane away from the gate. A highly paid mechanic drove a tractor pushing the plane's nose. Two lower-paid baggage handlers walked back with the wings to guide the tractor. At Eastern, the union insisted that three mechanics do the job, which meant that the baggage handlers just returned to the terminal to wait for the next flight. Borman suggested that Eastern get rid of the tractor and have each plane use the reverse thrust of its engines to push itself from the gate. A large crowd gathered at the Atlanta airport to watch the first test of this new procedure, which later became a standard industry technique known as a powerback. All that morning, Bryan tried to call Borman to stop the test, but his calls were ignored. Finally the union leader stalked out onto the runway and stood in front of one of the engines. A manager came out, yelled over the roar of the engines for Bryan to get out of the way. Bryan told him to go call a cop. The manager called John F. Peterpaul, the head of the machinists union's transportation division and Bryan's boss in Washington, D.C. Peterpaul, who himself had trouble dealing with Bryan at times, just laughed and said: "What do you want me to do? Run over the son of a bitch for all I care." Borman decided to take Peterpaul at his word. "So they put it in reverse and blasted the thing," said Bryan. "It knocked me down on the ground. I got sick afterwards from the kerosene fumes and was feverish for three or four days."

For much of his youth, Charles Eustice Bryan had drifted in and out of poverty. After high school he attended Ohio State at night to study engineering, but quit after several years to support his growing family. In 1956, when Bryan moved to Miami and landed a machinist's job at Eastern, the company already was caught up in its usual catfights between the unions and management.

Bryan worked in part-time union posts until 1972, when he was elected to a full-time position as general chairman of the IAM's District 100, which includes Eastern. (There are six

general chairmen who serve under the district's president.)
Over the years of Borman's stewardship, Bryan became convinced that the ex-astronaut was cooking up crises in order
to put the squeeze on employees and make them foot the bill
for his egotistical expansion plans. He also thought that the
union leadership did a lousy job of standing up to Borman.
Bryan agreed that Eastern had some basic financial problems.
But he believed that employees had to adopt a meaningful role
in the running of the company. It made no sense for employees
to keep giving concessions if management was just going to
fritter them away.

In 1980, Bryan ran for president of District 100 on a platform
that called for overturning a wage concession program Borman
had put in place several years earlier. After he won, Bryan
collected proxies from employees who had been given stock
in earlier concession plans. Then he marched into the annual
stockholders' meeting and nominated himself for a seat on
Eastern's board of directors. The move didn't sit well with
Borman or the board, and Bryan was rebuffed. The national
press, however, picked up the story, and Bryan thus attracted
the attention of labor-union activists interested in giving employees a bigger share in managerial decisions.

Over the next few years, Bryan assembled a team of advisors
to help him grapple with corporate finances. One was Randy
Barber. A heavyset, cheerful man with a pleasing smile and a
penchant for cowboy boots, Barber made a name for himself
in 1978 when he co-authored a book called *The North Will
Rise Again.* In it, he argued that employees should use their
billions in pension-fund money as leverage to gain ownership
or control over their companies. Barber was to become Bryan's
most trusted advisor.

Bryan's views fit in well at the machinists union. William
Winpisinger, the union's president for most of the 1980s, was
one of the most left-wing labor leaders in the country. But
Bryan, who doesn't like politics and doesn't think of himself
as a socialist, was developing in his own direction. Influenced
by the concept of passive resistance, he read Gandhi and Kahlil

25

Gibran and even got caught up in the defensive tactical ideas of Sun-tzu, the fourth-century B.C. Chinese author of *The Art of War.*

Bryan's tenacity and suspicious nature made negotiations a game of brinksmanship. Bryan wouldn't sign a new contract until he was convinced that his members wouldn't be cheated in any possible way. Since such assurances are nearly impossible to come by, he just wouldn't sign any deal. In addition to driving company officials to distraction, this caused friction with Peterpaul and the union leadership. Bryan's chronic unwillingness to sign an agreement often forced Peterpaul to step in and finish off Bryan's negotiations.

Bryan's style and personality compounded the problem. His slow and deliberate manner of speaking led some people to assume that he lacked intelligence. Sometimes colleagues would even ridicule him behind his back. Borman told his board of directors that Bryan was crazy. "Charlie hears voices," he would say.

"It's true that Bryan appears unable to make a decision," says Brian M. Freeman, an investment banker who has served as Peterpaul's close advisor for years. "But he knows that others will force his hand, like Peterpaul. Charlie is a lot smarter than he appears and than I thought in the early days. Then, I wondered about some of his positions. But he turned out to be right. Charlie appears plodding at times but he's a thinker. He's risk-adverse. And he knows the situation better than anyone else."

In 1983, during Eastern's first real brush with bankruptcy, Bryan proposed a sweeping and highly innovative reform plan that was largely the brainchild of Randy Barber. The outcome was one of the boldest and most far-reaching experiments in the history of labor-management cooperation in the country.

The idea got by Borman only with great difficulty. In early 1983, Borman called for massive cuts in pay and benefits. While the pilots and flight attendants consented to the cuts, Bryan threatened to strike. Borman asked Eastern's bankers for a $200 million line of credit, so he could keep operating during a walkout. When the banks turned him down, Borman, to stop the machinists from striking, agreed to give Bryan a stunning 32-percent increase over three years. The machinists, in exchange, promised to boost productivity.

By the fall, Borman was in trouble again. The pilots and flight attendants were furious that Borman had caved in to the machinists. They were even angrier at Bryan, whose refusal to compromise had put the company in jeopardy and then won the machinists a fat pay hike while other unions swallowed cuts. Both the pilots and the flight attendants were determined not to be made suckers again. Bryan, however, thought management was lying. After all, the company hadn't collapsed from the machinists' raise.

In January 1984, after complex talks, a historic pact was reached. All three unions agreed to concessions worth about $360 million for one year. This included immediate wage cuts of up to 18 percent, plus productivity improvements. Similar cutbacks were instituted for nonunionized employees, who numbered almost 18,000. In exchange, Eastern gave 25 percent of its stock and four seats on the board of directors to its 38,000 employees, union and nonunion alike.

The revolutionary aspects of the new agreement involved power-sharing. On the board of directors, Charlie Bryan represented the machinists. Robert V. Callahan, the head of Local 553 of the Transport Workers Union, which represented Eastern's flight attendants, took another slot. The pilots chose an outsider, and management picked another outsider to represent nonunion employees.

Perhaps even more extraordinary, Eastern gave the unions an unprecedented degree of input into managerial decision making. It opened its books to the unions, which is something most companies never do for anyone. Labor leaders also helped formulate Eastern's business plans, from the carrier's routes to its fares.

Borman didn't like the idea of employee ownership or board membership for union officials. The latter was a particular sore point because now Borman had to listen respectfully to Bryan. To assuage the chairman, the rest of the board voted to give Borman a five-year contract as Eastern's chairman.

Previously, he had had only one-year commitments. Still, Borman took a lot of heat from fellow airline executives who thought he'd given away the store and set a dangerous precedent for the industry.

Bryan and Peterpaul also fought the stock idea, which had come from the pilots. Bryan was adamant that the shares Eastern gave its employees be worth every penny of the concessions they agreed to. Bryan made the debate so involved that it was resolved only after the machinists met with Fred Bradley, a senior representative from Citibank, Eastern's major lender, and with Raymond J. Minella, a managing director of Merrill Lynch, Eastern's investment bank. Even then, the bankers only reached a deal when Brian Freeman came in and suggested the company give its employees a new issue of preferred stock in addition to common stock.

Despite the birth pains, power sharing worked wonders, at least for a while. Eastern's management seemed to value the opinions of the unions, particularly because they were backed up by solid advice from the financial experts. Most impressive was what happened to employee morale. After years of bitterness toward management, a new atmosphere blossomed.

The best stories came from machinists. In the early days of unions at Eastern, crews of machinists had worked under a lead mechanic, who was a senior union member with long years of experience. When the air conditioning broke down on a plane, the lead would instruct his crew on how to fix it. If a latch didn't work, he'd send someone out to put it right. But as strikes and job actions occurred, management had responded by hiring supervisors to make sure the work got done.

Over the years, a highly bureaucratic and inefficient system had evolved. By the 1980s, if a pilot had a problem with his control panel, he'd tell operations, which would assign a supervisor to the task. The supervisors, who were not themselves trained mechanics, would direct the union members. The lead mechanic continued to get higher pay to perform the oversight work now done by the supervisor. Now all this began to change, as Eastern cut back on supervisors and returned power to the lead mechanics. Union members took over such jobs as filling out flight forms and verifying planes' pre-takeoff weights. Leads even signed time cards for their crews.

These new roles threatened both supervisors and some union members, who didn't like their former colleagues telling them what to do. Still, the new arrangement began to work. It put a dent in the rigid bureaucracy and sped up some jobs. Employees began to look for ways to work more efficiently. The new pact gave them a financial incentive to do so: if the machinists boosted productivity by 5 percent, a new formula would raise their pay. In addition, management agreed to return work to Eastern's machine shops if the union could prove that it could do the job more cheaply than outside contractors.

The unions set up employee action committees to look for cost savings and new work. They found plenty. George Henderson, a mechanic in the engine shop, thought of a way to reweld and remachine old jet-engine fan blades. Normally, the company threw out the blades after they became nicked and burned. Henderson began fixing them at a cost of about $20 a blade. Total net savings: $306,000 a year.

Machinists even found a better way to fix the CF-6 engines on Eastern's big jetliners, which normally need rebuilding after 1,000 to 4,000 hours of flying time. A few years earlier, management decided that the work could be done at a lower cost by outsiders. So it subcontracted the work—and union jobs—to United. Mechanics in Eastern's engine group persuaded management to give them a shot at doing the work themselves again.

On the first go-round, the machinists took more than 400 hours to rebuild the engine, an embarrassing performance. Their pride stung, the machinists dug in and analyzed the problems. They wound up designing some 30 tools to do the job. They then asked their machine shop to make the tools, which turned out to be much more efficient than the ones they had been using. One example involved something called a jig. The factory-made jig, which sets ball bearings in place, had 16 settings and took two hours to use. The machinists devised a simple ring that dropped the bearings into their slots in seconds. On the strength of such improvements, Eastern soon was rebuilding the engines in 165 hours, faster than anyone else in the business. This saved more than $600,000 a year.

There were plenty of similar stories. An aircraft servicer discovered that Eastern paid $15,000 a year to have an outside firm clean its mops. He suggested buying a washing machine and doing the job in-house. Since the machine cost $10,000 and lasted about five years, that saved another $65,000. The machinists saved another $250,000 by printing all of the company's 170 forms themselves. One phone call saved $177,000 when a mechanic discovered that Eastern paid $1,640 for a barrel of Skydrol anticorrosive hydraulic fluid, while Delta paid only $1,400. In total, employee action teams saved Eastern some $30 million in 1984.

This extraordinary relationship began to collapse after just one year. The primary reason was economic. In late 1984, before all the cost savings could build enough protection to insulate Eastern, airline traffic turned sour. Management thought that the business outlook for 1985 was ominous. It asked union leaders to continue the initial 18 percent cuts past January, even though the agreement called for them to be restored. Since Eastern actually had the most profitable month in its history in November 1984, the unions felt that their members should get at least a token return on their investment.

Borman disagreed, and in December 1984 he sent a letter to Eastern's employees refusing to restore their wages. This was probably the worst way Borman could have handled the matter. Eastern's employees, whose trust had slowly begun to return, were stunned.

They reacted so bitterly to what they perceived as Borman's betrayal that Jack W. Johnson, the senior vice president of human resources, felt obligated to defend Borman in a letter to employees. "Frank Borman's integrity," wrote Johnson, "has been maligned over a decision by the company to continue a program in place that kept Eastern Air Lines alive in 1984. . . . Frank Borman signed the letter . . . but it was a decision made by all of the officers responsible for managing the business." A few weeks later, the company backed down and agreed to forgo the concessions. Then, after a few more months, when it became clear that things really were getting bad, employees finally gave in and took pay cuts.

By the middle of 1985, the productivity program had become a major bone of contention between the company and the machinists. In part, this was political. Other employees' jobs didn't lend themselves to such savings. Some pilots and flight attendants resented the pay hikes the machinists were getting in exchange for the productivity savings. Some managers harbored resentments, too. Many of the machinists' new ideas involved work for them, such as ordering the washing machines or negotiating an end to the United engine contract. Because the machinists' pay-raise formula didn't apply to them, they got nothing for their pains.

The main problem, however, lay in evaluating the savings. The company argued that many cost reductions were one-shot deals. The machinists disagreed. The company also claimed, with at least some justification, that the union sometimes padded its cost reporting. The machinists totaled the company's savings for April through June at $16 million; the company thought they came to $2 million. The union was caught off guard by the magnitude of the discrepancy. It agreed there was some cheating and thought they could compromise. After bitter feuding, both sides gave up and killed the pay-raise formula. The machinists agreed to a smaller wage hike than they could have gotten if the program had continued. Management agreed to pay it to them without more productivity improvements.

In the summer of 1985, Eastern's profits suddenly hit record levels. The company in its new era of cooperation became the toast of Wall Street. Management felt so flush that it actually opened up the machinists contract in September and restored the pay cuts agreed to just weeks before. It even tossed in 8-percent raises through 1987. In October, management restored full pay to the pilots.

No one noticed, however, that the entire industry was riding a national surge in passenger traffic that year. Nor did anyone much seem to care that Eastern was making out like a bandit from strikes at Pan Am and United. Then air traffic slowed and the strikes ended. Frenzied fare wars broke out. Eastern was forced to match the competition's discounted fares even though it couldn't afford to do so.

Before employees had time to spend their new paychecks, it was business as usual again. Talks about restoring the flight attendants' pay came to an abrupt end. Eastern showed a small profit for the three months ending in September, but only by fiddling with the books and taking $52 million out of an employee profit-sharing fund. Wall Street suddenly issued dire warnings that the company could go from a $74 million profit in the first nine months of the year to a $100 million loss by year's end.

Eastern's cooperative venture was about to fall apart. Because the company had never adequately dealt with its root problems of a poor route structure and an impossibly burdensome debt load, the entire edifice of cooperation started to collapse when the airline industry hit a particularly bad time. Management and labor went back to feuding, and the door swung open for Frank Lorenzo.

CHAPTER THREE
The Night They Sold the Company

In late 1985, Borman presented the union leaders with an ultimatum. If they did not agree to new concessions, he would sell Eastern. If he couldn't sell the company, he'd declare bankruptcy. Borman, in fact, had no desire to sell or go into Chapter 11 bankruptcy, but he reasoned that the choices before the unions had to be stark or they wouldn't listen seriously. The strategy became known as: "Fix it, sell it, or tank it."

The final threat was particularly tricky. Eastern had come close to bankruptcy before. Now the carrier was in danger of defaulting on its $2.5 billion debt. On January 1, 1986, it appeared Eastern would be in violation of the rules set by the banks that had loaned the company additional money earlier that year. If Borman threatened the unions with bankruptcy, the banks might believe he was serious and put the company into Chapter 11.

In November, Borman asked the bankers for help. Publicly, the company denied that this had anything to do with the union negotiations. Borman and his deputies declared that bankruptcy was not an option. However, everyone knew that if the bankers didn't give the company more breathing room, Eastern could be pushed over the brink. By publicizing his discussions with the bankers, Borman sent a message to the unions without threatening them directly.

With Merrill Lynch, Eastern's investment banker, Borman made the rounds to potential buyers: TWA, Northwest Airlines, Marriott Corporation, Hilton Hotels Corporation, and Texaco, among others. The Merrill Lynch bankers had come to the conclusion that Borman should sell if he couldn't get concessions. But Borman prevented them from arranging a real purchase. "Every time we made contact with a buyer, Borman would call us off," said Ray Minella, the Merrill Lynch banker who had helped to negotiate the 1984 power-sharing pact with Charlie Bryan. "He wasn't serious about selling, so of course no one was interested."

In early December, Borman got a call from Frank Lorenzo, who wanted to know whether Eastern would sell its computerized reservations system, which Continental didn't possess. Borman, who knew that his unions hated and feared the Texas Air boss, saw the opportunity he had been looking for. Here was a club to bludgeon Charlie Bryan into submission. Borman asked if Lorenzo had any interest in buying the entire company. Lorenzo, always interested in a cheap deal, said sure. Borman declined to start formal merger negotiations, but he told Lorenzo he'd call him if he wanted to pursue the idea. Borman then proceeded with the assault on the unions.

Most labor groups are free to strike when their contract ends. But airline and railroad unions are covered by a separate federal law that calls for a different procedure. If labor and management in these industries can't reach a new accord when the old one comes up for amendment, the government's National Mediation Board (NMB) steps in and attempts to bring the two sides together. When the NMB decides that the two sides are at loggerheads, it releases the two sides from mediation and declares a 30-day cooling-off period, during which the parties must continue to negotiate. Only after this period ends can the union strike or can management impose a new contract.

At Eastern, the flight-attendant and pilot contracts were open in late 1985. The machinists contract wasn't due to come up until the end of 1987. Management began with the flight

attendants, the weakest employee group. The company demanded 40-percent reductions in wages and benefits and more
flying time—a stunning request, even for Eastern.

Borman then demanded that the mediation board release
the flight attendants. Although the board is supposed to be
neutral, he got his way in a matter of weeks, a remarkably
short time. The board started the 30-day period. On January
20, 1986, the flight attendants could strike or Eastern could
impose the cuts it wanted.

The 4,200 pilots got a taste of the same medicine. The company called for 20-percent pay cuts as well as major changes
in benefits and work rules that would slice away another 13
percent of their compensation.

On the last day of 1985, Borman put the finishing touches
on his pincer play. He reached a new pact with his bankers
under which Eastern wouldn't be in technical default on its
loans. In return, Borman agreed to another deadline. He promised that he would have new labor agreements by February
28, 1986, not just from the flight attendants, but also from
the pilots, who hadn't yet been put on the mediation board's
30-day clock, and from the machinists, whose contract was
good for another two years.

Borman's ploy infuriated the union leaders. Bryan had no
intention of opening his contract and giving 20-percent wage
cuts simply because Borman claimed the banks wanted it.
Bryan sent an open letter to midlevel Eastern managers asking
them to support efforts "to reverse the suicidal course of action
of Eastern's current top management."

Borman's demands prompted Bryan to endorse an idea that
would influence Eastern's fate for years to come. Ever since
the unions had got Eastern stock in 1984, some pilot leaders
had been suggesting that the unions band together and buy
Eastern. In late 1984, Eastern's pilots hired Eugene J. Keilin
of Lazard Frères & Co., a prestigious Wall Street investment
bank, as an advisor. Keilin, who had helped to put together
one of the first major labor buyouts, at Weirton Steel Corporation in West Virginia in 1983, started looking for a partner
who could help the unions wrest Eastern away from Borman.

The employees still owned nearly 25 percent of Eastern's stock, and could build from that base to buy 51-percent control.

This was a bold idea. At the time, only a few unions in other industries, notably steel, had bought or tried to buy their companies. No union had succeeded in buying a company as large and as visible as Eastern, though at the time the pilots union was attempting employee buyouts at Pan Am and United. In addition, top machinist leaders such as Peterpaul and Winpisinger were skeptical of the concept, which they feared was a means of dumping failing companies on workers.

Although Bryan had opposed the notion of a complete buyout before, he now agreed to form a coalition with the pilots and the flight attendants for the purpose of buying Eastern. The coalition hired Skadden, Arps, Slate, Meagher & Flom, a corporate law firm known for its aggressiveness in takeovers. The pilots and the machinists both urged their members to buy Eastern stock. In late January, the unions filed an official notice with the Securities & Exchange Commission, informing the agency of their intention to boost employee stock ownership.

The outside directors, who are bankers or executives from other companies, prepared for battle. To protect themselves from possible lawsuits by irate shareholders, they ordered Eastern to put aside $20 million, in case the board's insurance was canceled. For added protection, they hired the Wall Street law firm of Davis Polk & Wardwell and later Salomon Brothers, the large investment banking house.

Then the mediation board intervened with the flight attendants in an unusual way. Normally, the board appoints a mediator to handle talks at each airline, and assigns one of its three members to oversee each set of discussions. To preserve impartiality and credibility, the board member lets the mediator handle the case, only getting involved at the last stages of negotiations. Even then the board goes to great lengths to ensure that it doesn't seem to be siding with one party or another.

This time, Walter C. Wallace, the board member in charge

of Eastern, held a press conference in Washington in mid-January to say that he had met with Eastern's bankers and that they were "prepared to take steps which I'm not at liberty to disclose." The message was clear: bankruptcy. Knowing that the lenders had set the February 28 deadline, Wallace took the extraordinary move of meeting with them to see, he claimed, "whether that date is flexible. To the best of my ability, I find it is not."

Wallace's statement was an effort to scare Eastern's unions. He and the banks had aligned themselves with Borman. Bryan and other union leaders didn't believe there was much chance that the banks would shove Eastern over the edge. Usually, bankruptcy offered them nothing but endless litigation and headaches. "No bank wants to run an airline," one lender said several days later. "What are we going to do with all those planes?"

Wallace didn't stop there. A week later, he started the 30-day clock for the pilots, conveniently ensuring that they, too, would face a showdown—two days before the bank deadline.

Bryan and Randy Barber formulated a counterattack. They decided to try to split the directors from Borman in order to push him out of the company altogether. To do so, they wanted to demonstrate to Eastern's board that the carrier's problems stemmed from Borman, not from the unions. Their first step was to show how a new business plan could reinvigorate Eastern. Barber drew up a four-page proposal that outlined suggestions division by division. They also wanted a committee with representatives from management and each labor group to supervise and implement the plan. In return, the unions would make productivity improvements designed to cut Eastern's losses. If all this medicine didn't work, Bryan would open his contract and take the cutbacks.

The two men hoped their plan would show Eastern's board that they were serious. Bryan and Barber didn't want to ask openly for Borman's head. They knew that if they did, the chairman's intense pride would cause him to dig in his heels and turn the issue into an all-or-nothing choice for the board. The only hope of dumping him, they realized, was to quietly

37

convince the directors that Borman was killing the company.

Bryan and Barber asked Michael Connery, a Skadden, Arps lawyer, to sound out leading members of the board. Connery flew to Boston to talk to John T. Fallon, head of the board's executive committee. Fallon rejected the unions' ideas.

Borman had gotten himself in a jam. Instead of knocking off the unions one by one, his deadline had united all three employee groups. The flight attendants' 30-day clock had run out and Eastern imposed the huge cuts. Since they were free to walk off the job any time after the 30-day period, Bob Callahan, the flight attendants' leader, announced that he was setting a strike date of March 1. This would fall just days after the pilots' cooling-off period ended.

Borman's biggest problem was the growing alienation of the pilots. Pilots can shut down an airline. Management can always hire new flight attendants, and usually it can contract maintenance work to outside machine shops. But pilots can't be trained overnight.

Airlines don't usually have to worry about pilots, who tend to identify more with management than with the other employees. But Eastern's pilots were fed up with Borman. Some of their disenchantment went back to September 1985, when Eastern decided it needed a two-tier wage structure from the union, in which newly hired pilots, who already start out at the bottom even if they come from another airline, would be paid on a lower scale than current ones. The idea, which had been initiated by American the year before, seemed especially suitable to Eastern, because it meant that new workers would bear more of the burden and existing employees would take a smaller pay cut. Then management had a further idea. Why hire any new pilots at current pay levels? Why not wait until the company could get the pilots union to agree to the lower rates? Eastern would stop hiring while management argued with the union.

The result was a minor disaster. Just when Borman shut the door, passenger traffic picked up. By the time he started hiring again, Eastern didn't have enough pilots, who require at least several weeks' training, to keep up with the demand. The company was forced to fly 5 percent fewer hours than projected and lost an estimated $250 million in revenue. Borman's move also sent a message to pilots. Not only was management willing to play politics with employees, it was also inept. The episode drove home the point Charlie Bryan had been making for years: many of Eastern's problems were created by the company itself.

By early February 1986, the pilots had had enough. The union began to gear up for a major confrontation. It organized a family awareness network, which the union had developed some months earlier during a strike at United. The union put on teleconferences in which union leaders kept the pilots and their families informed of events. This got families involved and helped to knit individualistic pilots into something more closely resembling a traditional union. The efforts worked well. In 1984, only about two-thirds of Eastern's pilots were members of the union. By early 1986, nearly 90 percent belonged.

The union's leadership, however, remained split on how far to push. A group of militants led by Charles H. "Skip" Copeland, a pilot leader from New York, wanted to hang tough. Other leaders, including Larry Schulte, the chairman of the Eastern pilot group, thought the company really needed help. But Schulte faced a severe political problem. Most of his members had bitter memories of the crisis that hit Eastern in 1983, when the pilots gave Borman concessions and the machinists wound up with 32-percent increases. This time, the situation was even worse. Because the pilots' contract was open and the machinists' wasn't, Bryan could insist that the pilots settle their dispute first. If Schulte gave in and Bryan then refused to follow suit, the pilots would be out for Schulte's head.

To circumvent this dilemma, Schulte wanted to put the squeeze on Bryan. In mid-February, he secretly asked his union's ruling Master Executive Council (MEC) to give him the authority to agree to 20-percent cuts. Copeland, a close friend of Bryan's, resisted. In the end, the MEC voted to allow Schulte to strike a deal, but only with Bryan, not the company. "If Charlie came around, I didn't want to have to go back to the MEC and let Charlie escape after he said okay," said Schulte.

Schulte's search for a compromise failed to prevent his members from turning against the company. On February 21, several days after the MEC's secret vote, the union polled its members to gauge the amount of sympathy for a strike. A stunning 96 percent said they were ready to walk off the job. The poll shook up the company, which had been convinced that the pilots would opt for the continued security of their high salaries over a strike. The same day the results were announced, the board of directors met with union leaders to announce formally what most employees already believed anyway: Unless the unions caved in, the directors would sell the company. And if they couldn't sell it, they'd declare bankruptcy.

Borman turned his attention back to Bryan. Eastern's chief executive had been dealing with Peterpaul for years and also had come to know Winpisinger, the national machinist president in Washington. In fact, Borman and Winpisinger usually went with a group to the Indy 500 every year, where the machinists entered a car. The week of February 17, Borman began asking both men to intervene. Peterpaul was in Fort Lauderdale at the Diplomat Hotel, where the machinists union holds many of its meetings. "I was in rail negotiations at the time and when I got back to the Diplomat, I found that Borman had called me six times during the day," said Peterpaul. "He calls my office, restaurants, everywhere. When he finally got me, he says: 'Are you going to help me?'

"Then he starts swearing: 'You don't give a fuck about my airline.' I said I'd been helping him for 10 years. I said, yes, I'll help, but not under the conditions you propose, not for 20-percent cuts. So he hung up. Borman is always trying to circumvent Bryan. He comes running to me or to Wimpy. There are seven other carriers [with machinists contracts]. No one else does this."

Borman saw little choice but to go for his ace in the hole: Frank Lorenzo. Ever since their initial conversation in December, Borman had kept in touch with Lorenzo. In January they had discussed the sale idea again. Borman allowed Minella and Minella's colleague at Merrill Lynch, Jeffrey Berenson, to stay in secret contact with Lorenzo. The weekend before the pilots' strike poll, Berenson called Lorenzo, who was vacationing in Acapulco, to tell him that he might need to "be ready" as early as February 21 to make an offer for Eastern. After the poll, Borman authorized Berenson and Minella to contact Lorenzo officially.

By calling in Lorenzo, Borman set in motion a rush of events that quickly gained a momentum of their own and spun out of his control. Borman had no desire to sell the company. He'd spent his whole career in just two places, the military and Eastern. The first had shot him to dizzying heights of fame. Civilian life proved much more challenging than anything deep space had to offer. Failure there would be a bitter end to what had been a successful climb to the top of the corporate ladder. What's more, if Borman gave up his command of Eastern, it was unlikely that at 57 he'd have anywhere else to go.

The team from Merrill Lynch had promised Lorenzo that they wouldn't allow Borman to use him as a stalking horse with Eastern's unions. Borman, knowing how much the pilots hated Lorenzo's tactics, tried the maneuver anyway. Lorenzo, however, called Borman's bluff. He told Minella and Berenson that he wouldn't make an offer for Eastern unless Borman personally supported the bid. Borman refused. The Merrill Lynch duo, who by this time had concluded that Borman could never put Eastern on its feet again, tried to go around the chairman. They asked Borman merely to present any Texas Air offer to Eastern's board of directors. He didn't have to support it himself. Borman went along with their compromise strategy, and so did Lorenzo. "That was the whole trick," said Minella. "I knew that if we could get an offer to the board, it would be out of Borman's hands."

Borman, figuring that Lorenzo couldn't negotiate a complicated merger with Eastern by the bank deadline on February 28, thought he could get away with the move. He was sure that by then, the unions would knuckle under, especially if faced with Lorenzo. Borman was right about the pilots. But he wasn't prepared for two other factors: the high-pressure tactics of Lorenzo, and the stubbornness of Charlie Bryan.

Lorenzo was aware of Borman's predicament and moved quickly to take advantage of it. To block Borman from using him as a club against the unions, Lorenzo added two stipulations to the Merrill Lynch plan. First, Eastern had to pay Texas Air a nonrefundable $20 million fee simply to make the offer. Second, he wanted an answer in two days, by midnight Sunday, or he'd withdraw. This was a ridiculously short time to sell the nation's third-largest airline. But Lorenzo knew exactly what he was doing. By setting his own deadline before the one called by Eastern's banks, he took control of events. "We were interested only if it was something quick," he said afterward. "We just did not want to get into a big public drama."

The deadline threw everyone at Eastern off balance. Although Borman didn't agree formally to Lorenzo's time frame, he called a meeting of Eastern's directors for Sunday. The board, which must approve any sale, had a rule that its meetings must be called at least 48 hours in advance. "We wanted to leave the option open," said Minella.

Late Friday evening, Borman called the leaders of each of the three unions to his office on the ninth floor of Building 16. He told them that the board had found a buyer. He didn't say who it was. He didn't have to.

Borman asked the union leaders to return on Saturday for a special joint meeting. When they convened the next day in the auditorium on Building 16's ground floor, he laid out the strategy that they knew he'd been following for months. "Fix it, sell it, or tank it." Then he gave them the zinger. The deadline was midnight Sunday, the very next day. It was time to act.

Eastern officials moved to nearby hotels and began negotiations with the pilots and flight attendants. Only Bryan, whose contract hadn't expired, didn't negotiate. Henry Duffy, the president of the national pilots union, came down from Washington, and both Winpisinger and Peterpaul remained in Miami.

Borman kept asking the two machinist leaders to talk sense into Bryan. Peterpaul, who promised Borman that he would help the machinists unit at Eastern come to an agreement, insisted that his members would never take concessions until after the pilots. Peterpaul knew that both Borman and Schulte, the pilot leader, were trying to use him to bypass Bryan. To force them to deal with Bryan, he decided to leave town. On Saturday afternoon, he returned to Washington for other negotiations. Peterpaul told Borman that he wouldn't return to Miami until Tuesday. Although this was after Lorenzo's deadline, he didn't think that Borman would take the date seriously. After all, Borman had set deadlines for years and no one paid attention. He even got other people to set them for him, as had just happened with the banks and Walter Wallace of the mediation board. In addition, Peterpaul said that Borman had sworn he'd never sell to Lorenzo.

Berenson also got to work Saturday morning. He called Lorenzo in Houston and started negotiating the terms of the offer. Later in the day, he, Minella, and several Eastern officials flew to Atlanta. There they met three top Texas Air officers: Robert D. Snedeker, the company treasurer and Lorenzo's right-hand man; Robert R. Ferguson III, the vice president for corporate strategy; and Charles T. Goolsbee, Texas Air's general counsel. As the two sides began working up a merger agreement, Texas Air pulled another trick out of Lorenzo's bag: a 1985 merger agreement Texas Air had completed in an unsuccessful bid for TWA. Texas Air and Eastern then set to work to amend the 100-page document, without which even Lorenzo never could have put together a deal in 48 hours.

On Sunday afternoon, February 23rd, Eastern's board convened in the auditorium. Bryan and Bob Callahan, the flight attendant leader, who still had their seats from the 1984 cooperation pact, attended as well. Outside in the anteroom, union advisors and bank representatives gathered. The crowd soon swelled as employees, lawyers, and security guards trickled into the room.

Company officials gave directors the general terms of Lorenzo's offer. Borman then told union leaders that each group had to cough up 20-percent cuts and agree to sweeping work rules changes. In all, he demanded $450 million in annual concessions.

The union leaders, who didn't believe Borman would sell his beloved airline, held firm.

Back in the hotel where the pilot talks were going on, Keilin, the unions' investment banker, and Connery, their Wall Street lawyer, were in a separate room. In recent weeks, they had found a few people who might make a bid with the unions. One was Don Burr, who was still running People Express. Another was Jay A. Pritzker, whose family owned Hyatt hotels and who had been a small investor in Jet Capital back in 1969. Pritzker had served on Continental's board of directors since the early 1960s, leaving only after he bought bankrupt Braniff Airlines in 1983. Now he was in the market for another airline. As the pilot executive council negotiated with Eastern officials, Keilin and Connery worked the phones, trying to put together a last-minute buyout.

At 7:30 P.M., the Merrill Lynch team showed up with a completed deal. The board reconvened, and Merrill Lynch went over the details. Knowing he had Borman over a barrel, Lorenzo offered a mere $615 million for the entire carrier. Moreover, only $256 million would come from Texas Air. The remainder would come from Eastern itself: $231 million from a new preferred stock that Eastern would issue; $108 million in cash that Eastern would reimburse to Texas Air; and the $20 million "inducement fee" that Eastern would pay Texas Air for the privilege of being purchased by Lorenzo. Texas Air would take over a carrier nearly three times its size for little more than peanuts.

The deal also gave Lorenzo an option to lock up 35 percent of Eastern's stock. Bankers call this a hell-or-high-water deal because it protects the buyer from the directors and offers from other bidders. "Our presentation lasted about a half an hour," said Minella at the time. "The board had questions. It was not an unemotional meeting. It is a topic about which people cared deeply. Selling a company the stature of Eastern is not an everyday occurrence."

Merrill Lynch said the offer was fair from a financial point of view. So did Lewis Kaden, the Davis Polk lawyer hired by the outside directors. Kaden went further. He told the directors that if they didn't take the deal, they could be left open to stockholder lawsuits if the company declared bankruptcy. Though Borman continued to assure the outside directors that the machinists' higher-ups would intervene, the board began to feel boxed into a sale.

The board broke for a recess after the Merrill Lynch presentation, and Borman asked Bryan to come up to his ninth-floor office for a private chat. The discussion didn't last long. Bryan, who had made up his mind that it was time for Borman to go, wouldn't budge. He also thought that neither Borman nor the directors would ever go through with the sale. Moreover, his union, with two more years on its contract, had little to worry about even if the company was sold.

Things were going better for Borman across town in the pilot negotiations. The buyout idea wasn't working. Burr decided that People Express had too many problems of its own. Pritzker continued to call Bruce Simon, the national pilot union's outside lead attorney, trying to work up an offer, but was making little progress. Moreover, Schulte, who had made little headway with his attempt to strongarm Bryan, was arguing for concessions as a way to avoid a sale to Lorenzo. So were Duffy, the pilot president, and Connery, the union's Wall Street lawyer, who stressed that even if the company were sold, the pilots would be much safer with a signed contract. Skip Copeland and the other militants still thought the whole affair was just another ploy by Borman. By nine P.M. the pilots' negotiators decided to pass the question on to the union's executive council. The negotiators didn't officially endorse or reject the pact, which contained the 20-percent cuts, the stricter work rules, and even the two-tier pay system. However, union leaders told Eastern's directors that the deal was probably in the bag.

Not long after Bryan and Borman came back down from the ninth floor, Borman asked the machinists' leader to meet with two directors. Bryan went back upstairs with Harry Hood Bassett and Peter O. Crisp, who had tried to reach a compromise with the machinists earlier in the day. They began talking, offering to let Bryan nominate a vice chairman in exchange for 20-percent cuts. Bryan, claiming that the union had just cut 5 percent out of the machinists' labor bill in productivity savings, refused. He offered to find savings worth another 15 percent. If he couldn't within six months, the union would take a pay cut. Bryan again laid out the idea—which he'd pushed through Mike Connery several weeks earlier—for a joint committee to solve Eastern's problems.

"We started hearing wild promises," said Barber. " 'We'll set up a committee like you wanted and Bryan can pick the head. There'll be a bonus program.' It was like people drunkenly throwing darts at a wall. It was clear they hadn't considered anything they had proposed. They started talking about compromising. But they also thought Peterpaul and Wimpy would intervene."

In the midst of the conversation, Borman came in. He'd been trying to track down Peterpaul in Washington. Having no luck, he finally called Winpisinger, the machinist president. "I've got Wimpy on the phone, he wants to talk to you," he told Bryan. The two walked back to Borman's office. Bryan went in and got on the phone as Borman paced the hall outside.

Bryan told Winpisinger about his talks with the two directors. He said the board was split and didn't necessarily back Borman. When Borman came back, Winpisinger told him there was nothing he could do. Borman knew it was over. Charlie wasn't going to give in. And no one could make him.

The only question now was whether Borman would step down or let the sale take place. Throughout the night, Borman told board members that he would resign if necessary, but it was clear he didn't mean it. He also told them he wouldn't work for Lorenzo.

Back downstairs, Bassett and Crisp told Bryan they wouldn't accept 15-percent cuts through productivity improvements. It had to be 20 percent, and it had to be real wage cuts.

When the board reconvened, the hostility toward Bryan reached the breaking point. One of the lawyers screamed at him. Bryan held his tongue, conferring under his breath with Connery and another union lawyer, who were sitting behind him. Finally Bryan spoke up. He offered to take 15 percent if the board would solve the company's problems. He looked straight at Borman.

Eastern's chairman erupted. He stalked over to Bryan. "Charlie, are you going to cooperate or not?" he demanded. Bryan just sat there. Borman pointed his finger at Bryan and snarled: "I'm going to tell the world you destroyed this airline."

"I'll tell them you did, so where will that get us?" Bryan shot back.

By 11 o'clock, the board still hadn't reached a decision. Then Salomon Brothers, the investment bank hired to advise the outside directors, dropped a bombshell. Claiming that it hadn't had enough time to study the proposal, Salomon announced that the firm would have no opinion on whether Texas Air's offer was fair or not.

This was a highly unusual statement. If directors accepted a lowball bid, stockholders might sue them for selling Eastern too cheaply, particularly if the unions agreed to concessions and costs were cut.

Bryan took comfort in the development. He was sure the board wouldn't sell the company without a fairness opinion. But Bryan misread Salomon's move. Although not all of the directors knew it, some Eastern officials secretly had asked Salomon to hold off its opinion in order to give the board an excuse to delay voting on Lorenzo's offer if it wanted a way out. "Salomon told us well in advance that the Lorenzo price was a good one," said a top Eastern official. "But they were set up to say no to give the board a basis for not acting."

Jack Fallon, the head of the board's executive committee, tried to take advantage of this opening. He asked everyone but the outside directors to leave the meeting, which meant both Borman and Bryan had to step out. For more than an hour, the outside directors debated what to do. Fallon knew that if the board agreed to take 15 percent from Bryan, it would have to lower the pilots' and flight attendants' cuts to 15 percent, too. Standing in the back of the auditorium, he asked Wayne A. Yeoman, Eastern's senior vice president for finance, if the company could live with 15 percent instead of 20 percent. Yeoman repeated Borman's position: it had to be 20 percent. Fallon then asked Borman, who had been called back inside, if the company could live without a deal from the machinists. Borman said no.

Outside, Richard Magurno, the Eastern general counsel and a loyal Borman fan, approached Bryan. "Charlie, I'm trying to control my temper right now, but you've just destroyed 40,000 jobs," he said. "I want them all to know that one guy destroyed their jobs."

"There are 15 guys inside who did it," replied Bryan, gesturing toward the closed doors where the outside directors sat.

"They're just doing their fiduciary responsibility," responded Magurno.

"It's awfully damn late for that," said Bryan, now angry himself. "They should have been doing it all along."

Around midnight, Fallon reconvened the entire board. "I think the board has deliberated long enough," he said, adding that they had no choice but to consider Lorenzo's offer. On the verge of tears, he asked for a prayer before the vote.

Just then, Howard Turner, an outside Eastern lawyer, broke into the room and announced that Lorenzo had extended the deadline by a few hours. The tension eased slightly. Soon word came that the flight attendants were willing to sign.

Over at the pilot's hotel, Pritzker made a last-ditch effort to put in a bid. He sketched out a several-page offer by hand, had it typed up, and telecopied it to Simon, the pilot lawyer. But Pritzker had run out of time. All night, Copeland and the dissidents had been blocking a vote on the 20-percent cutbacks by a slim margin. Schulte and other top pilot leaders were frantically trying to swing the executive council their way. Pilot negotiators were afraid that an offer by Pritzker would tip the scales in Copeland's favor, causing the council to vote down the cutbacks. So Simon never showed Pritzker's offer to the council; even Schulte himself didn't find out about it until years later. "They didn't want to complicate things and give the [executive council] an out," said Keilin, the unions' investment banker. "If there had been another idea on the table then, they never would have gotten an agreement."

Back at Eastern's headquarters at about one A.M., Bryan asked for a recess. He told Connery, the union's lawyer, that he would consider 15-percent wage cuts, but only if Borman was fired. "I didn't want to bring it up in the board meeting," said Bryan. Connery got together with Bassett and Crisp, the two directors, and told them what the union leaders proposed. They debated the idea, trying to develop a compromise.

As they talked, Fallon, the executive committee chairman, kept popping in, telling them they were running out of time.

Bryan stayed outside the room, consulting with Connery when the lawyer emerged. At one point, he took a stroll out of the building. A few minutes later, Borman walked by. "I understand you want me to go," he asked Bryan quietly.

"Yes, it's nothing personal," Bryan replied.

"I understand," said Borman, who then turned and headed back indoors.

Fallon returned again to Connery and the two directors. They seemed to be making progress. But Fallon, who was afraid that he would get blamed if no agreement was reached and Lorenzo pulled back his offer, wouldn't wait. He told them he was going to start the vote.

Borman went upstairs to the executive offices. He told a group of officers gathered there that the game was over. Then he shook hands with everyone except Minella, the Merrill Lynch banker, who was there, too.

As the board prepared to vote, Connery went in search of Borman. When he finally found him, he said: "Frank, you have to go in there and offer to resign."

"I already did," responded Borman.

"Go back in and make them take it. You don't want to be remembered as having your last act being that you sold the company to Lorenzo."

Borman, who's nearly a half-foot shorter than Connery, looked the lawyer in the eye. "Are you speaking on behalf of Charlie Bryan?" he demanded.

"Yes," came the reply.

"Then I'm not going to do it."

At 2:30 in the morning, the directors again prepared to vote. Borman, who had come back into the meeting, couldn't face the finale. He left again, visibly dejected. "It's out of my hands now," he told some of the crowd still gathered as if on a deathwatch outside in the anteroom. "I think it's sold."

Borman passed Minella and Berenson in the hallway and said bitterly: "Well, you finally got your deal."

On the other side of the doors, the atmosphere was one of resignation. The four union representatives voted against the sale. One director was out of the country, and another, Borman, was out of the room. The remaining 15 voted yes.

As soon as the voting concluded, Howard Turner, the company's outside lawyer, emerged from the boardroom. "They did it, they sold the company," he yelled. A minute later, Joseph B. Leonard, whom Borman had appointed as Eastern's president several months earlier, stepped out and called Borman back into the boardroom. All the board members gave him a standing ovation. Only Bryan refused to join in. Borman could barely contain his emotions. He walked out into the anteroom and told the group: "I'm sorry to tell you that as a result of our inability to reach agreements, the board did the only thing it could do and sold the company to Texas Air." Then, his voice cracking, he added: "I can't say anything more now," and ran to the elevators.

Pandemonium broke out as other top company officials discovered that the board had gone through with the sale. They realized that they'd handed Lorenzo two new labor contracts, which left the directors open to potential lawsuits. They scrambled to undo them. Leonard ran to a phone in the anteroom to call Robert J. Shipner, Eastern's vice president of flight operations, who was supervising the pilot negotiations. "Bob, do you have a deal?" he demanded. "Pull it off the table right now. Get it back, goddammit, get it back."

Leonard then rushed over to the hotel where the pilots' executive council was meeting. The council had fought bitterly since nine o'clock. Copeland argued that if the pilots rejected the 20-percent cuts and went on strike, Lorenzo would never buy the airline. Finally, just minutes after the board vote, Larry Schulte, the Eastern pilot leader, burst into the room. He had just returned from the directors' meeting and didn't know the company had been sold after he left. "Vote now or it's sold," he shouted. The council held an immediate vote, passing the contract with a slim 60-percent majority.

When Leonard showed up minutes later, he stormed in yelling. Shipner was standing in the middle of the room talking to Alan C. Gibson, Eastern's vice president for pilot administration. Schulte walked over at the same time and said to Leonard: "You're too late, Joe." Leonard turned purple with rage and screamed: "You son of a bitch, you wanted a new management, now you got it." He stalked over to Shipner, grabbed him by the lapel, and barked: "Where is it?" Shipner opened his jacket, where he had put the single signed copy of the contract. Leonard snatched it away and stalked off. Passing Schulte, he shook his fist and yelled at him again. Schulte lunged at Leonard, but Gibson held him back.

Management tried a similar tactic with the flight attendants. Leonard got the company negotiator on the phone just as he was about to initial their deal. When the negotiator got off the phone, he announced, "I've been told not to sign," and walked out.

When Leonard returned to Eastern's headquarters, Duffy, the national pilot president, persuaded Borman that he should sign the pilot's contract. Leonard and Magurno, Eastern's general counsel, insisted that Borman not sign. Finally Borman forced Leonard to surrender the contract and kicked him and Magurno out of his office.

In his final moments of power, Borman got what he wanted from the pilots: about $150 million a year in concessions. But he won it for Lorenzo. Schulte and the pilots' national leaders, however, were ecstatic. Despite the hefty cutback, they now had a new contract that the union-busting Lorenzo couldn't touch. "It was Frank Borman's finest hour," pilot attorney Bruce Simon said sardonically.

The sale of Eastern was a humbling experience for Borman.

Immediately, he tried to make amends to the pilots. On Monday, Borman and Duffy went to the pilots' building to meet with the executive council. Borman formally re-signed the contract that Leonard had tried to kill the night before. The council gave him a standing ovation. Schulte hugged Borman. They both cried.

Borman then set up a meeting for seven A.M. Tuesday with Lorenzo and Duffy. They met in the Miami Marriott, and both Borman and Lorenzo agreed that the deal reached with the pilots was valid. A few days later, Eastern finally agreed to honor the flight attendants' contract as well. "Lorenzo told Duffy that we wanted to more or less let bygones be bygones and begin anew," said Don Skiados, the chief spokesman for the pilots union in Washington.

In the end, two egos decided Eastern's fate. Bryan decided that he wasn't going to tolerate Borman's arrogance anymore, no matter what. And Borman couldn't overcome his blind hatred of Bryan, not even to save his company. "Borman's ego got in the way," says Lew Kaden, the lawyer for the outside directors, whose advice had a lot of influence on the board's decision to act. "He wouldn't tell the board he'd give way to Bryan's demand for his head."

The clash of personalities, moreover, was a metaphor for the power struggle between labor and management. "Borman didn't want to back down again," said Magurno. "If Charlie got 15 percent, it wasn't just financial. He would have beaten management. He would have set the tone for the company. The board felt the question was who was going to run the company, management or labor."

Borman agreed. "The board thought it was crazy," he said. "Here we have a union guy trying to tell us how to run the company. That's our job."

"What really happened was reverse solidarity," said Barber. "The board wouldn't axe Borman for a labor guy. If Bryan had been a banker asking to get rid of Borman, the board wouldn't have blinked an eye."

The machinists' leaders all put a brave face on what had happened. Bryan claimed that it made little difference whether

Borman or Lorenzo ran the company. "I think Mr. Lorenzo represents an interesting opportunity," he said. "We aren't intimidated, don't feel threatened, and are willing to deal in a businesslike manner."

Peterpaul, Bryan's boss, wouldn't admit that Bryan had made a mistake, either. "I don't think Charlie miscalculated," he claimed. "We thought they would sell it. Although we didn't like it, we thought we couldn't stop the board, unless it was with a formula for disaster, i.e., to continue running the company the way it has been."

Monday afternoon, Bryan sent Lorenzo a telegram. "I am at your disposal to schedule a meeting to begin exploring the challenges and opportunities that lie ahead." Lorenzo did not respond.

CHAPTER FOUR
"They've Got Ice Water in Their Veins"

A day and a half after he gained control of Eastern, Lorenzo flew from Miami to New York on one of his new planes, remembering that he had worked at Eastern after college. "You don't get sentimental over a deal like this," he said, but it wasn't long before he was gazing at the ceiling. "They really do a nice flight—just look at how clean it is up there." He fingered the seat fabric. "I like the feel of this cloth." Then he pulled out the plastic headphones and tried them on. He smiled broadly. "Aren't these just the greatest headphones?"

Snapping up Eastern was a classic Lorenzo move. He had tripled the size of Texas Air. With Continental and Eastern, Texas Air would employ nearly 50,000 people, fly 451 planes, and pull in nearly $7 billion in revenue. Together the two carriers would account for more than 15 percent of America's airline traffic. In just seven years, Lorenzo had catapulted from managing a dinky regional carrier nicknamed Tree Tops to become the boss of the largest airline company in the world next to Aeroflot, the Soviet government airline.

The purchase was also typical of Lorenzo because it was a bold, even cocky gamble. A world-famous astronaut had spent a frustrating decade trying to steer Eastern on an upward course. Its marketplace problems were overwhelming. Its feuds with employees were legendary.

Lorenzo wasn't worried. Borman never had the financial resources to go to the mat and take a strike. Lorenzo did. Continental had emerged victorious from bankruptcy: the unions were broken, its costs were rock-bottom in the industry, and its debtors were on the way to being paid off. Add the money Texas Air raised in stock and bond offerings to Eastern's own cash reserves, and Lorenzo had some $1 billion in the till. In addition, the 20-percent pay cuts pilots and flight attendants had taken were worth some $200 million in annual cost reductions. Moreover, if Eastern's unions didn't buckle under, Lorenzo could just repaint Eastern's planes with Continental's colors and hire new, nonunion workers.

Though Eastern had expensive unions—even now the company's labor costs were 37 percent of total expenses, while Continental's were only about 20 percent—Lorenzo made the picture out to be worse than it really was. Eastern had dropped to fourth in the industry in terms of labor expenses, and was increasingly being outspent by other carriers who were pulling out of the tailspin that had followed deregulation. At United, the industry leader, labor costs were 41 percent in 1986. Other carriers were even beginning to give raises again, thanks to improved efficiency.

Keeping pace with rising wages wasn't Lorenzo's flight plan. Lorenzo barreled into Eastern with the attitude that the fastest way to turn the company around was to reduce labor costs. Given Eastern's history of fractious interunion relations, the old divide-and-conquer strategy seemed the best way to do this. Texas Air officials knew they could use this method to play the machinists union off against itself, and to play all three unions off against each other.

The machinists, who hadn't taken cuts the night of the sale, came first. Texas Air officials were counting on two things. They figured that Bryan was a hothead. If Eastern pushed hard enough, he'd lose his cool and call a strike he couldn't win. They also believed that Bryan was more militant than many of his members. They thought, as Borman had, that Bryan adopted a tough approach because he craved the limelight. If Bryan went off half-cocked, Lorenzo and his team reckoned, the machinists probably could be split internally.

There was some logic to this. About half of Charlie Bryan's 12,500 members were highly skilled, well-paid mechanics who probably wouldn't find it difficult to land another good job. The other half were less-skilled workers: baggage handlers, stock clerks, janitors, and ground personnel. Many of them pulled in $15 an hour, a rate the union had achieved by piggybacking them with the mechanics. This was one of Lorenzo's biggest beefs with the machinists. Baggage handlers would have a hard time finding work elsewhere that paid anywhere near what they earned at Eastern. Texas Air reasoned that if the mechanics were offered small cuts, the baggage handlers' pay could be cut in half and the mechanics wouldn't join a strike.

The pilots and flight attendants had to be handled differently. Their internal divisions were primarily over tactics and politics, not pay, so buying off one faction probably wouldn't work. However, both groups blamed Bryan for Eastern's sale and were angry that the machinists never took the same pay cut they had. It was unlikely that they'd join the machinists in a strike. Though their recent 20-percent cutbacks made it impolitic for Lorenzo to ask for more immediately, the Texas Air boss knew they wouldn't be a problem after the machinists were broken.

Even though Borman was still at the helm and the sale to Texas Air wasn't due to go through legally for more than six months, Lorenzo wasted no time in setting the tone. In late April, he lashed out at the machinists at Texas Air's annual stockholders' meeting in Houston. Calling the Eastern machinists' leaders "fat cats," he said: "We've given the [machinists] every indication that its [pay] rates are absurd. Its attitude is intolerable."

In May, Lorenzo began sending in his men from Texas Air, although he continued to deny that he was calling the shots. Joe Leonard, the man who had been made Eastern's president not long before the sale, told Jack Johnson, Eastern's human-resources vice president, that Lorenzo wanted Johnson to go. Lorenzo sent over John B. Adams, the hard-line personnel vice president from Continental, to fill Johnson's shoes.

On June 31, the day after Borman formally resigned, Leonard called in Bob Shipner, Eastern's vice president of flight operations, who had negotiated the pilot's contract the night of the sale. Leonard told Shipner, a former pilot who'd advanced into management, that he would no longer be a vice president and would have to go back to flying if he wanted to stay at Eastern. Shipner, he said, would be replaced by Donald J. Breeding, Lorenzo's vice president for flight operations at Continental. When Shipner asked why he was being demoted, Leonard replied: "You don't have the stomach to do what we're going to do to the pilots."

Shipner pointed out that the pilot contract, which he personally had signed the night of the sale, was good for two more years.

"That fucking contract doesn't mean a fucking thing to me," Leonard shot back.

Leonard, who had to show that he was tougher than the rest of Borman's crew if he wanted Lorenzo to keep him on as president, never let up. He announced that Eastern planned to cut $160 million out of the budget. Leonard suggested that he might set up separate companies for baggage handlers, fleet maintenance, and other ground services like loading food. The machinists resisted, knowing that he'd try to take the jobs away by making the new subsidiaries nonunion. Leonard also demanded that the machinists reopen their contract. He wanted them to cough up the 20-percent cuts that Bryan had refused to give the night the airline was sold.

When Leonard's threats went nowhere, Eastern, without notice, announced layoffs of more than 1,500 people. When Bryan complained, company officials denied that the machinists were being singled out. But nearly 500 of those laid off were machinists. Leonard dismissed hundreds of managers as well, leaving Lorenzo a clear deck for a new management team.

Leonard didn't stop there. He trimmed Eastern's route system, cutting out the airline's Miami-to-London run and dropping 41 of its 53 flights out of Charlotte, N.C. Suspicious Eastern workers were convinced that Eastern was pulling out of the routes so Continental could pick them up. In September, when the repair warranties expired on 70 Rolls-Royce engines used in Eastern's jets, management gave the maintenance contract to the manufacturer. The machinists could only file a grievance to protest the 300-odd jobs it lost. "We are in the midst of an all-out war," Bryan wrote in a letter to his members.

Lorenzo personally took the reins of power in mid-October, a full month before Eastern shareholders were to vote on the sale. In a sweeping management shakeup in which he was made Eastern's chairman, Lorenzo completed Leonard's remaking of the corporate structure. Leonard himself was one of his first victims. Lorenzo demoted him to chief operating officer and replaced him with Philip J. Bakes, Jr., a former chief counsel at the old Civil Aeronautics Board who had been made president of Continental during its bankruptcy and had helped to steer it through the strike.

Lorenzo also pitted Eastern's new managers against each other. Not long after he installed Bakes, Lorenzo had breakfast in Miami with Richard Magurno, Eastern's general counsel, who had been a hard-line opponent of labor under Borman. According to Magurno, Lorenzo told him, "There are some things you tell me that you don't tell other people. You report to me." Magurno, who a short time later left Eastern after 17 years there, said, "This is an accepted part of Texas Air's structure. Here he is telling me not to talk to Phil Bakes, the president of the company."

Although Lorenzo kept the unions off balance by denying that he had any plans to strip away Eastern's assets, there was no doubt about what he was up to. On October 29, 1986, just days after Lorenzo took over as Eastern's chairman, a company official in Toronto named Guy Uddenberg sent out a confidential memo to his managers. The memo, which described a meeting Uddenberg had with John Nelson, an Eastern officer, gave the lie to everything Lorenzo was saying publicly.

"When we are on the same footing as [Continental on a cost and revenue basis, five years from now], we will be one airline," Uddenberg wrote. "If we can't cut our costs our aircraft will go to Continental. . . . The differences this year are that we have the cash by selling things—to prevent a strike. . . . We will not quit until we do it right . . . no need for a war with [machinists] as we have enough cash to bid out and hire people. . . . Our number one objective is to cut costs to make a profit . . . we have some internal dirty laundry to take care of. We know exactly what our priorities are . . . the new [Texas Air]–appointed people at Eastern have the ability to get things done—ice water in their veins."

Because the machinists contract didn't expire until the end of 1987, Lorenzo was blocked by law from imposing new wages and work rules. To overcome this, Eastern mounted a systematic war of nerves to make the union buckle. At the Eastern annual stockholder meeting in November of 1986, where the sale to Lorenzo became official, Bryan, who still held a seat on the board of directors, showed up, ready to confront Lorenzo. Lorenzo never appeared. When one stockholder spoke up in favor of the takeover, Bryan lost his temper and the two men stood up and began pointing their fingers and yelling at each other about who was really to blame for Eastern's problems.

Management knew how to handle that. The meeting was adjourned. Bryan's mike was cut off, and the lights were doused. Then the directors refused to renominate Bryan and Bob Callahan, the flight attendant leader, and they lost their seats on the board.

The machinists union struck back with a symbolic gesture of its own. The Miami machine shop held a meeting to present Bryan with a plaque for defending the union. Laminated on it was a picture of Bryan and the stockholder screaming at each other.

Eastern called the police, hoping to have Bryan arrested for holding an illegal meeting. The police sent out five squad cars of officers to watch the gathering, but refused to arrest anyone. When that tactic failed, Eastern attempted to humiliate Bryan personally. John Adams, the new human-resources vice president from Continental, sent a letter to Bryan calling the episode a "public soap opera." He added: "You will no longer be allowed unlimited access to company property because you have so abused that extraordinary privilege." Adams couldn't take away the union leader's right to fly free on Eastern planes, but he banned Bryan from flying first class and said that from then on, Bryan's tickets would have to be stamped COACH in large red letters.

Charlie Bryan, however, didn't react the way he was supposed to. He didn't explode. He advised his members that Texas Air was trying to provoke them into a strike that it then would try to break. He counseled patience, reiterating that the union was safe until the end of 1987.

In early 1987, Bakes announced that he wanted to chop 30 percent out of Eastern's $1.7 billion annual labor bill. Some $265 million would come from the machinists, whose costs had to drop almost in half. In addition, Bakes said Eastern wanted 30-percent cutbacks from the pilots and flight attendants. This move would come back to haunt Lorenzo, who was counting on the pilots to cross any picket line the machinists set up. Instead of playing the unions off against each other, he was giving them every reason to join forces.

At the time, Lorenzo assumed that he could push the pilots to the breaking point before they'd join the machinists. The pilots had never forgiven the machinists for their 32-percent wage hike in 1983. There was also a feud between Charlie Bryan and John J. Bavis, Jr., a pilot leader who had replaced Larry Schulte as the head of Eastern's pilots union unit after the Texas Air takeover. "If Jack Bavis and Charlie Bryan went into a room, you could soon measure the size of the room because they'd each be on opposite sides of it," said Raymond "Buzz" Wright, an Eastern pilot leader who was friends with Bryan and often acted as a buffer between the two men.

The antagonisms between Bavis and Bryan dated back to the second round of concessions that Borman had demanded in 1983, when Bryan proposed that the pilots give up 22 percent and the machinists give up 17 percent. "I blew up," said

Jack Bavis, who was in charge of negotiations for the pilots at the time. "He proposed that we give up more than him. That's when Charlie and I had our falling out. He's into sharing the wealth. Bullshit, they can become pilots if they want to make what we do.

"In the end, we gave 22 percent and the machinists gave 18 percent plus 5 percent productivity improvements. I called it even, and Charlie could say we gave more. But I was mad. Charlie is a socialist and I have a problem with that. Then he did the same thing in '86. We gave 20 percent and he didn't, in part because he's willing to push to the edge and he knows we aren't, and partly because he thinks we pilots are rich. The perception we had was that the pilots got taken advantage of by the machinists."

"Bavis and I really got in a tangle over something else in 1983," Bryan argues. "The pilots have two pension plans, which no one else did. I didn't knock them for it, but their second plan wasn't included in their 22-percent cut. I said we had to include it. When you stick in that pension, they took almost exactly 18 percent, too, just like us. . . . He told me he was elected chairman of the pilots in 1986 on a platform of not being controlled by Charlie Bryan. He wouldn't return my calls and got staff guys to call me back."

But Lorenzo's move angered the unions enough to draw them together. They refused to open their contracts to give Eastern concessions. When Adams sent the flight attendants a letter about their agreement, Callahan, their president, didn't even bother to formulate a reply. He just marked a few grammatical corrections on it in red ink and returned it to the sender.

The stalemate dragged on. For all its tough talk, there wasn't much Eastern could do. Lorenzo's threat to move Eastern planes to Continental had lost its power. Continental was having such a hard time integrating People Express and Frontier, the two airlines Texas Air had purchased shortly after it bought Eastern, that Lorenzo was afraid to load more weight onto the carrier. Moreover, Eastern's traffic had picked up a little, and it actually posted a $30 million profit in the first six months of 1987. Lorenzo had to wait for the situation to change.

All he could do was turn up the heat. Management pounded away at the unions, hoping to weaken their morale. Managers began firing and suspending machinists union members, making a particular target out of local leaders. "Lorenzo embarked on a campaign to break our resolve, and tried to wipe out the leadership so people would have no one to go to," said Bob Taylor, a machinist who had been with Eastern for 18 years, since he was 22.

"I was one of eight chief stewards in Atlanta, which meant I handled disputes and processed grievances. They walked into my office and said I was terminated. They said I was too influential with people. They never explained what this meant. I was one of the first to be fired in the [machinists]. I was off the job without pay for eight months. In August 1987, I was elected to the post of general chairman for Atlanta, which is a position paid by the union, so they couldn't fire me again. My case finally went to arbitration 23 months later, and I was given $21,000 back pay."

Management went after the pilots as well. Under federal regulations, the pilot in command of a plane has ultimate responsibility to accept or decline an aircraft for a flight. Even though mechanics or safety inspectors might render this unnecessary, many pilots take deep pride in the professionalism this power confers.

Company officials issued an order that any pilot who refused to fly a plane had to first explain his decision to the dispatcher, then talk with the regional chief pilot, and finally write a report. If the chief pilot wasn't satisfied, he could remove the pilot from flight status while the matter was investigated. Many union members said they felt humiliated by the procedure, which they saw as dangerous and demeaning.

Eastern's flight operations managers even told some pilots to ignore Federal Aviation Authority (FAA) safety regulations. In 1987, Captain Ron Russell was told to fly from Atlanta to Houston, even though it would put him over the FAA limit of 30 flying hours a week. Russell protested, and then called the FAA, which at first told him to stick to the rules and ignore the company. An Eastern official immediately phoned FAA to complain about its interference, and the agency backed off. Russell asked the union what to do. The unions told him to fly unless he wanted to get fired.

Shortly thereafter, embarrassed FAA higher-ups sent Eastern a warning to stop flouting the rules. Agency official's faces grew even redder when they learned that Eastern was telling pilots that the company would pay any fines the FAA levied against them for exceeding flight-time rules. In response, the administrator in charge of aviation standards wrote Eastern a letter rebuking it for the practice.

The company tried other tactics to humble the pilots. After complaining that the company had more pilot absences than other airlines, Eastern instituted a harsh new absenteeism policy. After three "occurrences," a pilot would get a warning and undergo counseling about missing work. A three-day suspension would follow the fifth incident, and termination could come after the sixth. Pilots complained that they were being forced to fly even if they were sick, which threatened safety. But Eastern enforced the policy even after it became apparent that the company's absenteeism rate wasn't improving.

Management established an absenteeism policy for machinists that was even tougher than the one for pilots. It automatically triggered Eastern's system of progressive discipline, which ends in firing, after three days of tardiness or absence. This was all the more surprising because the machinists had a low absentee rate of 2 to 3 percent. The Department of Transportation later reviewed the policy and stated: "The program has apparently not affected Eastern's ground employee absenteeism rate. . . ." The department also concluded that Eastern's motivation did not seem to stem from a genuine concern over chronically absent employees. "No documents were found indicating managerial concern over the absenteeism rate of ground employees."

The flight attendants received the worst treatment of all.

Some 600 were placed in immediate jeopardy of being fired for going óver their new absentee limits. Managers kept the union off balance by striking out haphazardly.

Michael H. Stubbins, a 35-year-old flight attendant based in New York who had flown for Eastern for nine years, was the recipient of such treatment. In 1981, Stubbins took a month's leave from work after his first child was born. When his second child was born in 1985, he called in sick for one day. "Two years later, under Lorenzo, they changed the rules," says Stubbins. "They put in the new policy and took it back two years. So when I missed a trip a few months after [the new rules were put in], they said I had gone over the limit and terminated me, because they counted the time I took off when my son was born."

Stubbins was out of work for 18 months, until his case came up for arbitration. The arbitrator ruled that he had the right to the day off when his child was born, and gave him his job back with full pay for the time he missed. "Lorenzo's whole creed is fine, sue me, take me to court, it will take forever," says Stubbins. "Meanwhile, he breaks the union and I'm out of a job. I was no big activist, but when I came back to work I spent two weeks on line and then went to work for the union. I was sick and tired of seeing people treated this way."

The campaign against employees didn't come only from high-level management. Lorenzo had put Eastern's managers and supervisors on a war footing. The managers used the new absentee policies, alleged drug abuse, and charges of phony medical claims and theft to fire a record 262 machinists union members in 1986. Over the next two years, that number swelled to 840, including 39 union stewards.

Managers became adept at psychological warfare. Flight attendants were forced to pick up trash on the planes, in violation of their contract. If they refused, they could be fired for insubordination. Adams, the new human-resources vice president, announced that employees suspected of theft would be searched, as would their work areas. A new auditing system for on-flight liquor sales spurred a wave of paranoia among flight attendants, some of whom were fired when their receipts showed $2 or $3 discrepancies. As Lorenzo's reputation grew, wild stories began to circulate about strip searches and about auditors disguised as nuns, pregnant women, and Sikhs.

Machinists got their share of mental intimidation, too. The company hung rotating video cameras in some machinist work areas. Although management claimed the cameras were installed simply to control petty thefts, they created an Orwellian atmosphere. One mechanic in the Miami machine shop became so angry that he began to take down the camera near him, only to be nabbed in the act by another one hidden close by.

There was little that didn't become an opportunity for confrontation. The company even cut off the phones of the union's efficiency team set up in the 1984 days of cooperation. A few weeks later the team's parking spaces were revoked. The team soon was evicted from company property.

The atmosphere became so confrontational that managers began to think in military terms. "On D-day, we will impose the new work rules and rates, do layoffs, and replace people with vendors where necessary," said another confidential memo from Guy Uddenberg, the Toronto Eastern official. The company put up barbed-wire fences around the entire headquarters building, hinting darkly that it expected union violence. The pilots found listening devices planted in their union headquarters. The FBI investigated but never tracked down the culprit.

Eastern also filed a multimillion-dollar suit claiming that the machinist leaders had launched a campaign to intimidate company managers. It alleged that Bryan and two of his officers had arranged for the distribution of inflammatory literature, which in turn had unleashed a wave of mail and telephone threats to Eastern officials. The suit became just one more battlefront in the dozens of legal skirmishes between Lorenzo and the unions.

Opposition carried a stiff price. Don W. Edgar, a chief steward in Eastern's components overhaul shop at the Miami airport, was fired for protesting when a manager ripped union literature off bulletin boards. An arbitrator finally gave him his job back with back pay two years later.

The unions filed grievances to protest every incident, firing, and suspension. But the flood of complaints overwhelmed them. "Each arbitration cost us $5,000," said Mary Jane Barry, who took over from Callahan as head of the flight attendants' union in 1987. "I believe Eastern used the system to deplete union resources. They lost 85 percent of their cases, but kept creating incidences anyway. So there must have been another motive besides enforcing discipline. They wanted to keep the union busy and off guard."

The stress began to take its toll on employees. A 1987 survey by Virginia Tech University showed that 23 percent of Eastern's pilots showed frequent symptoms of depression. More than 40 percent of their spouses reported similar psychological problems. Eastern pilots also sought medical help much more often than pilots at U.S. Air and Piedmont, the other two carriers surveyed. Only 2 percent of Eastern's pilots felt their jobs were "very rewarding," versus 85 percent at the other carriers. Company officials dismissed the surveys as self-serving. Employees, they charged, said they were unhappy because their union leaders told them to.

By September, Lorenzo had slashed Eastern's work force by nearly 4,000 people, to about 39,000. Many employees, including pilots, went looking for new jobs. In fact, more than 100 pilots, about half of them captains, had left by June. This was nearly triple the normal turnover rate before Lorenzo took over.

Shortly before the formal machinists contract talks were due to open in October 1987, the union held an election for officers. By now, hundreds of union members had been fired or suspended from work. Angry machinists delivered a clear message that Lorenzo had misjudged the internal divisions in their ranks, reelecting Bryan to an unprecedented third term as president of District 100. He chalked up a four-to-one edge over his opponent, his highest margin ever. Texas Air officials, like Borman, had believed that Bryan was out of touch. But he wasn't. In fact, even under Borman, Bryan had been under constant pressure from some members to be more militant. He had been elected in 1980 by taking a strong stance against management. After a year of Lorenzo, Bryan sometimes had to restrain his troops. It was rarely the other way around.

In October, Eastern finally was able to start formal wage negotiations with the machinists according to the normal rules laid down by the Railway Labor Act, which covers airlines as well as railroads. The company moved quickly to take advantage of the law. In most industries, union negotiations almost always begin the same way: One or both sides send proposals for how they want to change the current contract. Eastern, however, decided just to chuck the whole contract and start over. It sent off a 60-page proposal that rewrote virtually the entire machinists agreement. Lorenzo demanded sweeping work-rule changes that permitted extensive use of part-timers, and 40-percent wage cuts for baggage handlers. In fact, management demanded that the old contract be replaced by two new agreements, one covering mechanics and another covering baggage handlers and other ramp-service workers. It demanded a stunning 2,000 changes to the old contract.

Eastern's demands were so all-inclusive that it was difficult even to put a number on the total amount of concessions. "You couldn't tell how much they really wanted, because they made too many changes," said Harry Bickford, the mediator who had been handling Eastern for the National Mediation Board (NMB) for years. But it was clear that the amount was in the range of the $265 million a year that Bakes had asked for in the beginning of 1987.

Management did offer one enticement. To ease the hit to baggage handlers, it promised to set up a $100 million fund. This would go to retrain unskilled workers to be higher-paid mechanics.

An outraged Bryan issued a counter-offer calling for 10-percent pay hikes over two years. Bryan said he thought that Eastern's problems should be addressed the way they were during the 1984 year of cooperation, through joint efforts to find efficiencies.

Grounded

After less than two months of bargaining, Eastern told the NMB that the two sides were at an impasse. Management demanded that the board start the mediation, which must precede the mandatory 30-day cooling-off period before a strike.

"I read in the papers that they want a settlement," said Peterpaul, who was involved as the machinist union's transportation division chief. "But after eight meetings they ran to the board asking for mediation. Now they're asking [Senator Orrin] Hatch on the Hill to get the board to release them."

Management also fired off another broadside. To top up the war chest by cutting expenses, Eastern lopped another 3,500 people off the payroll. Employees were in shock. From the 42,000-plus employees who worked at Eastern the day Lorenzo took over, a little more than 35,500 now remained. In public statements, Bakes made it clear that there was more to come if labor costs were not reduced.

Then Bryan sent a bulletin to his members. "From this day forward, you must assume that Eastern Airlines intends to force a strike, and you must be prepared for the worst. . . . Arm yourself by putting your financial house in the best possible order you can."

Eastern made elaborate preparations for a strike. Initially, the company set aside $48.5 million to hire 2,500 mechanics, 300 security guards, and 6,000 airport-services employees to fill in on the day machinists went out on strike. Management also budgeted for 1,450 flight attendants, in case they walked out in sympathy. Eastern paid outside contractors to recruit, train, and hire strikebreakers. Later, the strike-insurance kitty was pumped up to $70 million.

Eastern's detailed strike plans called for what would be a new airline. Internal company documents showed that baggage handlers would earn $3.85 an hour in Orlando, Florida, and $5 at La Guardia Airport in higher-cost New York. Mechanics would get $8 an hour, less than half their pay at the time, in Miami, but $14 in Newark. Flights would be maintained at full strength in New York, Atlanta, Boston, and Philadelphia. Detroit and Buffalo flights would be cut sharply, and

Kansas City operations would be reduced to a shadow of what they had been. Service would halt altogether to Saint Louis, Seattle, San Diego, Dallas, and New Orleans.

Lorenzo was confident that he could buy off the pilots. But he went to great lengths to make sure Eastern could fly if they did walk off the job. The company signed a $5.5 million contract with an air cargo company called Orion Air to train 400 nonunion pilots, and arranged for Orion to use Eastern planes to train on. Lorenzo even brought Continental into the picture, transferring $22 million from Eastern to its sister airline to provide services in event of a strike.

All of Eastern geared up for D-day. In January 1988, the company's finance men drew up a bound booklet entitled: *Eastern Airlines: Cash Impact of Contingency Planning.* It projected the carrier's cash situation in six different scenarios: running at 60 percent , 40 percent, or 20 percent of capacity; and running at each level during a strike. The projections showed how much money Eastern would spend and need in each month, assuming a strike began in April 1988—the very latest Lorenzo expected to have to wait. During a 60 percent downsizing and a strike, for instance, Eastern would have to cough up $50 million in escrow deposits to American Express, Chemical Bank, and to outside vendors. It would lose $96 million in advance ticket sales, $56 million for refunds, and another $65 million in what airlines call "plating," bookings that travel agents would turn over to other airlines.

In February, Texas Air and Eastern officials briefed Wall Street analysts on their readiness for a strike. Bakes even sent an unusual letter to Eastern's frequent flyers, warning them to brace for the collision ahead. Assuring them of management's commitment to safety, he explained "the need to fix our labor cost problem. . . . The lengthy saga of financial losses requires a permanent fix to the fundamental Eastern problem—an inefficient labor cost structure." Eastern also drew up plans to spend $1 million on four mailgrams that would be sent to travel agents during a strike, to keep them updated on what was happening.

Worried employees heard rumors that Eastern was poised

to declare bankruptcy. Lorenzo considered it frequently. "We talked about bankruptcy several times," says Harvey Miller, the lawyer who thought up the Continental bankruptcy. "We were called down periodically to Miami for preventative maintenance, which meant we looked at Chapter 11."

The tension of not knowing what would happen caused even nonunion employees such as reservations agents to suffer under the strain. They knew that a showdown affecting everyone at the company was imminent. But no one knew when it would come or whether it would be a strike, a bankruptcy, more layoffs, or a dismantling of the company. In February, a reservations agent complained about Eastern's problems to a reporter booking a flight. "I'm sick of this job," she said, unaware that she was speaking to a member of the news media. "I hope Lorenzo puts us into bankruptcy, so I can get out of here. I've worked here for 22 years, but I can't get my pension for another year. I would in bankruptcy. We've been going up and down like a yo-yo and we're all tired of it."

Bryan, too, knew that a clash was inevitable. He had little choice but to stall the showdown as long as possible. It was clear that Lorenzo was no Frank Borman. "This is the kind of fight only one man walks away from," said Bryan."

CHAPTER FIVE
The Texas Air Chainsaw Massacre

Frank Lorenzo was growing desperate. He had mustered all his resources around the expectation that a showdown with labor would occur by April 1988 at the latest. But Charlie Bryan refused to be goaded into a strike, and the mediation board refused to declare impasse. Texas Air's financial predicament worsened by the day: Eastern was losing money again and Lorenzo kept spending millions of dollars a month on strike contingency plans. Lorenzo realized that he needed cash to keep going until D-day. It wasn't long before he began to dismember Eastern.

Lorenzo had, in fact, started to strip assets from Eastern almost as soon as Texas Air gained control of the company. He had bought the carrier with the long-term plan of merging it into Continental. Chopping off parts of Eastern, moreover, sent the unions an unmistakable message: Their jobs and Eastern's strength depended on obedience to Lorenzo's demands.

But as his battle with the machinists wore on, Lorenzo's cherry-picking of Eastern became a necessity. Instead of giving parts of Eastern to Continental, Texas Air had to sell chunks of the Miami carrier to raise cash. Phil Bakes, Eastern's president, called it the company's insurance policy. If Lorenzo couldn't break the unions, he could always dip into Eastern's assets.

Lorenzo's corporate structure enabled him to use Eastern as a kind of piggy bank that he could break open at will. It also allowed him almost unlimited room to shift money among his various entities.

With an empire as unprofitable and as highly indebted as Texas Air, such maneuverability was crucial. In 1988, Lorenzo's quest to run the country's biggest airline had saddled Texas Air with $5.5 billion in debt, making the company one of the country's most leveraged. Because it was a chronic money-loser, Texas Air also was vulnerable to bankruptcy. To avoid this risk, Lorenzo spawned dozens of subsidiaries. By 1988, the parent company had given birth to about 25, which allowed Lorenzo to parcel out the enormous debt among all his children.

This extended family created an effective buffer for Texas Air. If a debt payment couldn't be made, the lenders could send only the subsidiary into bankruptcy. Thus Continental could buy bankrupt Frontier Airlines and remain untouched by Frontier's liabilities because it was a different subsidiary.

When Lorenzo placed Continental into bankruptcy, he was able to use his corporate structure to keep Texas Air out of the courthouse. It was one of the rare instances where a company was in bankruptcy but its parent wasn't. Lorenzo then miraculously borrowed some $1 billion to buy Continental 38 planes during the company's bankruptcy. Almost all of the money came through Texas Air and New York Air. Since they weren't in bankruptcy, they simply bought the planes and leased them to Continental.

Likewise, when Texas Air bought People Express in 1986, the latter was an absolute financial mess. It was little better when Texas Air sold People to Continental the next year. To shield Continental, Lorenzo kept People as a corporate shell that leased planes to Continental. That way, if lawsuits against People got too burdensome, Texas Air could simply shove it into bankruptcy and keep Continental out of the fray.

This structure meant Lorenzo was always living on the edge,

constantly pulling money from one unit to subsidize another. When things flowed smoothly, the money would stream up to Texas Air, which accumulated hundreds of millions of dollars even though it was just a holding company. When crises developed, as they did incessantly with Continental, Texas Air could feed it money by taking cash from one pot, like Eastern, and putting it in another.

The system let Lorenzo do things most corporations couldn't. For instance, holding companies normally take money from a subsidiary through dividends paid on stock. But the banks that loaned Lorenzo's companies money put restrictions on such payments as a way of ensuring that they wouldn't be left holding the bag if Lorenzo took all the profits out of the company they had lent to and then put it in bankruptcy. Texas Air got around the banks through a variety of ingenious financial arrangements, such as charging its children fees for legal, banking, and management services.

Lorenzo had plugged Eastern right into the machine. Once the purchase was complete, Texas Air quickly had stripped out one of Eastern's biggest single moneymakers, its computerized reservations system. Known as System One Direct Access (SODA), this bank of computers gave more than 5,000 travel agents around the country instant access to Eastern's flights and fares. In the mid-1980s, major carriers had come to use these as a major tool to pull in the passengers—and the profits.

In March 1987, a new Texas Air subsidiary called System One Holdings Inc. bought SODA and a related software unit called EAL Automation Systems Inc. When Eastern's board sold the company to Lorenzo, Merrill Lynch, Eastern's investment bankers, concluded that SODA alone was worth between $200 million and $250 million. Another outside company estimated SODA's worth at $450 million. In late 1986, TWA sold a half share in its PARS reservation system, which linked 3,600 travel agencies, for $140 million.

Texas Air paid $100 million for both of Eastern's systems. Moreover, instead of paying cash, Texas Air gave Eastern a note for the $100 million that paid interest at well below market rates. Because the note didn't come due until 2012, it probably was worth less than $50 million.

Eastern was also required to pay to use what had once been its own reservations system. System One received a fee for every reservation made on Eastern, plus other fees. The total came to about $10 million a month. In the nine months after the Texas Air purchase, Eastern paid some $90 million for use of a service that it had sold for what amounted to $50 million. In 1988, Eastern spent some $120 million for SODA's services. Eastern would have had to spend much of this money even if it had kept SODA, in order to run the computer system. But when SODA became a separate company, its charges were structured so that it made a profit from Eastern's business. As a result, Eastern had to pay millions of dollars extra for a service it previously had provided for itself.

Lorenzo's financial moves were so convoluted that even Wall Street analysts had a tough time figuring out what was going on. The pilots union finally became so fed up trying to follow Texas Air's transactions that in January 1988 it hired Touche Ross & Co., one of the country's largest accounting firms, to help analyze Eastern's finances. Ironically, the pilots secured the services of Farrell P. Kupersmith, a Touche Ross partner who had represented Lorenzo during Continental's bankruptcy. Kupersmith even had testified in court against labor's motion to dismiss Continental's bankruptcy filing. "My role at Continental made relations with the unions quite awkward in the beginning," said Kupersmith. "But they saw that we had done well in court against the unions, so they wanted our expertise. I wasn't necessarily antiunion before, but I had never represented a union, and I had a general belief, just from reading the papers, that a large part of the problem at Eastern was the unions. But I met with Eastern's pilots in the latter half of 1987 and I didn't see guys with horns trying to destroy the company."

Lorenzo continued to spin off other parts of Eastern. In April, Eastern created a new company called Protective Services Corporation, whose 50 employees were guards already represented by the machinists union. Management served notice that a new labor agreement would have to be negotiated just for these 50 guards, who averaged $13.50 an hour.

Of course, a new labor contract would give management an opportunity to slash the guards' wages without waiting for the entire machinists union to agree to concessions. Union officials said they feared that Eastern eventually would try to dump all 6,000 of its baggage handlers and other fleet-service workers into the new company.

Two months later Eastern created Airport Ground Services Corporation to employ about 100 union baggage handlers and maintenance people in Fort Lauderdale. Leonard, Eastern's chief operating officer, announced that if the new venture was successful, it would spread to other Eastern locations.

Within days after Eastern announced the idea, the machinists' lawyers filed suit in the U.S. District Court in Washington, D.C. Almost immediately, Judge John H. Pratt issued a temporary restraining order against the spin-off. The machinists contract, the union argued, stipulated that any changes in working conditions had to be negotiated before, not after they occurred. Pratt agreed that this was probably the case and ordered a trial on the question.

Lorenzo, unfazed, kept up a flurry of sales and spin-offs throughout 1987 and 1988. Some moves stripped money or resources away from Eastern, often to the benefit of Continental. Others deprived the unions of jobs. Almost every time, Eastern wound up paying out cash or taking risky notes, even though it was mostly losing money. In total, Kupersmith, the Touche Ross accountant, estimates Lorenzo made off with a net sum of at least $750 million in assets, even when the cash Texas Air put into Eastern's purchase is factored into the equation. What follows is a sampling of Lorenzo's actions from the time Texas Air bought Eastern through 1988:

• In January 1987, Texas Air combined Eastern's sales force with Continental's to form a new company. Continental had 28 sales offices, mostly in locations where Eastern had little business. Eastern had 139, many located in the Northeast, where Continental had just expanded by buying People Express. Continental and Eastern each were given 50 percent of the new sales company.

• When Texas Air bought People Express in late 1986, it picked up $100 million in notes from the nearly bankrupt carrier. The notes, which carried no rating from Standard & Poor's, a company that rates bonds, were so risky that they probably would have fetched much less if sold on the open market. Texas Air, however, sold $30 million of them to Eastern for $25 million even though it had paid less than $21 million to buy this set of notes in the first place. Texas Air walked off with a $4.4 million profit. Eastern was left $25 million poorer, holding a piece of paper of dubious value.

• Eastern started a new, wholly owned subsidiary to take over its lucrative airport-lounge club chain, called Ionosphere Clubs Inc.

• Eastern sold Continental 11 airport gates at Newark for an $11 million note. An outside consulting firm had appraised the gates at twice that much. Eastern itself valued them at nearly twice as much as well. Earlier, Eastern had sold eight of its gates in Charlotte, N.C., a much smaller market, to Piedmont Aviation for $25 million. In cash, of course.

• Continental bought 50 percent of a small East Coast commuter airline called Bar Harbor Airways for just under $1.5 million. Eastern offered a hand, on the theory that many of Bar Harbor's passengers would be funneled its way. First, Eastern paid Continental a $1.5 million "inducement" fee to persuade it to buy Bar Harbor. Then it provided more than $30 million in added financial support for Bar Harbor, loaning much of the money at interest rates substantially lower than those Eastern itself had to pay to borrow on the open market. A year later, Continental restructured Bar Harbor's routes, cutting many flights to Eastern's hubs and increasing flights to Continental's. Eastern's share of Bar Harbor's feeder traffic fell to less than 40 percent.

• Eastern sold Continental six of Borman's fancy A-300 jets. Continental paid $162 million; $67 million of this was in a promissory note. Continental then sold the same planes to someone else for $169 million—in hard cash. This left Eastern

$7 million short and holding another note of dubious value.

• Texas Air created a new company called Texas Air Fuel Management Inc. to buy fuel for all its airlines. Eastern paid on the order of a million dollars a month for the service, which brought no apparent benefit to Eastern. Eastern paid Texas Air another half a million a month in management fees for legal and accounting advice, although Texas Air never proved that the services saved Eastern any money. These arrangements allowed Texas Air to take additional cash from Eastern by circumventing the legal restrictions that limited the stock dividends Eastern could pay to its parent.

These moves weren't just haphazard attempts to raise cash by a hard-up management. They were part of a deliberate and premeditated campaign to break the unions, damage Eastern, and help Continental. Nowhere is this intention better reflected than in a confidential memo entitled "Chunks," which the unions uncovered in the course of one of the lawsuits between them and Lorenzo. No one at Eastern ever admitted to writing the four-page missive. But the company conceded that it contained the thoughts of someone at Eastern that were forwarded to Texas Air. It's obvious from the memo's scope and tone that the person was a very senior executive.

The memo listed eight Eastern assets that could be cut. It described the number of aircraft involved for each one, the "IAM impact," and the pros and cons of the sale or transfer. Clearly, the effect on the IAM, the machinists union, was foremost in the author's mind. For instance, target No. 2 read as follows:

Sell Air-Shuttle
1. To Continental, if possible, or
2. To a competitor.
Number of aircraft: 14.
Visibility: Maximum.
IAM impact: Maximum.
Pros.   1.   Sends a message on our ability to spin off operations.

2. Maximum shock value.
3. If sold to [Continental] or to separate [Texas Air] subsidiary, integrated Air-shuttle product and [Texas Air] market base preserved.

Cons. 1. Reduces [Eastern's] dominant market position in the Northeast.
2. Very profitable [Eastern] operation.

It took Eastern's unions a while to realize what Lorenzo was up to. When they did, the struggle took on an almost ritual air. Texas Air would cook up an asset deal or announce a layoff. The unions would sue in court. Not long after the machinists won the temporary bar against the ground-services subsidiary, Judge Pratt found that the scheme did in fact violate their contract. He ordered Eastern to drop the whole idea. Then the pilots weighed in with a lawsuit against the transfer of the six A-300s to Continental. The two unions kept at it, hoping to block Lorenzo's machinations any way they could.

In February 1988, Lorenzo gave the first hint that he might consider easing up on the sales and layoffs. He expected the National Mediation Board to let him confront the machinists in a couple of weeks, and he wanted to make sure the pilots would fly through any strike the machinists mounted.

Bavis, the pilot leader, had been asking for a deal even before the pilots' executive council had elected him to its top post. After Lorenzo bought Eastern in 1986, the council had asked Bavis to lead a committee to track any Lorenzo move to merge Continental and Eastern. A medium-sized, dark-haired man whose quick mind and rather sharp features make him seem more like a lawyer than a pilot, Bavis seemed to enjoy the intellectual challenge of puzzling out Lorenzo's convoluted maneuvers. Bavis was convinced from the start that the best way to deal with the industry's chief union-buster was to extract guarantees that would protect Eastern pilots in a Continental merger.

In early 1987, as soon as Lorenzo began demanding concessions from pilots, Bavis asked Texas Air to open up "fence" talks. In other words, he wanted the parent company to put a legal fence around specific Eastern planes and jobs and agree not to sell them. Bavis also demanded that Texas Air reinstate the pilot union's right to represent Continental pilots. Only on those terms would Bavis agree to discuss the cutbacks Lorenzo wanted.

Not surprisingly, Lorenzo wanted no part of Bavis's ideas. He had worked hard to break the pilots union at Continental. Building a fence around Eastern, moreover, would prevent him from siphoning off its assets to help Continental or Texas Air. He also would lose a major weapon against the machinists.

But as D-day seemed to approach, Lorenzo decided it would be worth taking a closer look at Bavis's demands. If nothing else, he could see how little he could get away with. As a result, in early 1988 Eastern began secret fence talks with the pilots. These discussions were conducted separately from the formal negotiations held under the auspices of the mediation board.

Lorenzo made his first move in January. In a surprise offer, Eastern said it would guarantee the pilots their jobs and seniority even if planes were transferred to other Texas Air units. In return, management wanted pay cuts of 10 percent to 20 percent. The company agreed to extend the fence to all 264 of Eastern's planes, which would have protected the jobs of all current pilots.

The offer hit a political nerve in the pilots union. The union's executive council had long been split between two groups. One faction had run the council for years, first under Larry Schulte and then under Bavis, his successor. Another faction was made up of hard-line militants led by Skip Copeland, the pilot leader from New York who had wanted to go on strike the night the airline was sold to Lorenzo. Their differences over tactics also had led to political infighting over who would lead the council. Bavis had served for 12 years as the administrative aide to the national president of the union, until Hank Duffy took over the presidency in 1983. In 1986, Bavis put himself in the running for the national presidency when Duffy came up for reelection. Copeland decided to run for the job of chairman of the Eastern pilot council. But when

Duffy won the national job, Bavis decided to run for the spot at Eastern, and won it. Copeland felt betrayed. "I felt screwed by Bavis," said Copeland.

Copeland had been attacking Bavis ever since. Copeland charged that Bavis's fence talks were a sellout to Lorenzo. A silver-haired man with a deep voice and craggy features, Copeland had been a close friend of Charlie Bryan's for years. Despite the differences between pilots and mechanics, Copeland had admired the way Bryan stood up to Borman. "Copeland was the only pilot who refused to powerback his plane back in the early 1980s, when we first started doing it," said Borman. "He wouldn't do it because his pals in the machinists were against it."

Copeland now stuck up for his friend again. He argued that Bavis was just trying to get revenge on the machinist leader for the humiliation Bavis had suffered in 1983, when the pilots took a bigger cut than the machinists, and again in 1986, when the machinists took no cut at all. Copeland also pointed out that Bavis still had his eye on the presidency of the pilots union. If Bavis could unionize Continental again, he would be a hero throughout the union and indeed the whole industry. To achieve this goal, Copeland charged, Bavis was willing to make Eastern pilots sacrifice more than they should.

Copeland's charges gained validity among other pilots executive council members because of the secretive way that Lorenzo and Bavis negotiated. The two met frequently, one on one, to discuss the fence idea. As a result, many of the 21 members of the council were highly suspicious of any fence deal Bavis produced. They knew that if Lorenzo really gave ironclad job guarantees, many members would be tempted to take them, even though it meant selling out the machinists. But most council members also were anxious to avoid another pay cut. Nor did they trust Lorenzo—or Bavis.

"We know we have a pilot group with a variety of strongly held views," Bruce Simon, the pilots union lawyer in Washington, said at the time. "Some pilots have a really vigorous dislike for the [machinists]. Others say we can't let Lorenzo sharpen his teeth on another trade union. If he succeeds with them, we're next. I don't have a clear sense of which one will predominate. . . . But having said that, I don't think Lorenzo is wise enough to buy them off."

Simon was right in the long run. But that January, the secret talks with the pilots collapsed for another reason altogether: Lorenzo had badly misjudged when D-day would come. Bryan wouldn't be bulldozed into a strike. And the mediation board kept telling both sides to keep bargaining. As the delay dragged on, Lorenzo had to pull back from the fence talks. If Texas Air gave pilots a guarantee that assets wouldn't be sold, the machinists would just have that much less reason to strike.

This set up a pattern that continued throughout 1988. Lorenzo would sell Eastern assets, either to help Continental or to keep Eastern going as he waited for a machinists strike. Whenever he thought the showdown was near, he'd step up the fence talks with the pilots. When the confrontation didn't materialize, he'd sell off something else. "Lorenzo lost a lot of money in preparation for a strike," said Kupersmith, the Touche Ross accountant. "But he knew he would get a dividend of hundreds of millions of dollars a year in savings in the end as a payoff. So he kept waiting for a strike."

In February 1988, just weeks after Lorenzo told the pilots that he'd considered written promises to end asset sales, he launched one of the most ingenious of all his asset-shuffling schemes. As Texas Air announced that it had lost $466 million in 1987—one of the worst losses in airline history—the company announced a plan to sell the Eastern shuttle.

Lorenzo, as the "Chunks" memo showed, knew exactly how important the shuttle was to the company. After SODA, the computer reservations system, it was Eastern's best single moneymaker. Its Boston–New York–Washington corridor was one of the most lucrative routes in the country. The shuttle poured out profits of $50 million or more on sales of some $175 million. It also was one of Eastern's most vital strategic assets. Eastern's core markets lay in the Northeast. The shuttle served the very heart of this territory. It endowed Eastern with a two-decade-old brand-name presence that far outweighed its size and profits.

The proposed spin-off sent the unions into spasms. The pilots knew that such a deal would give Lorenzo several hundred million dollars to add to his war chest. He could use the money for his waiting game with the machinists, or, because he'd made off with Eastern's best assets, he could sell the rest of the carrier.

The plan also angered the unions because it was a real sweetheart deal, even better for Lorenzo than the SODA sale. As usual, the move involved a jungle of new companies. Texas Air planned to create five new entities, including two limited partnerships. The shuttle would be one partnership. It would be owned by another partnership, of which Texas Air would own 80 percent. Lorenzo recruited investors such as New York hotel magnate Donald Trump and Los Angeles billionaire Marvin Davis to take the other 20 percent. Lorenzo also convinced Bruce Nobles to quit his job as president of the rival Pan Am shuttle and go to work for the Eastern shuttle, offering him equity in the deal, too. For parting with its crown jewel, Eastern would get $225 million, of which $100 million was in the form of a note. Analysts thought the shuttle was worth twice that much.

The proposed setup brought several other benefits, too. Because Texas Air would own less than 80 percent of the shuttle, it wouldn't have to pay all of the taxes that a lucrative operation like the shuttle would rack up. Nor would the shuttle be liable if Eastern was shoved into bankruptcy. This was important, because Eastern's pension liabilities were so large that paying them off could require the sale of juicy assets like the shuttle. As an added sweetener, Jet Capital was to get 5 percent of the shuttle for its investment-banking services.

To further anger the unions, word of Eastern's contract with Orion Air leaked out just as news of the shuttle plan broke. The pilots union members who might have been willing to forsake the machinists for a fence deal were furious at the notion of Lorenzo spending millions of dollars a month so he could have nonunion strikebreakers on hand to replace them. No longer could Lorenzo take it for granted that most pilots would fly through a strike.

The unions sued on the shuttle and Orion deals—and won.

On March 10, Judge Pratt, who had ruled on the IAM baggage handlers, sided with the unions on the shuttle, pointing out that the spin-off was another form of the same basic plan he had enjoined the company against in his prior ruling. He slapped Texas Air with a contempt-of-court citation for violation of his former order. In a final hearing two weeks later, Pratt chastised Eastern for "its deliberate and intentional conduct" in violating his previous order. He told both Lorenzo and Bakes, Eastern's president, to write letters to all Eastern employees informing them about his contempt citation. Pratt even ordered the company to pay the union's legal fees.

Although the deal was dead, Lorenzo still got his licks in. Eastern paid $3.55 million to Texas Air and $1.5 million to Jet Capital for expenses in the failed deal. Not only had Lorenzo tried to grab Eastern's best remaining asset at a giveaway price, when he got caught, he had Eastern pay his other companies fees for having failed to pull the stunt off.

In the Orion case, the pilots union argued that under its labor contract, only union members could fly Eastern planes. On March 29, Judge Barrington D. Parker in Washington, D.C., hit the company with a temporary restraining order, preventing it from using Eastern planes to train non-Eastern pilots. This was a major victory. With no alternate means of keeping Eastern's planes aloft in a pilot walkout, Lorenzo, who couldn't risk having Eastern shut down like Continental at a time when the hiring market was plagued by growing pilot shortages, now had little choice but to buy off the pilots.

The unions kept up the pressure. They demanded that the FAA and Congress take a close look at Orion. After months of pressure, the FAA finally did investigate. It found a company whose safety program and training standards were in disarray. Many pilots were training with home-study courses rather than ground-school classes, which is against regulations. Lorenzo realized that the negative publicity would further damage Eastern's already dubious standing with passengers. Eastern announced that it was canceling its Orion contracts because it no longer expected the pilots to strike.

Meanwhile, the unions had thrown Lorenzo another legal curveball. Back in January, they had filed a petition with the mediation board to have Eastern and Continental declared a single carrier for labor-relations purposes. The unions argued that even though Texas Air treated the two companies as separate entities, Lorenzo was calling the shots for both in terms of labor negotiations. Because of this, they claimed, the unions should have one bargaining unit for each employee group at both airlines. By April, it had become clear that Texas Air would have to take the suit seriously.

This was a risky maneuver. If the NMB agreed, new union representation elections would be held involving all the employees at both airlines. Since Continental and Eastern had about the same number of employees after all the layoffs at Eastern, it was conceivable that the unions could lose if all the Continental employees voted against them. Many Continental employees were extremely dissatisfied with their jobs. But they were also the same strikebreakers who had been spit on by pilots at other airlines. It was a big question whether their hatred for Lorenzo outweighed their resentment of such treatment. And if the unions lost, they'd lose everything. They wouldn't represent employees at either Continental or Eastern. Lorenzo would have a union-free empire.

If they won, however, Lorenzo would be dealt a devastating blow. Continental, the only major nonunion carrier in the industry, again would be unionized. The suit also turned the tables on Lorenzo's asset-shifting, which now could be used as evidence that he really was running both airlines as one.

As an added benefit to the unions, the single-carrier suit stalled the negotiations at Eastern. Bryan knew he couldn't win a strike, and that it still was possible that the pilots might not honor his picket lines. The longer a strike could be delayed, the more cash Lorenzo would lose. "If we won, we might have to go back to square one and start the whole bargaining process all over again, because there would be more than just Eastern employees to bargain for," said Joseph Guerrieri, a lawyer for the machinists who helped to file the petition.

Texas Air, which kept up a good face throughout all the legal setbacks, was hurting badly. Despite the profits Eastern earned in the first six months of 1987, the constant asset sales and tough market conditions produced huge losses in the second half of the year. The resulting record loss for 1987 had nearly dried up its operating cash, and the company had been forced to borrow $200 million from the capital markets in February 1988. Knowing they couldn't go to the public for funds, Texas Air's investment bankers tried to sell notes to private individuals. After weeks of trying, Eastern managed to raise $200 million. But it had to pay 17.25-percent interest, more than twice the prime rate and an indication that Wall Street was losing faith in its golden boy.

By May 1988, Continental still was not making enough money to cover its expenses. Eastern's losses weren't improving, either. Worse yet, the public was becoming as nervous as Wall Street about whether the labor strife was jeopardizing safety. Passenger traffic fell 26 percent in May alone. The courts had blocked Lorenzo from selling assets to keep going. Most important of all, Bryan and the mediation board wouldn't permit Lorenzo to engage in the showdown strike he had geared up for. One day in June, aboard the seven A.M. Eastern shuttle flight from New York to Washington, Lorenzo expressed his frustrations. "If I had known that these negotiations were going to drag on and on like this, I never would have bought Eastern," he said.

Lorenzo had to change his tack. He developed a two-track approach. First, he would try to get the mediation board to declare an impasse with the machinists. Walter Wallace, who recently had taken over as chairman of the board and was in charge of the Eastern negotiations for it, had kept telling him that he wasn't bargaining in good faith because he wouldn't change his demands. It was time for Lorenzo to show a little good faith.

In case that didn't work, Lorenzo ordered as a backup another plan for a drastic downsizing of Eastern. This time, however, his reasons went beyond just showing the unions who was boss. Texas Air was bouncing on empty. It had to sell off more assets to raise cash. And it had to sell a lot. "The ability to downsize Eastern is easy," said a senior Texas Air officer in late June. "The whole plan is in place. It calls for selling up to 50 planes initially, and possibly 100 within a year. Lorenzo wants a settlement with the unions. But it has to be done quick or the airline will lose its ass. Lorenzo has to decide by around the end of July, because that's when the fall schedules go to travel agents."

In June, Lorenzo started his good-faith demonstration for the mediation board with John Peterpaul, the machinists transportation boss. Very quietly, Lorenzo called Peterpaul. "The first thing he told me was he wanted to get together and see if we couldn't settle the issue," Peterpaul said shortly thereafter. "That raised me off my chair six feet. But I said that Bryan had to be there and that we wouldn't talk about the specific negotiation issues. I know he wants to use me to go to the [mediation board] and say we're at impasse. But as soon as I insisted on Charlie coming, we began haggling about where to meet. I suggested a restaurant, but he refused. Finally, we ended up at a private club in Washington, where Lorenzo usually stays. He wouldn't meet in a public place, because he didn't want to be seen with Charlie."

Lorenzo didn't mind not talking specifics, however. If he did, the unions could use it against him in the single-carrier case to show that he was managing labor relations for both carriers. The three men met and talked for three hours. Soon after, Eastern's bargaining position began to change. Instead of cutting newly hired machinists from $9 an hour to $5, management offered to cut them to $6.50. Before, Eastern had demanded that top baggage handlers, who made $15.60 an hour, be cut to $10 right away, then $9 a year later, and then $8 in the third year. Now, the company offered to drop the second two years and just cut them to $10.

All told, Eastern asked for $150 million in annual concessions from the machinists. The number sounded much lower than the $265 million or so that Eastern had asked for on the day official bargaining started in October 1987. Most of the reduction, however, came because the company's asset sales and route shutdowns had cut the machinists' workforce by more than 3,000 people. Thus, the same percentage cuts of up to 40 percent were spread over fewer people, which lowered the total dollar amount of savings to the company.

In return, Eastern offered a variety of relatively minor job guarantees. Lorenzo also mulled over the idea of even stronger ones. "There are about 10,000 [machinists union] members now," said a Lorenzo advisor. "He's thinking of covering 85 to 90 percent of them. The others wouldn't necessarily be laid off, but they could be cut in bad times."

Next, Lorenzo quietly called Bavis and asked for a meeting to restart the fence talks aimed at protecting pilot jobs. Here he made the offer even better. All along, Eastern had demanded $114 million in savings from the pilots, including a 12-percent pay cut. Now, it dropped the pay cut, which was worth about $30 million. Lorenzo also offered to put the fence around 240 of Eastern's 260 remaining planes.

After almost two years, it looked like a resolution might really be at hand. "I think it's doable," Wallace, the mediation board chairman, said at the time. "It's pretty clear what Lorenzo wants, to reduce labor costs. And it's clear what the unions want, to be assured that the airline will be around. It's not a simple step, however, how to translate into specifics. We're not there yet."

The unions remained deeply suspicious. Bryan and Peterpaul knew that Lorenzo was champing at the bit for a showdown. They feared that Lorenzo was trying to lure them into a discussion so he could run to Wallace for a strike date. Bryan was willing to talk. But he didn't intend just to accept Lorenzo's new proposal without any debate. He wanted to do what would be normal in any labor talks: negotiate.

"They are still taking very draconian positions on the economic issues," said Bryan not long after he and Peterpaul met with Lorenzo. "And they're still advocating a lot of issues that would gut the union contract, like contracting out our work. Basically, they just moved off of the future cuts and they knew damn well they wouldn't get those all along. Those were just throwaway demands in the first place. And I don't know of any job guarantees. All they do is talk to me in generalities. My position is that we already have guarantees and they don't guarantee anything."

Bavis still felt burned from the fence talks earlier in the year, which had melted away when Lorenzo realized that he didn't need the pilots quite then. Now, he wanted to make sure he got two things. First, if Eastern and Continental were merged, either by Texas Air or by mediation board decision on the single-carrier case, Lorenzo had to recognize the pilots union without an actual election if it collected a majority of pilot signatures.

Second, Bavis wanted all of Eastern's parent companies to guarantee the fence agreement. That way, Lorenzo couldn't wriggle out of the deal later on through some clever corporate manipulation. "Under law, a merger with Continental would make our guarantees disappear," said Bavis during the discussions that summer. "So we won't do a fence with just Eastern, and Lorenzo's resisting doing one with Jet Capital and Texas Air. We need commitments from them. This is a deal-stopper."

These demands put Lorenzo in a dilemma. For one thing, if Texas Air guaranteed Eastern's jobs and later hit turbulence, it would have to lay off Continental pilots instead of Eastern ones. "Frank made a commitment to Continental pilots who came to work during the strike," said a top Texas Air executive during the talks. "He'll have a problem with them if he signs guarantees with Eastern."

All this came to a head when, in the middle of these discussions, Bavis was called to testify in the single-carrier case. He told of his meetings with Lorenzo on the fence talks. Texas Air officials, feeling he had betrayed a confidence, exploded. "They blew up because Bavis talked about what they thought was a private meeting," said one Texas Air insider. "It's not just Frank, but the guys around him, too. Now it's an emotional issue, because they feel they can't trust the unions. I think they're so close to a deal that it would be tragic to let extraneous events misdirect them."

The labor talks collapsed, but not from the flareup. The real problem was Wallace and the mediation board. Lorenzo felt that he wouldn't get enough money from the pilots alone to forgo the downsizing he had planned as a backup. He wanted the machinists' cuts, too. He didn't intend to sign any fence deal with the pilots until Wallace gave a clear sign that he would declare an impasse.

Wallace probably would have gone along if Lorenzo had played the game the way most airline managers do. But the two men had completely different ideas of what constituted bargaining. By this stage, Eastern and the machinists had been negotiating for six months under the guidance of Bickford, the mediation board mediator. Almost all of the 2,000 initial company demands for contract changes had been resolved. Most were relatively minor points compared to the wage and benefit cuts; in resolving these points, Bryan had agreed to give up about $9 million to $12 million a year. Now only the big issues were left. Lorenzo thought he'd moved plenty by lowering his demands to $150 million a year, but Wallace saw that as nothing more than an opening gambit. He expected the two sides to meet somewhere in the middle, as almost always happens in any labor negotiation.

But Lorenzo already had gone farther than he wanted. His new $150 million offer was Eastern's first formal stance in the negotiations. It was also his final offer. Lorenzo, who made little effort to pretend that the company really expected a settlement, figured that he'd done more than enough to satisfy the mediation board. Now, he thought, if he insisted that the two sides were deadlocked, he'd force Wallace into starting the 30-day clock. Instead, he angered Wallace by acting as if Eastern didn't have to bargain like any other airline. The mediation board chairman held Lorenzo's feet to the fire to try to force a compromise.

Lorenzo's hard line backfired in another way. Because Eastern formally called the $150 million demand its final offer, the law said that Bryan didn't have to make a final offer from the union. If Bryan had, he would have had to suggest a tremendous cut, like $50 million or so, to demonstrate real movement to the mediation board and avoid a declaration of impasse. Instead, Bryan was allowed to say that he would put Eastern's final offer out for a membership vote.

At first, Eastern officials could barely contain themselves. Bryan's move came late at night in mid-July. Bakes, Eastern's president, was on the phone early the next morning, calling the media in exultation. "We got a final settlement offer late last night from the [machinists]," he crowed excitedly. "What I hope is that there will be a deadline" from the mediation board, he added.

But Bryan fooled them. He stalled for time by delaying the membership vote. Within weeks, Texas Air's financial crisis forced Lorenzo's hand. Only two weeks after Eastern's final offer, before a vote date had even been set, Lorenzo moved ahead with his contingency plan to downsize Eastern. On July 22, the company announced that it was closing its Kansas City hub and eliminating flights to 14 cities. The move wiped out another 4,000 jobs, or about 12 percent of Eastern's workforce.

If any union leader had thought that the thousands of jobs already cut were just pinpricks, this time there was no mistake: Lorenzo was cutting bone. And not just union bone. Eastern as an airline now was being damaged seriously. Borman had opened the Kansas City hub years ago in an effort to offset Eastern's reliance on Florida tourist traffic. It and the hub in Atlanta were part of the reason that Eastern was more than just a regional East Coast carrier. Bakes acknowledged the extent of the damage and tried to put a positive spin on it by saying that Eastern was "returning to its roots."

The severity of the move shocked employees and observers alike. Wall Street analysts and the media began to talk openly about how long Eastern would be viable as an airline. Even Borman, who had been vigorously supporting Lorenzo's efforts to break the machinists, conceded that Eastern was being gutted, although he placed the blame on the unions. "The thing is being dismembered," he said. "The core of Eastern was Atlanta, which is why we opened a hub in Kansas City. But Lorenzo only got out because of the high union costs."

At this point, Lorenzo had done little but chop up the airline he had been so pleased to acquire. The 260-plane fleet he had bought had been reduced to 200. Eastern now flew 1,000 flights a day compared to almost 1,500 before the sale. The number of employees had fallen from more than 42,000 to 29,000. Essentially, Lorenzo had brought a corporate raider's mentality to bear on the running of a company. Most takeover artists are interested in buying and selling companies, not in running them. Lorenzo wanted to run Eastern. But to cut costs, he was willing to sell off hunks of the company and lay off thousands of workers, even if it meant butchering the very asset he was trying to run.

From a strategic point of view, Lorenzo's approach made little sense. Virtually every manager in the airline industry operates on the same maxim: Size breeds success. American, Delta, United, and other carriers had all dealt with the trauma of deregulation by building powerhouse carriers whose market dominance would generate profits in excess of the cost-per-seat mile. Lorenzo himself often repeated the view that he wanted to achieve sufficient "critical mass" to compete in the deregulated marketplace. Indeed, that's why he purchased People Express, Frontier Airlines, and Eastern.

At Eastern, Lorenzo's judgment became clouded by his fanatical hatred of labor unions. Despite all his complaints about high labor costs, it's not at all clear that Eastern needed to do much about them when Lorenzo took over in 1986. When combined with Joe Leonard's cost-cutting of that year, the 20-percent cuts given by the pilots and flight attendants the night the company was sold had put Eastern into the black almost immediately. In the last six months of 1986 and the first six of 1987, the carrier turned a profit. Eastern only started to spill red ink again after Lorenzo began cutting. Every time Lorenzo sold routes or planes or airport gates, Eastern became less able to cover its overhead. In the beginning, most of the asset sales or shifts to Continental were done to help Texas Air and to bludgeon Eastern's unions. By 1988, Lorenzo was acting out of necessity. Texas Air needed money.

This could have been a defensible strategy. Eastern's price-sensitive routes didn't enable the company to sustain its debt

91

load during normal market fluctuations; selling off some assets might have paid down the debt. Instead, Lorenzo used the proceeds from asset sales to fund the remaining operations while he waited for a union showdown. As a result, debt and expenses grew larger in proportion to the shrinking asset base. Lorenzo was burning up the furniture to heat the house.

The economic foolhardiness of Eastern's downsizing is revealed by comparing its passenger loads with its costs. Analysts use what they call available-seat miles (ASMs) to judge an airline's costs on a unit basis. This is a measure of the total number of miles an airline's planes can fly, multiplied by the total number of seats it has available to be sold. From February 1986, when the pilots and flight attendants took 20-percent pay cuts, to the end of that year, Eastern's costs plummeted, from 8.8¢ per ASM to 7.4¢ per ASM. Its capacity grew at the same time, from 14 billion ASMs to nearly 15 billion.

In 1987, within months after Lorenzo took official control, the picture changed. Over that year and the next, the steady sale and closure of assets slashed ASMs to 11 billion. This downsizing produced a relentless upsurge in costs, from 7.4¢ per ASM to more than 9.6¢ by the end of 1988.

The more capacity Lorenzo cut, the higher Eastern's unit costs rose. Finally, in a sort of self-fulfilling prophecy, the company became as sick and unprofitable as Lorenzo had alleged it was to begin with.

Nor was the downsizing a haphazard reaction to the battle with labor. The six scenarios Lorenzo had drawn up in January 1988 spoke volumes. The least drastic outcome called for an Eastern at 60 percent of its original capacity. From the beginning, he never seemed to have contemplated keeping the company at the size it was when he bought it. What's more, all six scenarios shared a common outcome: they all predicted a critical cash-flow problem by June 1988, three months after the April date when Lorenzo expected a strike. As he well knew, cutting back operations would precipitate a financial crisis, even without a strike.

Closing Kansas City was a turning point. If there had been any inkling of a compromise before, it disappeared like a mirage on a desert road. The unions rushed back to Judge Parker to stop the move. Parker, the judge who had ruled on the Orion contracts, had some harsh words for Lorenzo. "The record shows that Eastern has served as a lending institution to meet the needs of Texas Air and Continental." Parker blocked the 4,000 layoffs, ruling that the action had to be negotiated first with the unions.

In September, Bryan finally held the vote on Eastern's offer. Outraged members rejected it by 98 percent. Union leaders felt a bitter vindication. They had thought all along that Lorenzo's new cuddly image was merely a ploy intended to play to the mediation board. The closing of Kansas City had justified that view. Any thread of hope that Lorenzo would bargain or compromise now vanished into thin air.

By this stage, Lorenzo's ruthless behavior had built up such an extraordinary degree of mistrust that many members no longer believed a word he said. They wouldn't have voted for his new offer if Bryan had got down on his knees and begged them to.

Eastern stumbled along through the summer as it appealed Parker's ruling on Kansas City. In the fall, it got lucky and wound up with conservative judges on the U.S. Court of Appeals in Washington, who allowed the layoffs to go ahead. But by then, however, it was too late. None of Texas Air's airlines were doing any better, and with losses mounting daily, Lorenzo had to act again. This time, there were few alternatives. A major hub was gone and the carrier had been cut to the point where it stood a slim chance of ever being rebuilt to its former size.

CHAPTER SIX
Labor Looks for a White Knight

From the day Lorenzo bought Eastern, the unions began looking for an outside investor to help them purchase the company from Texas Air. Although this was an unusual role for organized labor to play, by 1986 the airline unions had begun to learn the ropes in the capital markets. The pilots union in particular had developed a modicum of expertise in using concession-funded employee stock ownership plans (ESOP) to wrest control away from managers it didn't like. Within days of the February 1986 sale to Lorenzo, the union leaders took their first stab at an Eastern buyout.

The plan was simple. The government had to approve the sale before Eastern stockholders could vote on the board of directors' decision. The unions knew that if they found a higher offer, the board could be forced to reverse its decision. It was a long shot, however, because Lorenzo had demanded several lockup provisions that gave him almost certain control over 35 percent of Eastern's stock, even if the sale fell through.

To challenge these clauses in court, the unions needed another buyer, to present the judge and Eastern stockholders with a concrete alternative. They also hoped that a fresh face would give the directors a graceful way to change their minds.

After all, everyone knew that the sale had been a blunder, a confrontation that got out of hand and spawned an outcome that no one, including most board members, really wanted.

"I started immediately looking for a buyer that March," says Bavis, the pilots union leader. The pilots still employed Gene Keilin, the banker from Lazard Frères, as well as Bruce Simon of Cohen Weiss & Simon, the New York law firm that does much of the pilot union's work. Keilin and Simon again began contacting possible buyers. They returned once more to Pritzker, the Hyatt hotels owner, who had just been negotiating with them a few days earlier about mounting a bid for Eastern to rival Lorenzo's.

The unions originally had approached Jay Pritzker through Simon, who had become friends with the Chicago millionaire when he bought Braniff, where Simon represented the pilots. In March 1986, after Bavis and Pritzker talked, Pritzker flew to Miami to meet him, Charlie Bryan, and the other union leaders. Peterpaul, the machinist official in Washington, was called in, as was Brian Freeman, Peterpaul's financial advisor.

For more than two months, the parties held secret talks. A host of ideas were tossed around. At one point, a proposal was worked up that called for the creation of a new company, called Mergerco Inc., which would buy Eastern. Mergerco would be owned in three equal parts by Pritzker, Eastern's unions, and Pan Am, which also had been brought into the deal. The plan called for Steve Wolf, a former Continental president and later the head of United Airlines, to take over as Eastern's chief executive.

The unions offered $500 million in concessions plus another $133 million from employee pension plans. A major bone of contention was how much of Eastern they would get in return. Pritzker proposed giving employees 60 percent of Eastern's stock and taking 40 percent for himself. Charlie Bryan held out for a 70-30 split. After much haggling, they got down to 65-35. Then Bryan insisted on 67.5 percent. At that point, Pritzker lost his temper and called the whole thing off. "Charlie always wanted more," said one of Pritzker's associates. "The unions had a big meeting and finally he came out and told Jay he wanted 2 percent more. So Jay said, 'Who needs this?' "

Although the deal fell apart, the unions had a firm sense of what they had to do. To fend off Lorenzo, they had to foot the bill for a buyout with deep concessions, perhaps even as drastic as those Lorenzo wanted. But they were game nonetheless. After all, employees would rid themselves of a future with Lorenzo. They'd also get a big ownership stake in their company, which Lorenzo would never give.

Bryan began exhorting his members to buy Eastern stock. He argued that the 25 percent employees already owned from the 1984 cooperation experiment gave them a head start. The unions could build off that to buy Eastern themselves through an ESOP. Even though he and Peterpaul remained ideologically opposed to the concept of ESOPs, Bryan felt driven to try anything. In late August of 1986, the Transportation Department denied Texas Air permission to go through with its purchase of Eastern. Bryan immediately called leaders of the pilots' and flight attendants' unions and asked them if they would join him in making an employee-led offer for the company. After getting their assent, Bryan, who was still an Eastern board member, made a formal proposal to the directors that said employees would pay $10.25 a share for Eastern. Although this was more than Lorenzo's $10 offer, the directors, claiming Bryan didn't speak for nonunion employees, and questioning the unions' ability to finance their offer, turned him down.

Shortly thereafter, the Transportation Department approved Texas Air's purchase of Eastern. But the unions were determined to pursue their own bid. Leaders from the three unions formed what they called the EAL Employees Coalition Acquisition Corporation, and began work on another buyout offer. They picked January 1, 1986, as the starting date for calculating how much each employee group had to contribute in concessions for a buyout. Over the next two and a half years, this became the basis for all the agreements they reached with future buyers. Then union leaders brought in several ESOP experts, including Kelso & Co., whose founder,

Louis Kelso, was the grandfather of the ESOP, and several other financial companies, to help them raise money for a bid. A flurry of activity ensued as they sought to line up loans from New York investment houses.

Eastern's board paid little attention. In October 1986, the union coalition made another offer. Two days later, Eastern directors voted Lorenzo in as chairman. Then, only two weeks before the late-November Eastern stockholders' vote that would finalize the sale to Texas Air, the unions announced that they had lined up more than $425 million in financing. Bankers Trust Company gave Kelso's company written assurances that it could raise money for a union bid. The coalition then made another offer, raising its bid to $11.50 a share in cash. Eastern's directors voted it down. Soon thereafter, Eastern's stockholders—including Texas Air, which had purchased more than 51 percent of Eastern's outstanding shares by this point—ratified the sale to Lorenzo.

The unions' desperation intensified after Lorenzo formally took over. Throughout 1987, they kept spending to hire anyone who sounded like they could help, including F. Lee Bailey, the famous trial lawyer. One of the more ironic efforts came in March 1988, when the pilots approached T. Boone Pickens, the corporate raider. Pickens had earned a name for himself— and tens of millions of dollars—by mounting hostile takeovers. Eastern's unions thought it would take someone with Pickens's reputation to fight off the likes of Lorenzo.

Pickens helped, all right, although in the end his suggestion turned out to be so risky that even Eastern's unions didn't have the stomach to try it. For $500,000, Pickens put Boone Company, his personal investment advisory company, to work on the problem. Soon he had an elaborate strategy that involved a hostile takeover not just of Eastern, but of Texas Air. The entire Lorenzo empire.

The scheme was bold to the point of foolhardiness. Lorenzo had an almost watertight lock on Texas Air through Jet Capital. Pickens told the unions that there was a chance Lorenzo's corporate safeguards had a chink. Essentially, Pickens suggested that if the unions bought almost all of the publicly held

Texas Air stock, they might be able to dilute Lorenzo's voting shares.

The risks were enormous. Lorenzo could mount a counterattack by digging into Texas Air's many pockets to bid on the open market for some of those shares himself. In addition, Texas Air's $5 billion debt meant that it already was leveraged to the hilt. The unions probably would have to borrow more to buy Texas Air, making the company even more vulnerable to failure than it already was.

Pickens suggested offering $1.2 billion for Texas Air, which would have been about double the company's stock price at the time. The unions were supposed to come up with $400 million. "Boone guaranteed a bridge loan for the $400 million until the deal was done," said Robert T. Brophy, a former pilots union official who orchestrated the Pickens deal for the unions. "He also guaranteed that he would finance the rest by getting bank loans."

The easiest place for the unions to get $400 million was their pension funds. The pilots were willing. But after much debate, the machinists decided that it was too much to ask employees to bet their retirement on such a chancy idea. Besides, Continental had entered another bad spell at the time. The unions comforted themselves with the thought that Lorenzo's financial troubles had him on the run. "We all met yesterday to hear their presentation," said Randy Barber. "Pickens wanted us to use pension funds. That was a show-stopper for the IAM."

Union leaders hit up plenty of other famous business leaders in their search for a white knight. Bavis talked to J. Willard Marriott, Jr., the head of Marriott hotels, whom Borman had approached in 1986 before Lorenzo appeared on the scene. Marriott told Bavis that he was no longer interested in buying the whole airline. However, Marriott, whose company had lost Eastern's catering contract when Lorenzo took over, said he might be interested in investing in an Eastern buyout in order to get the catering back.

It wasn't long afterward, in June of 1988, that the Eastern pilot union's office in Miami got a call from an Atlanta businessman named Larry Spivey. He said he wanted to help the unions buy Eastern from Lorenzo. Spivey talked to several pilots union officials, and eventually wound up on the line with Jack Bavis. When Spivey said that one of his associates was a friend of Lorenzo's wife Sharon, and that Sharon was pushing Frank to sell Eastern, Bavis was all ears. In no time, Spivey was on his way to Miami to talk to the unions.

The tale of Loehr H. (Larry) Spivey is one of the strangest chapters in the saga of Eastern Airlines. Union leaders knew little about him at the time and it was many months before they found out more. A small, thinly built man with a sincere air and a proclivity for saying embarrassingly personal things about himself, the 45-year-old Spivey was an unlikely candidate to become a middleman in the war between Lorenzo and labor.

"I was born in Augusta, Georgia, and lived in New York during the war when I was a very young child," Spivey said some months after he first contacted the unions. "Then we moved to Greece and then Turkey. My father was in the tobacco business and imported Turkish tobacco. I grew up in Turkey and spoke Greek and Turkish. I still speak the latter fluently. I live in Atlanta now. I'm in real estate, construction, and the electronics business. I own a few companies. I'm not rich. I could write a check for a few hundred thousand and it wouldn't break me. That's all."

Spivey left out a few colorful tidbits that he hadn't bothered union leaders with either. In his early twenties, he had been arrested on moonshining charges in Columbia, S.C. Two years later, he got five years' probation in Saluda, S.C., on a worthless-check charge. All together, he had been arrested five times, including once on felony charges for aggravated assault on Charlene Spivey, who was divorcing him at the time. He also had declared personal bankruptcy in 1973 and again in 1982.

Spivey, however, had a talent for self-promotion. In 1975, he contacted the Georgia Bureau of Investigation (GBI), a state counterpart to the FBI, saying he had been approached by two acquaintances who wanted his help in a drug-smuggling scheme. The GBI, which didn't bother to check out his background, hired him as an informer on a contract basis and twice paid him $860 for information. According to GBI officials, Spivey worked for the GBI for two months, during which he helped on two or three cases in Atlanta. Spivey claims he spent time in Guatemala, Mexico, and Jamaica in pursuit of drug-smuggling leads.

After he left the GBI, Spivey got a writer to write a book about his experiences. The result was *The Spivey Assignment: A Double Agent's Infiltration of the Drug Smuggling Conspiracy*. The book, which is full of corrupt officials, jungle airports, daredevil plots, sex, and death, reads like a fiction thriller. Spivey recounts how 18 people died during his escapades, including two assassins he killed in self-defense. In the book-jacket photo, Spivey stands framed against a heavy growth of bushes, dressed in black pants and a black turtleneck and sporting a thick beard, full-length hair, and a lightweight automatic rifle.

According to Robert Coram, a journalist at the *Atlanta Constitution* during the time Spivey's tale allegedly occurred, much of this seems to be fiction. "I was covering drug busts in Georgia at the time," says Coram, who now writes books and magazine articles. "The paper asked me to review [Spivey's] book. I got three chapters into it and said, What the fuck is this? I knew that none of the busts he claimed credit for he had done." Robert Rosenberg, who wrote Spivey's book for him, says: "It was murder getting the story out of [Spivey]. I ended up sitting down with him and saying, 'What happened next?' He came over every day, put a gun on the desk, and talked. When he was telling me about the Mexico part, he gave a very detailed description of the place. Then later he gave me an *Esquire* article about Mexico and drugs. His description came right out of that article. I don't know that anything in the book is true."

This didn't seem to bother GBI officials. As Spivey began to promote himself in New York and Washington, the GBI told inquirers that Spivey indeed had worked for the bureau. Although GBI officials later told Coram that they knew Spivey was making up tales, they said that they were pleased as punch about the positive publicity Spivey brought to their agency.

Authenticated by the GBI, Spivey talked his way before a congressional committee. In the summer of 1978, he testified before the House Subcommittee on Coast Guard and Navigation, which was investigating drug smuggling at the time. Spivey told a dramatic tale that included names of his alleged contacts, such as Henry Kissinger, fugitive Robert Vesco, and Omar Torrijos, the former president of Panama. Spivey even read the committee a letter he had written to Griffin Bell, the U.S. attorney general under President Jimmy Carter. He told representatives that the president himself was briefed on the drug snatches he had masterminded. No one seemed to notice that Carter hadn't even been president in 1975, when Spivey alleged all the intrigue took place.

Soon, Spivey was on *Good Morning America*, telling his tale to host Sandy Hill and her millions of viewers; Time-Life Films optioned the book to make a movie. In early 1979, Spivey even landed a job as an assistant producer at a movie production company in New York, although after a few weeks he was fired and physically escorted out the front door. "That was a rather melodramatic book," admits Spivey. "That was a time in my life I'd rather forget."

Nonetheless, Spivey would play a significant role in a national labor battle, helping to bring into the picture several of the dozen or so potential buyers that Eastern's unions dealt with from 1986 through 1989, including John D. Backe, a former president of CBS Inc.; former baseball commissioner Peter Ueberroth; L.A. billionaire Marvin Davis; Texas billionaire Ross Perot; and former White House chief of staff Howard Baker.

One of Spivey's first moves was to call Perot, the founder of Electronic Data Systems Company (EDS), who had sold his company to General Motors in 1986 for a staggering $2.5 billion. Spivey had called Perot out of the blue a few years earlier, when he got involved in a campaign to raise money to save Radio City Music Hall. This time, he asked if Perot wanted to help save Eastern.

Perot said the unions should call him. Bavis, whose son worked at EDS, did. Perot refused to make a bid, but he did offer the services of his advisors to help the unions devise a strategy for buying Eastern. Bavis then asked Farrell Kupersmith, the Touche Ross accountant the pilots had hired to help the union on Wall Street, to meet with J. Patrick Horner, the president of Perot Systems Corporation in McLean, Virginia. Little came of the meeting.

"Larry Spivey called me once," said Perot. "I never could figure out who he was. Then the union guys called me and said, 'Would you be our representative on [Eastern's] board?' I said, 'If you could convince me it was good for the company and the industry, I would.' It kind of drifted off after that."

Spivey didn't, however. He leveraged Perot's slight involvement to the hilt, telling everyone from Backe to the unions that Perot might be an investor. Spivey also called nearly everyone else under the sun. Every once in a while, they'd get involved, even if only to the extent Perot did. At times, the links among the players at Eastern became so intertwined that it made the British crown's family tree seem easy to follow.

For instance, Bavis told Spivey that the pilots had used the Wall Street law firm of Paul Weiss Rifkind Wharton & Garrison to assist Bruce Simon's firm, which handled most of the pilot union's legal work. One of Paul Weiss's most prominent partners is Arthur Liman, who served as the lead prosecution lawyer for Congress during the Iran-contra hearings and later became the chief counsel for key Lorenzo supporter Michael Milken. Bavis told Spivey about Paul Weiss because the firm also represented Equitable Life Assurance Society, which just happened to be the second-largest stockholder in Texas Air after Jet Capital.

Armed with this information, Spivey called Paul Weiss and arranged a meeting at the firm's New York offices with a half dozen people: Liman, Horner, Kupersmith, and Marian S. Rosen, a Houston lawyer Spivey knew who was a friend of Sharon Lorenzo. But Paul Weiss turned out to be of no more help than the Perot people. "They told us we needed Lorenzo to want to sell in order to do anything," said Bavis.

Although the advice wasn't news to the unions, it went straight to the heart of the matter. For more than two years, the iron grip of one man on the lives of 40,000 people had been a central issue in the battle of Eastern Airlines. The unions became obsessed with trying to get Lorenzo to sell out. Lorenzo, whose hold was very nearly airtight, was obsessed with breaking the unions. He also had purchased Eastern at such a good price that there was little financial incentive for him to sell.

The few times he did say he might sell, Lorenzo demanded $1 billion for Eastern, enough to let him pick up a new sister airline for Continental and preserve his dream of ruling the skies. The unions didn't have that kind of money. Nor would any sane investor pay anything near that price for a company that had lost money for most of the previous decade. In the summer of 1988, Lorenzo explained why he didn't want to sell. "Listen, Continental's net asset value is about $1 billion," he said. "Eastern's is about $3 billion. It makes no sense to sell Eastern."

The unions could do nothing but wait Lorenzo out. They knew that the mediation board's Wallace was angry with Lorenzo for not bargaining. And Texas Air's financial strains were painfully clear. Bryan's tactic was to stall at every opportunity, hoping that Lorenzo would give in before Eastern was ruined. The union leaders also hoped for intervention from Lorenzo's backers in Texas Air and on Wall Street, who might force Lorenzo to sell. As early as the beginning of 1988, they picked up fuzzy but steady signals from the financial community and from various directors of Eastern and Texas Air that some board members wanted Lorenzo to wash his hands of Eastern.

Those signals were real. Lorenzo's all-or-nothing attitude was quietly losing favor with his key backers. Because of the way Lorenzo had centralized all power in his hands, there were precious few people he felt obliged to listen to. Among his multitude of board members, only Carl Pohlad, the Minnesota Twins owner, played a key role throughout the Texas Air empire. After an initial fight with Lorenzo over Texas International, Pohlad had stuck around and become a director at

Jet Capital, Texas Air, Continental, and Eastern. The two men had become friends. After Lorenzo, Pohlad was the second-largest stockholder in Jet Capital, owning 12 percent of its shares. If Pohlad ever pulled out, Lorenzo's protective corporate armor would have a big hole in it.

The other person Lorenzo had to worry about was Drexel's Mike Milken, who had helped Lorenzo raise more than $1 billion in a blizzard of stock and bond issues. The credibility he lent to Lorenzo had as much to do with Lorenzo's golden boy status on Wall Street as anything Lorenzo did himself. Milken couldn't take away the money he had found for Texas Air. But he could make others nervous about loaning to Lorenzo.

Neither Pohlad nor Milken, who were both big fans of Lorenzo's, were the type to come out publicly and tell Lorenzo what to do. They consistently had supported him at Continental and at Eastern. But by early 1988, they were growing squeamish.

Slowly, each separately came to the conclusion that Lorenzo's single-minded desire to crush the unions was self-defeating. They worried that he was endangering his whole empire. Pohlad in particular was concerned that Lorenzo was devoting so much of Texas Air's resources to the Eastern wars that he ran the risk of dragging Continental down as well. Lorenzo was a prickly character, not the kind of guy to be pushed around. But independently of each other, both Pohlad and Milken began working on him, quietly planting the idea that he should think of getting out of Eastern if his sledgehammer could not solve the carrier's problems.

Union leaders heard enough about these maneuverings to keep their hopes up. Bryan and Bavis continued the search. The pilots even went so far as to draw up a corporate-organization chart, which they hung in their headquarters building in Miami. They put the names of pilots union friends or members in many of the organizational slots, in anticipation of the day when employees would own at least part of the company they worked for.

In the late summer of 1988, Spivey resurfaced. By now, he

had formed a company, Grandview Acquisition Corporation, as a vehicle for helping the unions buy Eastern. Grandview consisted of Spivey, Sharon Lorenzo's friend Marian Rosen, and three people Spivey knew from California, where he had lived at one point: Dr. Dennis A. Casciato and his wife, C. Joy Casciato; and Dr. Jeffrey E. Galpin. The two doctors put up about $250,000, and Spivey went looking for more investors. This became the fund used to pay Grandview's expenses. Then he began to work the phones, looking for big names to join Grandview. Spivey, who knew he needed to get all three unions working together, with each other and with him, invited them on a fishing trip.

On Labor Day weekend 1988, about two dozen people from Eastern's three unions showed up at the Marriott Courtyards hotel near the Miami Airport. They came for a party Spivey arranged. The next day, most of the crew headed down to Islamorada, one of the Florida Keys, and stepped aboard a fishing boat Spivey and the two doctors had chartered. Bavis came, bringing two other pilots union officials, as did Mary Jane Barry, the new leader of the flight attendants. Bryan showed up with his daughter and granddaughter.

Spivey handed out T-shirts that said: MY HAT'S IN THE RING. It was a nice touch. Eastern employees got a kick of nostalgia from the slogan, which had been favored by the famous former chairman of Eastern, Eddie Rickenbacker. The group headed out into the keys and spent the day fishing. They caught 33 fish, mostly snapper, and talked with Spivey and his partners about how to buy Eastern.

"We kind of fell in love with the union guys," Spivey said not long after the fishing trip as he sat in the restaurant of the New York Marriott Marquis, proudly displaying snapshots of the fishing trip. "We got emotionally wrapped up in what the unions want to do. I was never much of a fan of organized labor and I'm not sure I am now. But I like Charlie. He got a divorce 12 years ago that didn't work. He's been dating Rita [his former wife] ever since. I got divorced 15 years ago and I'm remarrying my former wife next Saturday. Charlie's coming to the wedding, in Atlanta, and so are a lot of the other union guys. Charlie also had cancer seven or eight years ago, and so did I. All of this brought us together."

"The fishing trip," Spivey added, "was the first time the leaders of all three unions got together. I got everybody in the same boat rowing together in the same direction."

It wasn't long before Spivey had union leaders in sometimes ridiculous situations. In October, he held a party for about a dozen union officials and their wives at the Marriott Marquis to introduce them to Grandview's officers. Spivey announced that he was taking everyone to dinner at Sardi's, a New York restaurant famous for its theater clientele. Afterward, they would go to *The Phantom of the Opera*, the hottest play in town. Spivey, using Grandview funds, paid $200 apiece for scalped tickets for the sold-out show. Buzz Wright, the pilot leader who often had played a buffer role between Charlie Bryan and Jack Bavis, remained in the suite Spivey had rented at the Marriott, drinking gin and tonics. "We had to give his ticket away literally to someone in front of the theater," said Spivey.

Difficult as it was for the union leaders to figure Spivey out—they knew nothing of his background at this stage—he did seem to be connected to Lorenzo. Marian Rosen, the lawyer whom Spivey knew from Houston, was good friends with Sharon Lorenzo, and had agreed to help him pursue the idea of arranging a purchase of Eastern. In the spring of 1988, she had called Sharon to run the idea by her. Not long after, Frank called her back. He told Rosen that Eastern wasn't officially for sale, but that a sale might be possible, in the right circumstances. Two weeks later, Rosen got a call from Stephen D. Susman, a lawyer at the Houston law firm of Susman, Godfrey & McGowan that did work for Lorenzo. Susman's wife, Karen, had worked with Rosen at one stage, and the couple was good friends with Rosen. He told her that Lorenzo had said that it was okay for her to try to put together a purchase, but only under two conditions: that her group didn't talk to Eastern's creditors; and that they didn't enter negotiations with the unions.

Rosen's conversations convinced the doctors to put up seed

money for Grandview. Her talks also sold the union leaders on Grandview. After several rounds of meetings with Spivey, Rosen, and the doctors, the unions agreed to work with Grandview. Spivey then began scouring the country for investors willing to join labor in a buyout of Eastern. He also was on the prowl for airline executives who would give the company credibility if Lorenzo agreed to sell.

Meanwhile, the other union players were still busy working up buyers, too. One of the most serious was Brian Freeman, Peterpaul's financial consultant. A Harvard MBA who spearheaded the Chrysler bailout in 1979, Freeman began working for Peterpaul in 1982, helping him in labor negotiations and in financial deals in railroads and airlines. Along the way, he had come to know Carl C. Icahn, the chairman of TWA. The IAM represented the machinists at TWA, who in 1988 were in the midst of their own labor talks. Around Labor Day, while everyone else was fishing, Freeman suggested to Icahn that he ought to consider buying Eastern to merge with TWA.

The idea was fraught with difficulties. To begin with, Icahn and Lorenzo had a combative history with each other. Their feud dated back to 1985, when Icahn, who had made his money as a corporate raider, tried to buy TWA. When the carrier's board rebuffed him, Texas Air jumped into the bidding. Lorenzo actually signed a tentative agreement that would have given him 100% of the company. But TWA's unions were so anxious to ward off Lorenzo that they offered Icahn $300 million a year in concessions to help him outbid Lorenzo. Icahn agreed. Then he went to Lorenzo and offered to step out of the picture if Texas Air would buy Icahn's stock in TWA for a $12 million premium. Lorenzo countered with an offer of $5 million, but Icahn turned him down. They went around several more times, with Icahn raising his price on each occasion and Lorenzo getting increasingly angry. In the end, Icahn snatched TWA out from under the very nose of an outraged Lorenzo.

But the basic notion of merging TWA and Eastern made sense. In fact, Borman had thought of the same thing in 1985. Icahn also liked the idea. The media and Wall Street had

107

heaped abuse on Icahn because they assumed that he had little interest in actually running a company. They predicted that he would rip apart TWA and sell off the pieces for a profit. But Icahn never seemed to make up his mind what he wanted to do with TWA. First he looted the till by taking out $468 million in cash. Then he began to make gestures toward building up the carrier. Critics still charged that he planned to dress the airline up so he could sell it. And people who worked for him agreed that he'd sell in a minute if the price was right. But Icahn himself insisted that he wanted to keep TWA. He seemed thrilled with the glamour of owning an airline. Right after he won the battle to buy TWA, he donned the flight jacket of Harry R. Hoaglander, then head of TWA's pilot union, and danced around the room.

But TWA needed help if it was to be built up. The carrier had been an industry loser for years. Most analysts said it needed to be merged with another airline to make it stronger. Eastern was a perfect fit. TWA flew primarily east-west routes across the country and international routes to Europe. Eastern flew north-south routes and to many northeastern cities that were gateways to Europe. Like most airlines, TWA makes most of its money in the summer, when people take vacations across the country or overseas. Eastern's moneymaking season is the winter, when people on the East Coast fly to Florida and the Caribbean. Combining their operations would offset the cyclical performance slumps of each airline, and Eastern would feed passengers to TWA's overseas routes. The two airlines would complement each other.

Icahn decided to pursue the idea. On September 13, 1988, he called Bryan and then Peterpaul to sound them out. Icahn asked Bryan to fly to New York for lunch the next day, which he did. Icahn also called Lorenzo. At first, Lorenzo told Icahn to stay out of Eastern's labor situation. Lorenzo didn't want anyone giving the unions the idea that there was a savior out there who could help them buy the company. He knew a serious bidder would prompt them to stall negotiations even longer. Then he'd never get the mediation board to declare the cooling-off period.

A week later, Lorenzo called back and gave Icahn his approval to work out a deal with the unions. He even gave Icahn Bryan's home phone number. Labor leaders were ecstatic. At long last, Lorenzo had given a tangible sign that he might release his grip.

By early October, a complex series of negotiations were under way involving six union groups. For TWA to buy Eastern, Icahn and Eastern's three unions had to agree on the level of concessions employees would give, and how the ownership of the new company would be structured. TWA's three unions, which already held some TWA stock, also had to reach agreements with Icahn. Then Icahn and Lorenzo had to agree on a price.

The talks were tortuously intricate. The machinists and the pilots both represented the same groups at Eastern and TWA, but Eastern flight attendants were members of the Transport Workers Union, while those at TWA belong to the International Federation of Flight Attendants. The TWA attendants had been on strike since March 1986, after Icahn took control of the company, slashed their wages, and hired 20-year-old replacements at about $11,000 a year. Icahn already had been asking for concessions from his machinists, whose contract was due to expire at the end of the year. They were extremely suspicious of Icahn's intentions. Any merger of TWA and Eastern would involve pay cuts by the machinists at Eastern. The machinists at TWA suspected that Icahn was just using the merger idea to put the squeeze on them, too.

In addition, TWA's pilots were suing Icahn in the Supreme Court of New York. The pilots felt Icahn had reneged on a promise he had made to rebuild TWA. Though they were willing to accept less pay in exchange for stock, they weren't desperate like their brethren at Eastern.

By the weekend of October 8, Icahn was closing in on a deal with the machinists and pilots. Eastern's unions had agreed to come up with about $200 million in annual concessions. Bryan knew that the other two labor groups still resented the machinists for not taking cuts when the company was sold to Lorenzo—not to mention his refusal to do so during the battles with Borman in 1983—so he agreed that his members would take a majority of this cut. Privately, he thought this would amount to about $125 million. But the union leaders decided to wait until they had a real deal before they got more specific about exactly how to split up the concession.

In return for the $200 million, Icahn promised them stock in a company composed of a merged TWA and Eastern. TWA's unions already held 10 percent of their company's stock. He was vague about how much he would offer to Eastern's unions, primarily talking about something on the order of a 20-percent stake. Icahn agreed to the TWA machinists' demand for $3-an-hour raises, although they hadn't settled whether it would be in stock or cash. Either way, it would bring them in line with the $20 an hour that the union's mechanics had just won at United and Northwest. Icahn added to the bait by saying that he intended to take Eastern and TWA private after he merged the two airlines. Then in a few years, he'd sell shares to the public again and the unions could do the same. If the airline prospered, the employees would make a killing. "It looked like a very good deal for us," said Bryan.

"You could just see the dollar signs rolling around in Charlie Bryan's head," said one participant. "He no longer had any interest in Lorenzo."

Early on the evening of Sunday, October 9, Lorenzo placed another phone call—a very secret call, to Charlie Bryan. It was the first time he ever had talked with his chief adversary. Lorenzo told Bryan that he wanted to start a dialogue about alternatives at Eastern. Lorenzo called back the next morning. Bryan told him that an employee buyout remained his primary interest. Lorenzo seemed willing to go along with a sale. But he said that a deal had to be worked out fast, in 24 hours.

Icahn and the unions negotiated like crazy. They didn't finish in one day, but by the end of the week they were inches away from an agreement. Bryan and Bavis flew to New York with Randy Barber, Freeman, and other union leaders, where they entered intensive discussions with Icahn and his representatives. William O'Driscoll, the machinist leader at TWA, negotiated with Icahn on Friday at Icahn's sumptuous offices in Mt. Kisco, N.Y.

On Saturday, October 15, Icahn announced abruptly that the deal was off. The union leaders insisted they had reached a workable compromise. Icahn claimed, however, that there had been a misunderstanding between the two sides: no agreement had been close, he said. In reality, he was just engaged in more of the brinksmanship bargaining that had made him millions as a raider. He was playing poker both with labor and with Lorenzo.

Icahn brought the unions right to the edge of an agreement in order to sound out their true bottom line in terms of what they'd give up in concessions and how much stock they expected in return. These readings told him how expensive it would be for him to run Eastern. Icahn knew that if he told Lorenzo the truth about how much the unions were willing to offer, the Texas Air chairman would hold out for a higher price. So Icahn broke off the talks at the last minute and then made his move.

Icahn offered Lorenzo $350 million for Eastern and part of System One, the reservation system Lorenzo had stripped away. This wasn't a bad price, given the $256 million Lorenzo had paid for the airline and the hundreds of millions of dollars in assets that Texas Air already had walked off with. Lorenzo, however, held out for $800 million to $1 billion. Icahn tried to talk him down, saying that the unions were asking for too much. The two men haggled over the price, using the union talks as a bargaining chip. "I was sure I could have pulled off a deal with the unions," said Icahn. "But I wanted to get a deal with Lorenzo first. He started at big numbers, but eventually came down quite a bit."

Lorenzo had his own game going, too. While Icahn was shuffling the deck, Texas Air quietly had put the Eastern shuttle on the block again. An appeals court had overruled Judge Pratt's blockage of the earlier shuttle spin-off effort, so Lorenzo felt free to try again. This time, however, Lorenzo proposed an outright sale. He went back to Donald Trump, who had been one of the original partners in the aborted spin-off idea. Even though Texas Air had tried to walk off with the shuttle for $225 million, Trump was willing to pay $365 million. All of a sudden, Lorenzo had a much stronger hand to play against Icahn.

Now there were three card sharks sitting at the table. Icahn might have carried the day if he ponied up the $1 billion or so Lorenzo demanded for all of Eastern. But the TWA boss wouldn't offer even half that amount. The airline industry knew no two sharper-eyed dealers than Icahn and Lorenzo. Neither would compromise on a price in the middle. Lorenzo, who desperately needed cash for his faltering empire, pushed ahead with the sale of the shuttle to Trump. "Lorenzo and Icahn were highly antagonistic," said one intermediary. "Icahn played the part of a spoiler, because he wanted to see Lorenzo come apart at the seams. And they're both greedy beyond belief."

On Monday, October 17, Bryan called Icahn, who told him that TWA had dropped the idea of a purchase. The machinist leader called Lorenzo to continue their discussion about alternatives for Eastern.

To Bryan's surprise, Lorenzo asked him to come to Houston the following day for dinner. Bryan agreed. The two met for three hours. Bryan said he still wanted employees to buy the company. Lorenzo discussed the idea. He also suggested that there might be a way to give the unions stock in return for cuts. Lorenzo even managed a warm arm-around-the-shoulder gesture as the two left the restaurant.

Lorenzo swore Bryan to secrecy about the talks. The machinist leader dutifully kept his side of the bargain and never breathed a word to the media. Bryan habitually played his cards too close to the vest to do that, anyway. But word did leak out. The next day, Lorenzo was asked to confirm the story; he had a fit. "Damn, how did you find out about that?" he demanded. "Did Charlie tell you?" After he calmed down, he said: "I know Charlie didn't tell you. I know him better than that. Charlie has done a lot of good for his members. I'm hopeful we can work something out. I'm optimistic. I sense from all parties that they want a settlement. The odds of the unions putting something serious together are low, in terms of a buyout. We're not talking about a buyout or a sale to the unions. We could do something that might involve giving the unions stock. But I'd still be in control. Selling Eastern doesn't make sense. [After the shuttle sale], Eastern now has a lot of cash to begin the rebuilding process."

It was the first time Lorenzo had met with Bryan since the union leader had sent him a telegram more than two and a half years earlier, asking to talk. This may not sound like a big deal, but it was. To begin with, Lorenzo had bungled his relationship with Bryan. Lorenzo got off the phone and immediately called Bryan to tell him the news was out. But Bryan remained suspicious for months thereafter that Lorenzo had done the leaking himself, just to let the mediation board know that progress was being made. In addition, Bryan was embarrassed. Earlier in the day he had denied the meeting. Now he felt that Lorenzo had made him look like a liar.

More important to Lorenzo was the potential impact the dinner might have on the single-carrier case. It was one thing for Texas Air's boss to call Peterpaul and discuss generalities, as he had done in the summer. Peterpaul was a high union official who stayed out of the nitty-gritty bargaining until the very end. If Bryan accompanied Peterpaul at some of the meetings, Lorenzo could argue that such informal contacts didn't mean he was engaging in labor talks at Eastern. But this time he had been talking directly to the local labor leader. This was direct involvement, potentially damaging evidence that Lorenzo was in charge of labor relations at both of his airlines.

The single-carrier case was only half the problem. Lorenzo and his management squad from Continental had spent years psyching up Eastern's supervisors and midlevel managers for combat with the machinists. They had turned Bryan into the bogeyman. Now Lorenzo was chumming up to the guy. "I can tell you that the morale of Eastern's management went from zero to minus-50 when they heard that Bryan met with Lorenzo," said a close advisor of the Texas Air chief. "They thought Lorenzo had caved in. They feared that Lorenzo would

113

do the same as Borman did, and back down. In a traditional labor situation, you don't have the chairman and chief executive officer of the company negotiating with the lodge president in an adversarial relationship."

Phil Bakes, Eastern's president, conceded the same thing a few days later, although he tried to put a positive spin on the affair. "Talking to Bryan isn't Lorenzo caving in," he argued. "It should be looked at as a positive thing, not somebody wins or loses. I got a lot of feedback from managers here about the talks. But I take people talking as a good sign."

In the end, the talks between Bryan and Lorenzo led nowhere. The battles with labor never stopped, and Texas Air continued its sale negotiations. Icahn and Lorenzo sparred for another month or so while Lorenzo and Trump haggled over the price of the shuttle. Even after Lorenzo signed the tentative agreement to sell the shuttle to Trump, Icahn figured that he could wait a little longer and see if the courts pulled the Trump deal apart. If so, Lorenzo would have to drop his price for the whole airline.

On November 11, at a press conference at Trump's Plaza Hotel to formally announce the shuttle sale, Lorenzo conceded that he had discussed selling Eastern to Icahn. He added that a sale was unlikely and that "it isn't our preferred course."

Lorenzo was telling the truth. He always had been ambivalent about selling Eastern. Losing the company would almost certainly cost him his entire strategy. With Continental alone, Texas Air would never be the country's biggest airline. The shuttle deal gave Lorenzo some breathing room, but it also triggered another problem he hadn't anticipated. The proposed sale angered Wallace once more. "I'm still talking privately to Lorenzo," said Wallace, the mediation board chairman. "In fact, we talk frequently, although we disagree on a lot of things. He hasn't stopped banging on my door for a release. But now I'm concerned about what we're bargaining about. We were talking about wages, cuts, and so on, and then Lorenzo sells the shuttle, the guts of Eastern. So now the question is, what is the nature of bargaining with relation to the shuttle?"

Lorenzo had landed in a mess all over again. Wallace had seen through Lorenzo's springtime offer to lower his demands. Now it was November, almost a year after the machinists contract had come up for renewal, and nine months after the date set for a showdown in Lorenzo's original game plan, and he faced yet another delay.

Lorenzo's headaches didn't stop there. Like the proposed shuttle sale, the Icahn maneuver triggered a chain of events he couldn't control. Rather than convincing Bryan and other union leaders that they couldn't get a better deal with anyone else, the talks whetted their appetites. After more than a year of trying to convince Lorenzo to sell, they now thought he finally was getting to the point where he would consider it. "We knew one of the risks of the Icahn talks was that it would let the genie out of the bottle," said Bakes ruefully. "The company is not for sale. The Icahn situation was unique. We went ahead because he was a logical buyer, so we didn't want to deny the opportunity to the unions. But now we think the solution has to be to have serious negotiations" with the machinists.

Unfortunately for Texas Air, the union officials didn't feel that way. Bryan followed up his talks with Lorenzo by writing him an 11-page letter suggesting three alternatives. Either the unions could buy Eastern with an outsider; or Texas Air could merge it into Continental and hold union representation elections; or Texas Air could give employees strict job protections and seats on Eastern's and Texas Air's board in exchange for a machinists agreement to cap its labor costs at a specified percent of Eastern's revenues. "Bryan has this overriding idea that he wants to buy the airline," Wallace said at the time. "I'm not sure that he has many machinists with him. Bryan likes the publicity."

Meanwhile, Freeman stayed in touch with Icahn, who repeated that he was game if the price came down. Throughout October, Icahn phoned Lorenzo several times, trying to bargain with him. Freeman also found another possible investor, a New Jersey trucking and real estate magnate named Arthur E. Imperatore. The machinists represented some of Imperatore's trucking employees and had known him for years. Imperatore, who was worth on the order of $200 million, was interested. Freeman and Imperatore went to Goldman, Sachs & Co., the Wall Street banking firm, to explore the idea of putting together a bid for Eastern. Goldman called Bob Ferguson, Texas Air's corporate strategist, who eventually met with Imperatore at Goldman, Sachs's offices in Manhattan. In the middle of the meeting, Lorenzo arrived, unannounced, to discuss the idea. Nothing was resolved, but Imperatore came away ready to pursue a bid.

For a time it seemed as if the Icahn talks had unearthed everybody who ever had dreamed of owning an airline. The unions sent a delegation to Toronto to meet with a group of Canadian-based investors. Joseph Corr, who had just quit as TWA's president (and later wound up as president of Continental), was working with a group of St. Louis businessmen to make an offer for both Eastern and TWA at once. Gene Keilin, the Lazard Frères investment banker, began discussions with Jerry Kohlberg, a founding member of one of the country's biggest buyout firms, who had left to form his own company.

Also, by November, Spivey had managed to turn Grandview into something approaching a real company. He had signed on several credible people, including John J. Casey, a pilots union advisor who had served as chairman of Braniff and had held posts at Pan Am and American; John Scherer, a management pilot from Eastern; John McLaren, a former president of CBS Inc.'s old music division; and Aaron Gelman, a Philadelphia aviation consultant.

The unions also had helped Grandview to pick a candidate to be Eastern's chief executive after a buyout. With strong urging from Bryan, they settled on Morton Ehrlich, who had just left a job as an executive vice president at TWA. The unions liked Ehrlich, who had risen to be senior vice president of planning during the 15 years he spent at Eastern and wasn't a big fan of Borman's. Ehrlich had thought Borman promised him the job of president in 1985, but at the last minute, Borman had brought in Joe Leonard to fill the job.

Not long after his infamous dinner with Lorenzo, Bryan told Grandview and Imperatore, the New Jersey trucking magnate, that Lorenzo was willing to allow a buyout proposal to be presented to his board of directors. Bryan also flew to New York and met with Trump, trying to convince him to buy all of Eastern while he was at it. Trump refused.

In early November, Bryan called Merrill Lynch's Ray Minella. Bryan asked if Merrill Lynch would help the unions and Grandview make a bid for Eastern. Minella was a little surprised that Bryan would turn to him, of all people. After all, Minella had pushed Borman to sell to Lorenzo and bore a lot of responsibility for the sale. But Minella agreed to help. He asked Texas Air officials for permission to meet the group. After getting approval, representatives from the unions and Spivey met in Minella's offices in New York.

The next day, Monday, November 7, Lorenzo exploded and ordered Merrill Lynch not to work with Grandview. He called Bryan and told him Eastern was not for sale. In response to a call about all the activity, he got on the phone, angrier than ever.

"Whoever's feeding you this stuff is using you to put Eastern into play," he snapped. "They're trying to create an environment that there is a feeding frenzy going on . . . we didn't release Merrill Lynch. There's been some confusion. They were not released."

Once again, Lorenzo had outsmarted himself. He had learned that Wallace couldn't declare an impasse while any merger talks were going on. Lorenzo was willing to let the unions distract themselves by trying to find a buyer. But his primary goal remained busting the machinists. Nothing was going to shake him from it. Even if it meant angering everyone from Bryan, who was livid, to his own banker.

"Bullshit Lorenzo didn't release us" to work with Grandview, Minella said shortly thereafter. "Lorenzo has been getting quite concerned about the level of cash at Eastern. His whole strategy was to build up big liquidity to last through the labor strife and get released. That's been the game plan for two years. He was quite confident it could work. But the

117

unions showed themselves far more adept at fending him off than he had anticipated. Bryan called me and said that Frank told him he would treat the unions like any other buyer. He asked if we would help him. This was on Thursday. On Friday, we called Snedeker and asked if we could be released to help the unions. He said he would check with Frank. He came back the same day and said: 'Okay, we'll release you.' So on Saturday, I called the unions and we met Sunday. Then on Monday, Snedeker said he changed his mind, we're not released. It seemed clear that if we got involved with the unions in active negotiations to buy the company that the arbitrator would say they were still in negotiations and not at impasse. Lorenzo wanted to release us, but not if it meant derailing his main strategy."

Lorenzo's abrupt about-face did little good. The union leaders and buyers, who figured that Lorenzo was trying to get Eastern's price up, kept right at it. Lorenzo himself didn't help matters. He was so obsessed with keeping his options open that he refused to shut the door on a sale to TWA. "TWA has east-west routes, and Eastern has north-south ones," he said at the time. "They make a good fit." When asked if he would refuse to entertain another bid from Icahn, he dodged the issue, merely saying that "we've gotten no indication from him that he plans to make another offer."

Toward the middle of November, Freeman went back to Imperatore, the New Jersey trucker who had dropped his effort after Lorenzo's pronouncement. Imperatore agreed to give it another try. Freeman, the machinists financial advisor, made another appointment with Charlie Bryan in New York. Then, on November 18, a few days before the meeting date, "Arthur got a call from Ferguson, Texas Air's strategist," said Freeman. "He says the meeting's off and don't mess around with the unions or we'll slap you with a lawsuit."

Icahn didn't let up, either. He figured Lorenzo was merely posturing over the price. He called Lorenzo several times to discuss an offer for Eastern. Lorenzo wouldn't have it. He repeated as often as he could: The airline is not for sale. But few people believed him at this point. "I had a hot conversation on the phone the other day with Frank," Wallace said in mid-December. "He was denying that he had any talks on a sale, and said that if I don't take his word for it, I'm calling him a liar. But I know these talks are on and off."

Try as he might, Lorenzo couldn't put the genie back in the bottle again.

CHAPTER SEVEN
The Most Hated Man in America

The battle for Eastern airlines didn't overtake the national consciousness overnight. As early as 1987, the unions had gone to the public to counter the daily warfare that Lorenzo had unleashed on them. As the battle progressed, however, their strategy changed from a defensive stance to an active effort to force Lorenzo out of the airline industry altogether.

It's unlikely that Eastern's labor contracts would have become a national issue if Lorenzo had been a normal business executive. In the 1980s, many industries, particularly the airlines, went through raging labor battles without hitting the front pages for more than a few days. Even the uproar surrounding Borman, the famous astronaut, hadn't propelled Eastern into the public arena the way Lorenzo did.

Lorenzo and labor had taken their dispute to the mediation board, to Wall Street, to Washington, and to the public. As they did, their fight took on a significance that extended far beyond Eastern. Everyone in the airline business had known all along that this was a watershed battle for the industry. Both the national and the Eastern branches of all three unions were determined to halt Lorenzo's march. After more than a year of constant headlines, a good part of corporate America and most of the labor movement had come to see the confrontation as a turning point for the get-tough labor policies of management in the Reagan era.

The struggle at Eastern grew into a national issue in part because of the nature of the airline industry. Virtually every decision-maker in the country flies. The middle class flies as well, primarily for leisure—and the unions were helped immeasurably by the impact that deregulation had on the industry. By the late 1980s, deregulation had thrown air travel open to public scrutiny. The intense competition among carriers had transformed airlines into businesses that depended on the confidence of their customers for success. When Eastern's unions took their case to the court of public opinion, they were able to press their charges before a jury of travelers that barely had existed ten years before.

Labor mounted one of its first demonstrations less than two months after Lorenzo took over. Eastern just had instituted its new absenteeism policies and new procedures requiring pilots to defend their decision not to fly a plane for safety reasons. ALPA charged that the pilots were being intimidated into flying unsafe aircraft. To dramatize their claims, the union called out pickets in about a dozen large airports where Eastern operated. Several hundred pilots in full uniform donned signs with warnings like: EASTERN AIRLINES MAY BE HAZARDOUS TO MY HEALTH.

For the traditionally sedate airline industry, even these initial steps were rather extreme. Pilots don't normally picket, particularly when they're not on strike. Nor does any airline union casually bring up the sensitive question of safety. Everyone knows that if passengers turn away in fear, no one works. Naturally, Eastern responded by blaming the union. Eastern sent its managers a six-page memo claiming that the pilots' actions "are really a smoke screen to divert attention from [the pilot union's] campaign to preserve its $124,000 to $157,000 a year captain jobs at Eastern."

This wasn't wholly untrue. The campaign did have a political purpose. But in early 1987, the pilots were nowhere near contract talks. Although Lorenzo had laid out his demands, the pilots knew they didn't have to make up their minds for many months—certainly not before the machinists went to the mat. Nevertheless, the new regime really had brought serious worries that pilots on the line had to confront on a daily basis.

It wasn't long before the machinists chimed in. Bryan argued that the wholesale firings, absenteeism policies, and drug searches were creating inordinate stress among his members. Mechanics couldn't fix planes or do safety inspections properly if they were worried about their jobs. Soon, both unions were complaining not just to passengers but to the FAA. In March 1987, the pilots developed a campaign called Max-Safety, to channel complaints formally to the FAA.

There's no doubt these tactics had dual motives. The union wanted to show the FAA how bad things were. It also wanted to inflict a little pain on Lorenzo. MaxSafety functioned as a classic work slowdown. The union issued pilots a long list of "safety tips," some of which were frivolous. Safety tip no. 77, for instance, advised pilots to write up any insects on the plane, which could force the aircraft to be grounded until fumigated.

Employees, however, did have plenty of legitimate complaints. Some pilots said that potentially serious problems, such as stuck safety doors or partially inoperative fire-detection systems, went unattended.

One such pilot was Captain John P. Vandersluis. Vandersluis was in command of a 757 that was due to leave Washington, D.C., for Kansas City and then San Francisco. "The plane had no auxiliary power unit, which meant only one air-conditioning pack was working," recounted Vandersluis. "Normally there are two. They provide air for breathing. It's normal throughout the industry, when something breaks at a place with no maintenance facilities, to fly on to a maintenance base with passengers on board as long as it's a minor item and you can operate safely.

"In this case, I said I'd go to Kansas City. But I told them I wouldn't go on to San Francisco. If the other air conditioner blew, we would have lost pressure and have had to go down to 14,000 feet at least, maybe 10,000 to be safe. You can do that to Kansas City, but to San Francisco there are the mountains. The pressure to take these planes was unbelievable after Lorenzo took over. The company threatened me and said I had to take the plane. But I said it's not fair to the people in the back of the plane.

"Then they lied to me to try to get me to go. They said there were no other planes coming into D.C. that I could swap with. Just then, another captain, a good friend of mine, came walking in. I said, Where are you going? He said Boston. I asked him to take my plane and I'd take his. He said sure. But they didn't want to bother changing passengers and cargo. I absolutely refused to fly it, and they finally let us swap planes and I went on to San Francisco. It was really a crime. I filed a MaxSafety card but didn't put my name down because you weren't supposed to. I've been flying since I was 16 and I have 32,000 hours of air time. I taught acrobatic flying in the air force and still do shows on my time off, and instruct, too. I'm not afraid to fly any plane. But when I get a plane that's not safe, I'm not going to fly it, no matter what. That's what those punks at Texas Air were trying to do."

When pilots first began making such allegations in early 1987, Lorenzo blamed the whole thing on "union agitators" and urged the FAA to pay no attention. But the unions had struck a nerve. In June 1987, the FAA announced that it would hold a special inspection of Eastern to see if the adverse labor relations were affecting safety.

Later in the summer, the FAA released a study that said Eastern had the worst repair record of 11 airlines. The report looked at the number of items in need of repair on what's called the minimum equipment list. Eastern averaged 55 unrepaired items a day, compared with an industry average of 29. A House subcommittee held hearings on the report, during which Eastern unions and management officials argued over its merits. No real conclusion was reached, but the publicity hurt Eastern.

For the next two years, the unions used every opportunity to pound away at Eastern's safety record. Every time a flight experienced a safety-related problem, the pilot mailed a MaxSafety postcard citing the lapse to the FAA and to members of Congress. They mailed more than a thousand postcards.

Eventually, the volume began to worry decision-makers. In October 1987, two veteran Eastern pilots testified to a Senate committee that they had been pressured into flying unsafe planes. Both said that Eastern managers recently had disciplined them for refusing to fly.

In January 1988, the machinists and the flight attendants sat down to map out an anti-Lorenzo public-relations strategy. Randy Barber, Charlie Bryan's advisor, and Joseph Uehlein, who headed an AFL-CIO unit that helped unions mount campaigns against companies, suggested in a 10-page memo that the unions "make Frank Lorenzo the issue. Personalize the conflict to one between him (i.e., the man who's the pillager of the American Dream; the man who'd cut any corner to make a buck; the man who's a brutal, unscrupulous corporate autocrat) and us (ordinary working people, fathers and mothers; people just like you and your neighbors)."

The unions did all they could to implement Barber's strategy. At the AFL-CIO's winter gathering in Miami that February, federation president Lane Kirkland charged Lorenzo with endangering safety. Kirkland said that Lorenzo had shown "unprecedented contempt" for his employees. The federation scheduled a series of nationwide rallies by union members to join Eastern employees in publicizing their charges. They picketed, demonstrated, and gave speeches at airports and at Eastern and Continental ticket offices. The campaign pushed right to the edge of calling for boycotts of both airlines.

Around the same time, seven prominent individuals, including Joan Claybrook, the former head of the Consumer Products Safety Commission, and Eleanor Holmes Norton, a Georgetown University professor who had been a head of the Equal Opportunity Employment Commission, formed a self-appointed "commission" to investigate Texas Air's labor and safety record.

The unions also took full advantage of the 1988 presidential campaign, which was coming into full swing by that February. Representative Richard Gephardt met with union officials and blasted Eastern for going after "quick paper profits." The Reverend Jesse Jackson denounced Lorenzo. Governor Michael Dukakis went so far as to promise that he'd make a machinist secretary of labor if he were elected president. Even Georgia representative Newt Gingrich, the Republican leader of the ultraconservative new right in Congress, came out against Lorenzo; Atlanta, a major Eastern hub where employees had suffered many cutbacks, lies in the middle of his congressional district.

By March, more than 120 congressional representatives had backed a resolution by California Democrat Norman Mineta calling for the Department of Transportation (DOT), which oversees the FAA, to formally investigate Texas Air. The unions lobbied intensively, adding more representatives' names to the resolution every day.

There was nothing unusual about the unions' strategy. Personalizing issues, they felt, was a way of swinging public opinion back in their favor—and Lorenzo made their job easier. By the time it was over, the union campaign succeeded beyond Randy Barber's wildest dreams. The media came to see Lorenzo as Darth Vader. *Playgirl* magazine named him one of the 10 unsexiest men of 1988, which put him in the company of such other objects of national scorn as former attorney general Ed Meese, televangelist Jimmy Swaggart, and the Reverend Al Sharpton. At one stage, Barbara Walters asked Lorenzo on national television if he knew that he was the most hated man in America. He denied that he was and blamed the unions for his bad press.

But Lorenzo was stung by the negative publicity. He seemed never to comprehend the impact his behavior had on the rank and file. He saw his actions at Continental and Eastern as simply following the dictates of the marketplace. Lorenzo's failure to grasp the effect of his actions on others was so complete that he hired psychiatrists apparently to help him understand why unionized employees hated him so much. He told students at Stanford University, after protestors had thrown eggs at him as he entered the auditorium: "We have, in fact, a meeting going on today in Washington, D.C., by a bunch of psychiatrists and psychoanalysts who are going through the propaganda materials that these people are being sent. This is brainwashing in the style of the '40s. What is being put into their heads gets them excited about giving up their jobs." Later, in 1989, when asked by *USA Today* what he'd done to create such antipathy among employees, Lorenzo replied, "Nothing. The problem," he continued, "is they have created a public relations monster. Has anybody put together a case that I do insider trading, that I'm a bad guy, that I'm anything other than a guy who happens to have a family and is working hard to build a family?"

"Still," the interviewer countered, "you are perceived as one of the nation's toughest bosses, a man who is feared by your employees."

"I'm not paid to be a candy ass," Lorenzo responded. "I'm paid to go and get a job done. I could have ended up with another job, but the job I ended up with was piecing together a bunch of companies that were all headed for the junk heap. You know, everything's wonderful when you've got $600 million a year cash flow. That wasn't our lot. I had to draw charts that said, 'This is when the cash runs out, fellows, and unless we do something we're going to have to make changes pretty quickly.' I've got to be the bastard who sits around Eastern Airlines and says, 'Hey, we're losing $3 million a day or whatever the number is and bang, bang, bang, bang, what do you do?' So, some jobs are easier than others."

Lorenzo's belief that he was the victim of a union plot was fortified when Texas Air uncovered Barber's confidential strategy memo. He fought back hard. Lorenzo and Phil Bakes gave speeches arguing that the safety complaints were a union conspiracy. Texas Air's political action committee swung into overdrive, even though it already had doled out twice as much as the next largest airline PAC in 1987. Texas Air's lobbyists won over many in the Reagan Administration, including James H. Burnley IV, the secretary of transportation. Burnley resisted union calls for an investigation, arguing that the government should stay out of labor disputes.

Texas Air scored points in the press with the argument that Eastern machinists made far in excess of what the market would bear. One favorite company statistic was that Eastern baggage handlers earned $47,000 a year. This was misleading. Eastern actually started ramp-service personnel at $19,000 a year and brought them up to a maximum of $31,000, which wasn't over the industry average. The average ramp-service pay among the top ten airlines—including Continental—started at $17,000 and topped out at $29,000.

Texas Air twisted the figures, however. Sometimes they pushed the cost up by referring to compensation, such as health care and Social Security taxes, rather than pay. Other times they added in overtime. While some baggage handlers did earn $47,000 a year in pretax income, it was because management had refused to hire enough people to ensure everyone worked a normal eight-hour day. In fact, some machinists were disciplined for refusing to work more overtime.

After months of skirmishes, several events pushed the union campaign over the top. First, ABC's *20/20* news program ran a piece examining Eastern's safety problems. *The Wall Street Journal* ran a front-page article on the corporate house of mirrors that Lorenzo had created. The *Journal* argued that Lorenzo's arcane financial structure allowed him to milk Continental and Eastern while avoiding all the risks if they went belly-up.

The political heat grew too hot even for Burnley to ignore. In early April 1988, the Department of Transportation announced an unprecedented "fitness" investigation into Texas Air, to be conducted by Rosalind A. "Lindy" Knapp, the DOT's deputy general counsel, in only 30 days. The department had conducted dozens of similar investigations in previous years, but never of a major airline. The probe's stated goals were: to see if Texas Air followed government regulations; to see if it had adequate financing; and to see if it had competent management. Department officials specifically said they were worried that Texas Air might be diverting resources from its subsidiaries. The same day, the FAA slapped Eastern with an $823,000 fine for safety violations and launched a separate safety inspection of every one of the carrier's planes. The investigations made headlines around the country and made passengers more nervous than ever.

When it was released at the end of May, the fitness report appeared on the surface to be a model of political compromise. The DOT concluded that Texas Air passed all three tests. It then added that the protracted labor disputes could endanger safety at Eastern. This seemed to be cutting the baby in half. Union leaders branded the report a whitewash. Representative Mineta, who had sponsored the original congressional resolution calling for the investigation, said it ignored important issues such as whether Texas Air mistreated its employees. Lorenzo tried to seize the opportunity by arguing that he'd been vindicated, and declared victory.

In fact, the investigation played into Lorenzo's hand. It avoided precisely the issue that apparently had triggered it in the first place: Texas Air's asset-stripping from Eastern. The report didn't study this subject directly. Instead, it looked at Texas Air as a whole, to see whether the asset moves had damaged the entire entity. Of course, when seen from this perspective, the damage to Eastern became irrelevant.

Though the DOT report stated that it wasn't an attempt "to assess the wisdom of business decisions per se," Texas Air officials repeatedly cited the document as evidence that they hadn't ripped off Eastern's assets. For months afterward, they would claim that the government had looked into the matter and exonerated them. In truth, it had done nothing of the kind.

In part, the report's conclusions may have stemmed from what seemed to be an instinctive tendency on the part of some FAA inspectors to side with management. Many union members complained that nothing ever happened when they called the FAA about safety violations. In one highly publicized case, an Eastern mechanic named Joseph Hudak delayed a flight about to take off from Atlanta because of a broken floor panel he found in the first-class cabin. His boss screamed at him and threatened to fire him. An FAA safety inspector working on the 30-day fitness probe happened to be nearby at the time. Hudak asked him to come over and verify that the floor panel was indeed broken. "I don't want to get involved in a labor dispute," came the angry response.

Adroit and well-funded lobbying by Texas Air may have helped, too. Over the years, Lorenzo had proven singularly adept at cultivating government officials. In this case, he won over Secretary Burnley heart and soul. The very day the fitness investigation was announced, Burnley repeated his attacks on Eastern pilots for their MaxSafety campaign, saying they were trying to turn safety into a political issue.

In public and in private, Burnley stressed that only six of the 1,300 postcards received by the FAA at that point had produced proven safety violations. He insinuated that most of the complaints were concocted, citing the fact that many cards were mailed in unsigned. In December 1988, when the pilots union asked the DOT to initiate a second investigation of Eastern, Burnley rejected the request, saying that the union's demand was "a transparent attempt to put pressure on Eastern by raising new safety concerns," and that it "borders on abuse of the department's process."

As he was lambasting the union, the secretary was also negotiating for a job at Shaw, Pittman, Potts & Trowbridge, a corporate law firm in Washington that does business for Continental. The unions wouldn't find that out until February 1989, shortly after Burnley left his cabinet post. When they did, the pilots called for an investigation. Burnley denied any wrongdoing. The DOT investigated and concluded that Burnley had acted properly because in December he had cleared his involvement in the pilots' second petition with the DOT's ethics official—who, it turned out, was none other than Lindy Knapp, who headed the department's original fitness probe of Eastern.

Texas Air enjoyed similar good fortune on many occasions. T. Glover Roberts, the judge who presided over part of Continental's bankruptcy proceeding in 1985 and 1986, ruled that ex-Continental pilots couldn't sue individually for loss of their jobs, and delivered several pro-Lorenzo statements. Responding to a question about Lorenzo's purchase of Eastern, he said: "Who do you know with the guts to put half a billion dollars on the table and say he can do a turnaround" of a company that is a prime candidate for bankruptcy? Not long after Roberts allowed Continental to emerge from bankruptcy in the summer of 1986, he took a job with one of Continental's law firms. The judge had authorized the same firm to collect millions of dollars of fees for the work it had performed for Continental during the bankruptcy case before his court. The pilots protested then as well. Roberts denied any impropriety.

Lorenzo had kept his hand in government for years. Not only was Bakes the former chief counsel for the old Civil Aeronautics Board, but Texas Air senior vice president Clark Onstad had been the chief counsel of the FAA. Passing through the other way, a former lawyer for Texas Air named Robert Davis worked at both the Labor Department and at the DOT. In 1989, Frederick McClure, a Texas Air vice president, would become President George Bush's assistant for legislative affairs. He was replaced at Texas Air by Rebecca Range, who had been President Reagan's assistant for public liaison.

"There are strings of people like this on Frank's payroll," said Gerald Gitner, a former president of Texas Air. "All of them had been guardians of the public weal whose job was to protect the public."

Whether or not such links affected the DOT investigation, Burnley made a gesture to defuse charges that he was in Lorenzo's pocket. The same day the results were released in May 1988, he announced that he'd asked former Labor Secretary William Brock to talk with Eastern's unions and management to ensure that the labor conflict didn't affect safety. Brock, who spent about a month negotiating with the two sides, convinced the parties to form several safety committees designed to debate differences over issues such as sick leave policies and grievances. Still, the national publicity hurt business, driving more passengers away from Continental and Eastern. It also further harmed Lorenzo's reputation on Wall Street.

This was a mixed blessing for labor. Union leaders wanted to dry up Texas Air's ability to tap the markets for money: they hoped that, as Lorenzo began to gasp for air, he would give up on his wait for D-day with the machinists. But Lorenzo's lack of liquidity, combined with this inability to lure investors, also made it likely that he would dip more frequently into Eastern's shrinking pool of assets.

In September 1988, the pilots rented out a room at the Harvard Club in New York and invited Wall Street analysts to a briefing on Texas Air's finances. The union sent in an Eastern pilot named Wright George, who, like Lorenzo, had received an MBA from Harvard. He was accompanied by Farrell Kupersmith, the Touche Ross accountant.

Texas Air officials snickered at the bizarre idea of union types telling Wall Street pros how to do their business. But more than 100 people showed up. George and Kupersmith ran through a detailed analysis of Texas Air's intricate finances. They argued that Lorenzo had miscalculated by betting the house on a showdown that was nowhere in sight. Then they delivered the punchline: Texas Air bond holders, they suggested, might have to take a "haircut." All those Frank Lorenzo fans who had snapped up billions of dollars in bonds and notes from Texas Air might lose money.

That hit home. Many Wall Street professionals had already harbored growing doubts about Lorenzo's blizzard of bonds and notes. Many had spent mind-numbing hours puzzling over inch-thick financial documents, trying to follow Texas Air's convoluted moves and to assess the risk involved. George and Kupersmith cut through the numbers and pointed out the obvious: Lorenzo was going for broke, and if he lost, anyone along for the ride could go broke, too.

Investors and money managers got nervous when they heard such unsettling talk, even from such obviously biased sources. The next day, *The Wall Street Journal* kicked up a fuss over the heretical representation, which the paper found unsettling. The laughter from Texas Air began to ring hollow.

CHAPTER EIGHT
A Small, Obscure Bureau

By the end of 1988, Lorenzo's plan to bust the unions was more than a year behind schedule; public opinion had swung against him; Wall Street had lost faith; creditors and board members were complaining; and Charlie Bryan sat—as impassive as a stone statue—while the blows rained down on his head. If Lorenzo couldn't get his hands around the machinist union's neck, and fast, he risked losing everything.

Lorenzo knew what his real obstacle was. "He doesn't really see Charlie Bryan as his problem anymore," said a confidant that December. "It's Walter Wallace that's the problem." Indeed, Wallace and the mediation board had turned out to be as stubborn as Bryan. If Wallace would declare an impasse and start the 30-day clock, Lorenzo could take on the machinists and show everyone that his two-year wait had been worth it. But Wallace wouldn't budge. With growing desperation, Lorenzo struck out at Wallace with everything he had.

In truth, Lorenzo had mostly himself to blame. The mediation board chairman was hardly the pro-union shill Texas Air painted him as. If anything he was a lifelong promanagement type who, like Burnley and other conservative government officials, seemed a perfect candidate for Lorenzo to win over.

But Lorenzo had got off on the wrong foot with Wallace. Then, instead of trying to mend fences, Lorenzo chose to hit him harder and harder. Wallace, not surprisingly, dug in his heels. In the end, he came to see Lorenzo, not the unions, as the primary problem at Eastern.

A Republican lawyer from New York who had spent most of his life working for big companies, Wallace had served as chief of staff to James P. Mitchell, secretary of labor under President Dwight Eisenhower. After 11 years as vice president for labor relations at Hudson Pulp & Paper Company, Wallace signed on as the chief negotiator for the coal industry, which had experienced some of the toughest and most violent labor battles in American history.

In 1982 Wallace was appointed to the mediation board, and from the start he wasn't shy about angering labor. Pan Am's unions, which are branches of the Eastern unions, were furious when he tried to wring large concessions from them. The height of his disfavor came at Eastern itself, where in the last months before the sale to Lorenzo he held the press conference to say that he'd talked to the banks and that their deadline for union cuts was real. When Lorenzo took over at Eastern, Wallace was willing to help him get concessions, just as he had helped other airlines weather the deregulation and labor wars of the 1980s.

But Lorenzo didn't try to make his case to the board—he made demands. And he didn't even bother to make his demands directly to Wallace. Not long after the machinists talks began in November 1987, before the board had even appointed a mediator, Lorenzo flew to Washington to meet Helen Witt, who was the mediation board chairwoman before Wallace. He told Witt that he wanted to be on the clock—start the 30-day countdown that must proceed a strike—by Easter.

Meeting with Witt was a mistake. The machinists distrusted Witt because of a case she had handled several years earlier involving El Al, the Israeli airline. Moreover, Lorenzo made it seem as if he'd circumvented Wallace, who had been in charge of Eastern negotiations for the board since 1983, in order to cut a deal with the machinists' enemy. "It was a signal to the unions that the fix was in," said Wallace, who took over the mediation board chairmanship from Witt in June 1988. "That pissed me off." Wallace felt he had to bend over backward to show the machinists that the board wasn't biased against them.

It only got worse after that. Mediator Harry Bickford refused to release the two sides from mediation. "The company asked for a release a few weeks after I got there," said Bickford, who had been a board mediator for 20 years. "I told them that with 2,000 issues outstanding, I wouldn't even be able to get to the bottom of everything for at least a month or so. It wasn't even a question of recommending against a release. It was simply out of the question." Wallace agreed.

Texas Air requisitioned Frank Borman, still a Texas Air director, and William J. Usery, Jr., a former U.S. labor secretary whom Borman had hired in 1983, to lobby Wallace. Eastern even organized a group called PEACE, for Positive Employee Action Committee at Eastern. Although ostensibly this was a neutral group of employees, PEACE was run out of the office of Thomas J. Matthews, a Continental executive whom Lorenzo had drafted to replace John Adams as vice president for human resources at Eastern. The company paid for the committee to fly to Washington, where they lobbied congressmen for a release.

Eventually, the political pressure began to make Wallace uncomfortable. By September 1988, Bryan at last had held the membership vote on Eastern's final proposal. When the unions rejected the offer, Wallace seemed ready to release Lorenzo, even though he still didn't think that Eastern had engaged in real collective bargaining.

Then the machinists acted. On October 7, John Peterpaul, the machinist vice president in Washington, had lunch with Wallace. Peterpaul, who had been around the track with the board many times, concocted a maneuver for delaying a showdown. He told Wallace that the machinists were so angry at Lorenzo that the union had decided to call secondary boycotts if a strike at Eastern finally occurred.

This had major implications. In a secondary boycott, a union strikes companies that it's not bargaining with. The machinists had about 95,000 airline members, mostly at United, Northwest, TWA, and USAir. If the pilots and flight attendants at Eastern and other airlines honored the machinists picket lines, most of the nation's airports would be empty. Peterpaul also told Wallace that the machinists would set up picket lines on most of the nation's railroads, where the union represents 18,000 more workers.

Now Wallace had a much bigger problem on his hands. If the rail unions walked out, it could cause mayhem on the East Coast. The unions could shut down both Conrail and Amtrak. Without the Metroliner or the Eastern shuttle, Washington would be in a real jam. And because Amtrak controls a lot of the signaling and dispatching for New Jersey Transit and the Long Island Railroad, those commuter lines could grind to a halt as well. There would be an absolute mess in New York, where tens of thousands of commuters take the train to work—and, because Conrail is a major bridge for freight traffic between the East and the West, the rest of the country would be affected as well.

Peterpaul knew all this, and he knew what Wallace might have to do if secondary boycotts occurred. Under the Railway Labor Act, the board isn't required to start the 30-day clock and let a strike proceed. If the board, after it has started the clock, concludes that a strike could cripple national transportation, it can ask the president to appoint a three-person presidential emergency board (PEB) to take charge of the negotiations. The PEB can extend the no-strike period to 60 days while it tries to devise a compromise and avert a walkout.

If either side rejects the emergency board's compromise, the matter goes to Congress. Usually, Congress imposes the emergency board's suggestion on both parties, who must by law abide by the terms of the compromise. Peterpaul knew that an emergency board would delay a strike and almost certainly would result in a political compromise that would chop in half Lorenzo's demand for $150 million in cutbacks.

An emergency board would be a drastic step. It would drag the White House into what was fast becoming a messy and very political labor struggle. If Wallace asked for one, it was likely that the president would assent. In the previous 60 years, the mediation board had requested 211 emergency boards and had never been turned down. But emergency boards, which are used fairly often in railroads, are unusual in airlines. The mediation board hadn't called for one in the airline industry since 1966.

Peterpaul had trapped Wallace. Congress was about to adjourn for the November presidential election. After that, the holidays would keep the House and Senate out until late January. If Wallace declared an impasse and started the 30-day clock, President Reagan would have to recall Congress to a special session to decide what to do about Eastern. Even if he wanted to, the mediation board chairman couldn't move to declare an impasse until January.

Wallace was stuck another way as well. Because Peterpaul had told him of the union's intentions in confidence, Wallace was bound by the agency's tradition of impartiality not to disclose the strategy to Texas Air or Eastern. Lorenzo, hoping for an impasse, was frustrated. He had Tom Matthews, Eastern's labor-relations executive, send a blizzard of letters to Wallace, outlining the airline's case. The letters accused the board of dragging its feet.

Wallace only got more irritated. "I get these goddamn letters from Matthews, I don't even read them," he said one day in late October from the mediation board's headquarters in Washington. "He was in here yesterday and I told him this."

The unions did all they could to prevent the board from giving in. Hank Duffy, the pilot union's national president, called out his troops. The union began buttonholing people in the corridors of Washington, too, rebuffing Texas Air's arguments. The union's officials began to call it the lunch wars: every time Texas Air lobbyists would take a political bigwig out for a meal and a chat, the pilots would do the same.

Texas Air must have ponied up for fancier meals. It wasn't long before politicians and editorial writers around the country began complaining bitterly about the mediation board. Many took up the Texas Air line that the agency was a relic of the 1930s, when airlines first were brought under its jurisdiction. They argued that this obscure agency was blocking management's efforts to streamline the airline industry. Its cumbersome bargaining procedures took forever, they said, pointing to the Eastern dispute.

Few bothered to point out that for most of the 1960s and 1970s, the shoe had been on the other foot. In those days of steady growth, new contracts almost always meant big pay hikes, not cuts. Airlines were only too glad to delay negotiations and put off the day when they had to give out raises. They had used the mediation board just as shamelessly as Eastern's unions now were using it to delay cutbacks.

But Wallace brushed off the criticisms. He grew so impatient with the pundits who'd just discovered what they kept referring to as his obscure agency that he threatened to make up T-shirts that said S.O.B. across the front, for "Small, Obscure Bureau." In any event, Wallace planned to retire in about a year, so he felt he could resist Lorenzo's assault.

Lorenzo fired wildly at the board. Texas Air even tried to sponsor a bill in Congress that would have expanded it from three to five board members and put a 90-day limit on the length of board-supervised mediation. Lorenzo aides hinted that he was mulling over whether to sue the board for blocking an impasse. But while all his combative instincts may have told him to unleash the legal Dobermans, even Lorenzo could see that a lawsuit would only put off D-day. Instead of an impasse and a strike, he'd spend forever in court, snapping at Wallace's heels.

Lorenzo's life was not made easier by the fact that union lawsuits had tangled up the sale of the shuttle to Trump. "Frank has told us he wants that money by December 31," said a Trump Air official. "He's busting our ass to get it over to him." It was easy to see why. The company already had convinced a consortium of European banks to ease up on the requirements attached to a $300 million loan, which stopped Eastern from falling into technical default. Now Eastern's auditors said that it needed another waiver or it would again be in danger of default. Lorenzo had to go back to the banks again.

Worst of all, several of Lorenzo's colleagues were losing their patience. Some Texas Air officials began to refer to Eastern as Lorenzo's Vietnam. They said that by continually selling assets to keep fighting, he was engaging in scorched-earth tactics. If he couldn't win, he'd burn Eastern to the ground so the unions couldn't win either. They began to urge him to sell, to Icahn or to anybody else.

The most troubling critics among Lorenzo's backers remained Pohlad, the Minnesota Twins owner, and Milken, the Drexel banker. They both felt that the war against the unions had gone on too long. Milken gave Lorenzo sermons about how he was killing Continental with all the bad publicity from Eastern. Pohlad fretted about Continental, too. "I have a great deal of respect for Lorenzo," said Pohlad. "But he's controversial as a result of his relations with various labor unions."

"Pohlad thought Eastern was a cancer and should be given immediate surgery to get rid of it," said Harvey Miller, Texas Air's chief bankruptcy attorney. "A lot of people were working on Frank. I was, [Texas Air treasurer] Snedeker was, and others."

Pohlad and Milken wanted to give Lorenzo a face-saving exit. Enter Peter Ueberroth. Both Pohlad and Milken knew Peter Ueberroth, the baseball commissioner who had made a name for himself as head of the 1984 Olympics in Los Angeles. Milken and Ueberroth had lived in the same area of Los Angeles some years earlier, and Pohlad had come to know Ueberroth through his ownership of the Minnesota Twins. Ueberroth, whose term as commissioner was due to expire in April 1989, was on the lookout for something to do after baseball.

Ueberroth also knew Lorenzo independently of Milken and Pohlad. The two had met in the late 1970s, when Ueberroth was president of a group called the Young Presidents' Organization. They had met again in 1985, when Ueberroth joined the board of TWA as Lorenzo and Carl Icahn were fighting over which one of them was going to buy the company. Although the board wound up selling TWA to Icahn, Lorenzo didn't blame Ueberroth. The Texas Air chief and the baseball commissioner didn't cross paths again for the next two years. But in 1987, Pohlad arranged for Lorenzo, Ueberroth, and himself to get together socially. They would have dinner, usually in Los Angeles. The informal meetings continued in 1988, when Pohlad finally broached the idea of Ueberroth's buying Eastern. "I know Ueberroth," Pohlad said later. "He has experience in running airlines. I guess I made the suggestion that he would run Eastern."

Lorenzo wasn't about to remove his teeth from the prize that he'd so proudly dragged home two years earlier. Besides, Ueberroth had no money. But Milken thought it was a great idea as well. So Lorenzo decided to offer Ueberroth a job. In November 1988, the two met for dinner in New York, where Lorenzo raised the possibility of bringing Ueberroth aboard.

"The board is very dissatisfied with Lorenzo," said a senior Texas Air executive not long after that dinner. "Pohlad in particular is very unhappy. There are a lot of complainers. A lot of people are questioning Lorenzo's strategy. They're looking for him to take some action. Most of them want him to cut his losses and get out. But Frank is in the bunker. He wants to hold out."

Spivey, the colorful character from Atlanta, was also hard at work. From his "war room" in the New York Marriott Marquis, a suite staffed with a fax machine, a computer, a copier, 10 telephones, and a document shredder, he searched for backers to join Grandview, the company he'd set up to buy Eastern. "We have a lot of financing," he said that November. "Bill Marriott is one. Sam Walton is interested. It's remotely possible that Lee Iacocca would serve on the board—one of his board members is an acquaintance of mine." Then a bit later: "Grandview has a directors' meeting Friday afternoon. We'll add Joe DeLuca, a former general. We're still talking to John Backe, the former CBS president. And Marriott is now recommending our company as an investment to his friends."

Spivey had begun to sound like the self-imagined character he'd created in his book. "We'll be going under wraps next week or the week after," he said. "I won't be able to talk for a while. We'll do electronic sweeps of the rooms at the Marriott, to make sure no one's putting a bug on us."

It all seemed somewhat silly. What's more, some of Spivey's partners had come to see him as a hustler. Aaron Gelman, the aviation consultant, had set his firm to work on a detailed financial analysis of how to merge Eastern and TWA, which was what Grandview still was trying to do. Spivey claimed he'd already raised the funds to pay Gelman's consulting firm, but the money was nowhere in sight. Still, Spivey's hustle and the glamour of owning a major airline kept sucking new players into the act.

Spivey called former CBS president John Backe. Spivey had met Backe once or twice in California a few years before, when Spivey had attempted to get into the documentary film business. Backe, an amateur pilot, was intrigued by the idea of buying Eastern. He soon began negotiations with Grandview to become the group's president and chairman.

Spivey also hooked up with Louis Kelso, the father of the employee stock ownership plan, whose company had helped the unions in their aborted attempt to make their own bid for Eastern in the months just following the sale to Lorenzo. Kelso and his wife agreed to invest $100,000 of their own money in Grandview. They saw a union buyout of Eastern as the culmination of everything they had fought for in the past 20 years.

Bill Marriott, the Marriott hotels owner, also expressed an interest in joining Grandview's effort. After his initial talks with Bavis, the pilot, about his airline-catering company, Marriott had made inquiries about Spivey to his acquaintance Mort Ehrlich, the former Eastern executive who was Grandview's choice to head the company.

Spivey also talked to John Casey, the former Braniff chairman who had joined Grandview. Casey knew a person named Robert Booth, who had worked with him at Braniff. Chewing over their plans to help the unions buy Eastern one day, Booth suggested that Spivey and Casey call Peter Ueberroth, who was an old friend of his from the travel industry in California. In a move completely unrelated to the efforts by Pohlad and

140

Milken, Booth called Ueberroth's office the next day and then faxed him a note that said: "We have an airline situation that you ought to know about that's an exciting opportunity."

Ueberroth called Booth back in 30 minutes. In late November, Grandview and the unions sent a four-person delegation to meet with Ueberroth in the commissioner's Manhattan office: Larry Spivey, Charlie Bryan, John Scherer, the Eastern pilot who had joined Grandview, and Jack Suchocki, an Eastern pilot union official. After they recovered from Ueberroth's admission that he had just had dinner the week before with Lorenzo, Spivey and the union representatives told the commissioner about Grandview's plans to buy Eastern and TWA and merge the two carriers. Ueberroth told them that Lorenzo was thinking of offering him a job, but that he wouldn't get involved without labor's blessing. He said he loved the idea of employees owning a stake in their company, and would be glad to join their team. But, he said, he wouldn't get involved unless Lorenzo was willing to sell.

Spivey and the unions were back where they had started. Lorenzo owned almost nothing, but his octopuslike corporate structure gave him an unbreakable grip on Eastern. Ueberroth signed baseballs for the four men and they left. Secretly, however, the commissioner encouraged the unions to pursue the idea. Several days later, he and Bryan spoke by phone, and Ueberroth told the union leader to call him any time and that he would tell his secretary to patch Bryan through no matter what he was doing.

Ueberroth was extremely concerned that word of his involvement not get out. But a few days later, he admitted that the meeting with the unions had occurred. "I don't want to add any fuel to the situation," he said. "But I think the company, Eastern, needs to be rescued. It's a people business, and I think highly of the labor leadership. I've had a chance to meet with them. But they've got their own problems. I met with them because when people want to talk to me, I listen."

Not long after his encounter with the unions, Ueberroth met Lorenzo for dinner again. This time Lorenzo formally proposed that Ueberroth come in as chairman or president at Texas Air, Continental, or Eastern. Ueberroth declined, saying that he wasn't good at working for anyone else.

Eastern's unions weren't about to stop trying to buy the airline just because Lorenzo said he wouldn't sell. Despite the secrecy Lorenzo enforced on his boards, word continued to leak out about the troubles he was having. The unions had heard as far back as March that Pohlad was unhappy. Then, after Grandview's November meeting with Ueberroth, Gelman, the consultant working with Grandview, learned from a fund manager with holdings in Texas Air that some institutional investors had told Pohlad of their unhappiness with Lorenzo's policies. "So," said Gelman, "I suggested that Larry call Pohlad."

That November, Spivey did call Pohlad, using Ueberroth's name as an entree. Spivey claims that Pohlad returned his call one day when he was up in the war room with Buzz Wright, the pilots union official, and a few other people. Pohlad, says Spivey, said that if they got a credible offer together, the board might listen to it no matter what Lorenzo wanted. "Pohlad told me: 'Don't call Frank, call me, I'll take it to the board,' " says Spivey. "He kept referring to the scorched-earth policy. He got so mad that he kept calling me Peter, because I had told him that Ueberroth suggested I call. The more exercised he got, the more he called me Peter. He's obviously getting old."

Pohlad, who's in his mid-seventies, at first denied that he even remembered Spivey. Then he said: "I had all kinds of tire-kickers calling me. I refused to talk to them. I said, get an offer, present it to Frank, and he can take it to the board. It's a bunch of bullshit that I was going to go around Lorenzo." Whether Spivey was telling the truth or not, everyone believed him, including the union leaders who heard his end of the call in the war room, Backe, Gelman, and just about everyone else the unions were working with.

Bryan also pursued any avenue he could. Just after Thanksgiving, the machinist leader got a call from a friend of Jay

Pritzker's, the Hyatt hotels owner, whom he had come to know back in 1986, when Pritzker had made his two aborted efforts to buy Eastern. The friend asked Bryan if he wanted to meet Pritzker again. Bryan agreed and the three arranged to meet at a vacation home Pritzker owned on Williams Island, in north Miami. Before they met, Bryan called Ueberroth and asked the commissioner if he should tell Pritzker that Ueberroth was available to run Eastern if the unions bought it. Ueberroth said go ahead.

Pritzker told Bryan he was interested in making another effort to buy Eastern with the unions. Afterward, Bryan told Gelman about the meeting. It turned out that Gelman had himself known Pritzker years before. Gelman contacted Pritzker, and the two groups, Grandview and Pritzker's, began discussions to see if they could join forces.

The idea of an employee buyout had gained ground in the pilots union, too. For much of 1988, Bavis, the pilot leader at Eastern, had been talking to Lorenzo off and on about a fence agreement to protect his members' jobs. But Lorenzo's actions spoke louder than his words: it was all too clear that he'd abandon the pilots if he could, as his contracts with Orion to train replacement pilots had demonstrated. Such behavior had increased skepticism among pilot leaders about Lorenzo's promises for a fence deal, and more members of the union's executive council had swung behind Skip Copeland, the militant pilot who had run against Bavis to be council chairman.

The council recently had held elections for its officers, and Bavis had squeaked by with a one-vote margin. One seat on the council went to Buzz Wright, who, although he wasn't a Copeland follower, was quite enthusiastic about a buyout. Bavis asked Wright and Suchocki, the other pilots union officer, who eventually became a Copeland supporter, to take charge of the buyout effort.

"The [council] wanted to teach me a lesson," Bavis said later. "They wanted to get rid of Frank. But I didn't credit the buyout plan because I didn't think Lorenzo would sell. He wanted to get rid of the [machinists], then us, and then merge a nonunion Eastern into Continental. We had an internal struggle over priorities, so I gave Buzz buyout power to take the heat off of me." This swung the pilots solidly behind the buyout idea. Wright and Suchocki began to work closely with Bryan to work up other potential buyers.

But Lorenzo would have none of it. He and Bryan had proved to be equally stubborn. With Wallace holding fast, they became like two generals who held each other's armies hostage. Because neither could best the other, they kept fighting a devastating war of attrition. Lorenzo slashed jobs and his managers fired or suspended workers at the slightest excuse. The number of machinist members given the boot in 1988 represented a tenfold rise since 1985. Bryan, for his part, did all he could to stall a showdown. As they fought, Eastern was chopped gradually into a smaller and smaller company.

The directors of Eastern and Texas Air thought Lorenzo had carried on long enough. At this point, he had few backers left on the inside. Lorenzo, however, denied that there was any dissent on his board of directors.

"We have a board that is concerned and properly so," Lorenzo said one day in mid-December. "But we're very united. It's bullshit that they're complaining. No one is thrilled with how Eastern is going. I'm sure that the directors would be thrilled to have Icahn come along and pay $1 billion. But that's not happening." When asked about getting a release from the mediation board, he said: "Read the law. They're law-abiding citizens. If you don't think we'll be released, you need patience."

At the end of 1988, though, it began to look as if Lorenzo's patience would be rewarded at last. Wallace informed both sides that on January 6 he planned to step personally into the negotiations. Until this point, he had followed the normal mediation board procedure, leaving the actual negotiations in the hands of mediator Harry Bickford. Only toward the very end, right before the final decision about the 30-day clock is made, does the board member assigned to the case actually sit in on the bargaining.

Eastern officials were suspicious. They feared that this might be just another trick by Wallace to stall. Wallace did want to try one last time to pull both sides back from the calamity a strike would bring. But he had little hope. If it didn't work, then he would finally let Lorenzo have the showdown he'd been itching for during the past two years.

CHAPTER NINE
D-Day

Texas Air officials could barely contain themselves as January 6, 1989, approached. Wallace had announced that he intended to oversee the talks personally. Hoping that he could convince the warring parties to cool off, he tried to get the combatants away from the glare of the public spotlight by insisting that the meeting be held in a confidential location.

But Texas Air executives suspected that Wallace's intervention had been spurred by their lobbying fusillade in Washington, not by any real desire to bring their feud with the machinists to a head. So Lorenzo moved to ensure that Wallace couldn't wriggle out of anything by hiding from the media. Quietly, Texas Air officials alerted the press to Wallace's itinerary. When the chairman stepped off the plane in Miami, where the talks were to be held, the media was waiting at the airport, asking whether his presence at the bargaining table meant that a strike was in the offing. Needless to say, Wallace knew who had leaked news of his arrival time to the media, and was furious all over again.

Lorenzo didn't stop there. When the meeting convened, Eastern's negotiators dropped a bombshell. Privately, they told mediators that the company intended to sell Eastern's Philadelphia gates to USAir. This was yet another asset Lorenzo had put on the block to tide him over until the money from Trump came through. Eastern officials added that they also planned to sell six A-300 aircraft. Company negotiators said piously that they hoped this wouldn't screw up the negotiations.

When the machinists heard all this, they felt sandbagged all over again. Wallace abruptly broke off the talks and waited a few days for tempers to cool. Then he scheduled another round, in Savannah, Georgia. This time, the press didn't track them down. Eastern and the machinists went at it around the clock, with Wallace and Bickford trying to prod their talks along. No one budged. The unions sensed that the board was closing in on declaring an impasse.

Knowing that time was slipping through their fingers, union officials redoubled their efforts to find a credible buyer while the talks continued. Icahn continued to express interest to Freeman, the machinists investment banker. Sensing that Eastern was heading for a strike that could cripple the airline, the TWA chairman lowered his price even further. The unions turned their focus to Grandview.

Grandview was in a muddle. By late December, Spivey had become embroiled in a power struggle with other Grandview directors. Casey, the former Pan Am executive, Gelman, the aviation consultant, and Scherer, the Eastern official, were fed up with Spivey. He, in turn, felt that they were trying to squeeze him out. So Spivey maneuvered to have them tossed off of Grandview's board of directors. He kept bringing in new players to replace them, such as Lieutenant General Joseph R. DeLuca, a former comptroller of the U.S. Air Force, who agreed to join Grandview's board.

But Spivey had run into even bigger trouble with Backe, the former CBS president. At the end of December, Backe still had been negotiating to become Grandview's chairman and president. However, he wanted written guarantees that he would be in charge of Grandview, as well as clauses protecting him from lawsuits by Grandview shareholders if the deal went sour. "I was dealing with a very litigious guy, Lorenzo, not to mention the unions," Backe said.

Spivey, however, didn't want to let go of his baby. As a result, he and Backe were at each other's throats. Finally, on New Year's Day 1989, Backe told Grandview that he was dropping out. Spivey promptly tried to find a replacement. He did some fast footwork, and soon was angling to give Grandview's chairmanship to former Tennessee Senator Howard Baker, who had just left his post as White House chief of staff. Through Louis Kelso, Spivey got Baker interested in the idea. A few days into the new year, just before the negotiations with Wallace and the company began, Baker sent a representative named William E. Anderson to Miami, where the unions had convened a meeting to discuss Grandview.

This time, Spivey went too far. Most of the union leaders had come to respect Backe. Bryan, in particular, had spent many hours with him and had come to trust him. When they saw Spivey fighting to keep control from someone they perceived as bringing crucial credibility to their efforts, the union leaders threw up their hands in disgust. Most of the union leaders already had come to see him as a manipulator. The incident with Baker pushed them over the edge. "Spivey talks too much and everyone got sick of his big mouth," said Barber, Bryan's financial consultant. "So he was told by everyone that he no longer represents them, the unions, or Grandview's board." Buzz Wright, who still was in charge of the buyout effort for the pilots, decided to stop dealing with Spivey and passed him over to Wright George, the pilot who, with Farrell Kupersmith, had put on the September 1988 financial presentation to Wall Street analysts at the Harvard Club in New York. "My wife told me not to go on that fishing trip of Spivey's," Bavis recalled. "She said he was a hustler. But I went anyway."

Finally even Bryan, who had formed a close relationship with Spivey, put his foot down. Bryan called Backe and asked what it would take to get him back into Grandview. "I want Spivey out of my life," Backe told him. Backe suggested junking Grandview and starting another acquisition company. Bryan and the other union leaders agreed.

Bill Anderson, Howard Baker's representative at the meetings in Miami, soon had realized that Spivey was persona non grata, and had decided that Backe made more sense as the person to take charge of Grandview. So Baker had pulled back, agreeing that maybe he would join the company later as a director, after it bought Eastern. This left Backe firmly in charge. The unions kept negotiating with Backe, who formed another company, called First Flight Acquisition Corporation.

Spivey tried to put a good face on events. "I was just the recruiter," he said at the time. "Now I've stepped out. I was never trying to build a power base. I was just trying to save an airline." But after he formed another company, which he named Highland Capital Corporation, Spivey let on how he really felt. "Backe was greedy, shortsighted, and cheap. He wanted to be cook, chief bottle washer, and everything. He didn't want Spivey around. He was an arrogant asshole. So he told me to get lost."

Throughout the negotiations with Grandview (the name everyone continued to use to refer to Backe's group), the unions consistently had said that they would make whatever concessions were necessary to buy Eastern. Gelman's financial analyses of the company projected that the unions would be expected to kick in $200 million to $250 million a year. As he had done back in October 1988, during the discussions with Icahn, Bryan now agreed that the machinists would take the biggest chunk. Although the machinists might have to kick in almost as much as the $150 million Lorenzo wanted, union members would get Eastern stock in return. Besides, no one wanted to work for Lorenzo anymore. Backe began approaching investment banking houses to arrange financing for an Eastern buyout.

Throughout all these maneuvers, Charlie Bryan kept calling Ueberroth every week or two, telling him what was going on. True to his word, Ueberroth took his calls no matter what he was doing, and he assured Bryan of his continued interest in Eastern.

As the machinists and Eastern continued their secret talks in Savannah, Lorenzo, sensing that he was closing in on the kill, fired up the fence talks with the pilots. The pilots union, however, was more divided than ever. The faction led by Skip Copeland, Bavis's rival, and Buzz Wright, the pilot in charge of a buyout, was hotter than ever on the idea of purchasing Eastern. Wright was working closely with Bryan and Grandview, trying to scrape an offer together before the mediation board declared an impasse. The group was extremely suspicious that Bavis would cut a deal with Lorenzo behind their backs. Some pilot leaders actually called reporters to see if they could sniff out whether their own leader had been meeting secretly with Lorenzo.

To further muddy the waters, the single-carrier case was coming to a head almost a year after it was filed. The mediation board had nearly finished hearing evidence on the matter, which Wallace had maintained was unrelated to the Eastern mediation efforts. The final briefs, over 90,000 pages in all, were scheduled to be delivered to the board in Washington by February 6. The machinists asked Wallace to delay the clock until the board had ruled on the single-carrier issue.

Wallace played his cards close to the vest. When the talks in Savannah broke off on January 22, Wallace made up his mind to declare an impasse within the following week. But he didn't tell any of the parties. "I had lunch with Wallace today and he didn't mention it," said Peterpaul two days later. "I assume the clock is coming shortly, but I don't know when."

The machinists were as eager as ever to avoid a strike. In fact, Bryan's predicament hadn't really changed in two years. The real question mark was the pilots. Despite the internal tension between Bavis and other pilot leaders, most union officials were fairly sure that many rank-and-file pilots would cross a machinists picket line if Lorenzo came through on a fence deal. Then the machinists would be left out on a limb. Although Eastern was suffering badly, they knew Lorenzo would do everything in his power to keep flying without them.

With pilots to run his planes, there was a very good chance he'd pull it off.

So the machinists union set to work on its backup strategy. Its leaders in Washington got together with pilot officials and the AFL-CIO, which had assigned a staff support group to Eastern. The machinists told them about Peterpaul's secondary boycott and emergency board (PEB) plan. The idea of bringing everyone into the battle against Lorenzo wasn't exactly new. In 1983, when Lorenzo declared bankruptcy at Continental, the pilots had toyed with a plan to mount a national airline strike. But at that point, the union hadn't achieved sufficient solidarity among its members to carry out the idea. Now, six years later, pilots everywhere knew how much damage Lorenzo had inflicted.

Even so, national union leaders were reluctant to call a secondary boycott. Lorenzo's public image was so bad that even many Republicans were sympathetic to the unions. After a decade of falling membership and negative press that had left labor reeling, union officials were leery of any steps that might place them in a bad light again.

By this time, Texas Air had gotten wind of what was up. Wallace had spent much of the previous October and November trying to get Transportation Secretary Burnley to discuss what to do about the possibility of a secondary boycott. But Burnley wouldn't meet with him, apparently because he was negotiating the job he later took at Continental's law firm—and because, according to Brian Freeman, who had known Burnley for years, he wanted to force a strike. Finally, the day after the presidential campaign was over and Bush had won, Ann Dore McLaughlin, the outgoing secretary of labor, arranged a meeting between Wallace and C. Boyden Gray, Bush's key aide. Just before Christmas they met at the White House with A. B. Culverhouse, Reagan's general counsel, whose job Gray was designated to take when Bush took over as president. Wallace laid out the problem at Eastern. Over the next few weeks, Wallace and Gray continued the discussion on the phone. Finally, Gray told Wallace where the administration stood: with Lorenzo. "I made it clear that [Bush's] advisors were leaning against" the appointment of a PEB, said Gray.

On January 5, 1989, William Winpisinger, the machinist union president, in a letter to the mediation board, promised to call secondary boycotts on airlines and railroads. This was an extremely unusual move. Although Peterpaul had brandished this stick privately in October, the union's president now was committing himself publicly. It indicated what a watershed the union thought the battle with Lorenzo to be. After all, what did railroad employees have to do with airline workers? If the union's members at other air carriers went on strike, they knew that shooting down Lorenzo would have a direct beneficial impact on their lives. But Winpisinger would have to expend a tremendous amount of political capital to ask rail workers to make a sacrifice that would never benefit them.

The prospect ignited a new round of furious political maneuvering. After all this time, Lorenzo was not about to be cheated out of his showdown. Besides, he couldn't afford to wait. He still didn't have his money from the shuttle, whose sale continued to be tied up in court by union lawsuits. And Continental had lost $315 million in 1988. Texas Air's lobbying cadre flooded back into the halls of Washington. Senate Minority Leader Robert Dole and Republican Senator Phil Gramm of Texas called Wallace in for a meeting and laid into him for blocking a release at Eastern.

Lorenzo even brought Kay McMurray in to be a new director on Eastern's board. McMurray had all the credentials necessary to legitimize Lorenzo's lobbying battles. Former head of the National Mediation and Conciliation Service, a federal board designed to help solve labor disputes, and the mediation board, McMurray dutifully joined in to oppose an emergency board. Texas Air's battalions of lawyers were put to work to scrutinize the major machinists union contracts. They quickly inundated the mediation board with documents to demonstrate that secondary boycotts would be illegal at other carriers.

The AFL-CIO began to get involved, too. Although the national labor movement often lends a hand to the battles of individual unions, the action rarely moves beyond verbal support and perhaps a little cash. The case of Lorenzo was different. Labor leaders in a host of unions felt he had to be stopped at almost any cost. They recalled all too well how they had stood by in 1981, when Ronald Reagan had summarily fired striking air traffic controllers. The president's move had legitimized a resurgence of confrontational labor relations, and helped to usher in years of weakened clout for unions. Most union presidents saw the Eastern dispute as a similar watershed. They were determined to prevent Lorenzo from giving another boost to the get-tough style of management.

The unions that counted the most were the rail workers. And they were as solid as ever. "If they put up picket lines, we would respect them," said Richard I. Kilroy, the president of the Railroad Labor Executive Association, a body representing all the rail unions. "We see reruns not just of the PATCO [air traffic controllers] strike but of Continental, too. It affects everyone if a company can go bankrupt and avoid unions. It's not just one union but everyone who's involved here. This is a test for labor."

Many in corporate America agreed that the battle was a watershed. To them, Lorenzo represented a new breed of managers with the strength to break the unions and restore America to its rightful prominence. Some executives were torn between this view and the new alternatives of cooperative management that had begun to spread across U.S. industry. A Lorenzo victory would go a long way toward validating the confrontational wisdom that had served the U.S. so well for so many decades. "This struggle is greater than just Eastern," said Borman. "Labor is trying to reassert the momentum it lost under Reagan."

On January 31, the mediation board finally moved. Wallace sent out an official proffer to Eastern and the machinists, suggesting the board arbitrate their labor dispute. Eastern rejected the offer within hours of receiving it. Wallace began the 30-day countdown the next day.

D-day was set for 12:01 A.M., March 4. Company officials were thrilled. "We intend to operate if there is a strike," said Matthews, the labor relations vice president, that day. "We have the experience to do so. And we're making progress with the pilots. We met yesterday on the fence talks. I think they will go with Bavis."

Other groups leapt into action. Icahn already had reopened talks with Lorenzo, and went up to have dinner with him in January at restaurants near the TWA owner's home in Mt. Kisco, New York. With a showdown looming at last, Icahn decided it was time to bargain seriously. The two men met for dinner again in February and haggled over the price. Finally, on Thursday, February 16, Lorenzo agreed to an offer of $350 million. This was slightly less than the $365 million Texas Air would get if the sale of the shuttle to Trump went through. But by surrendering the rest of Eastern, Lorenzo would also be getting rid of the company's $2.3 billion in debt, which potentially could engulf Texas Air and Continental if a strike turned into a disaster and the company went bankrupt. Lorenzo and Icahn shook hands on the deal, and Lorenzo left Mt. Kisco.

The next day, Icahn gathered some two dozen lawyers in Manhattan in preparation for signing an agreement to buy Eastern. They sat around waiting as TWA and Texas Air officials began hammering out the details of a contract. Then a problem developed. Lorenzo was nowhere to be found. At last his aides tracked him down—on the ski slopes, where he had headed after he had left Icahn the day before. When he and Icahn finally got on the phone, each was hopping mad, with Icahn yelling: "This is why you can't make deals," and Lorenzo screaming back, "Don't tell me where I've got to be."

When the two calmed down, Lorenzo played hardball and raised the price for Eastern. The $350 million agreement they had reached the day before included provisions that called for Texas Air to pay back about $200 million of Eastern's debt. Telling Icahn that he had found a liability from Texas Air to Eastern that already had been repaid and that he therefore didn't owe, Lorenzo demanded that Icahn pay an extra $40 million. Icahn refused. Lorenzo wouldn't budge, either. He told Icahn to call him if he changed his mind, and the two hung up, the deal dead at the last minute.

"I had second thoughts the night before, right after we made the agreement," said Icahn. "But I gave him my handshake, and I was committed. He did me a favor with the $40 million. Maybe I could have said, Let's split the difference. But I didn't want to negotiate anymore. I felt relieved to be out of the deal."

While all this had been happening, other buyers were getting serious, too. Right after the mediation board had started the 30-day countdown, Backe, the former CBS president, quickly realized that he had no time to go the traditional route of raising money through a Wall Street investment bank. He had begun working with Donaldson, Lufkin & Jenrette, a Wall Street firm, which had approached Texas Air on the Backe group's behalf. Lorenzo sent word back that they should work through yet another investment banker, Smith Barney Harris Upham & Co., which Texas Air had hired to represent it as a supplement to Drexel, its normal investment house.

On February 13, Backe and his aides met with Smith Barney officials in New York. Smith Barney, however, told Backe that Lorenzo refused to open up Eastern's financial books unless he knew who was putting up the money for the purchase. Backe was in a catch-22. He needed the books to know what kind of offer to make, and he couldn't raise money on Wall Street without an offer. He had to change tack. "We needed a deep pocket, and fast," said Backe.

Charlie Bryan suggested that Backe try Jay Pritzker again. Throughout December and much of January, the Hyatt hotels owner had expected Grandview to get back to his aides. Grandview, which had been in turmoil during this time, had been waiting for a call from Pritzker. Finally, Gelman, the Grandview consultant, and the Pritzker group began talking again. In mid-February, Backe and Pritzker finally met each other for the first time, in Chicago. The two hit it off, and agreed to form an alliance.

Pritzker worried that Lorenzo wouldn't sell to him. The two

155

had clashed on several earlier deals, including Lorenzo's purchase of Eastern. The Texas Air boss saw Pritzker much as he did Icahn: as a rival to be bested at any opportunity. "Jay thought it could be a macho thing with Lorenzo if he got involved," said Backe. So Pritzker called Pohlad, whom he knew from Continental's board, to ask for advice. Pohlad told him to link up with Peter Ueberroth. On February 24, Pritzker called Ueberroth. The two of them and Backe then began talking about putting a deal together.

Pohlad was still trying to talk Lorenzo into selling Eastern to the baseball commissioner. So were other Lorenzo backers, such as Drexel, which had asked Ueberroth in January if he was interested in running Eastern. But no matter how hard everyone pushed, they all faced the same problem: Ueberroth didn't want to go to work for Lorenzo, and he didn't have enough money to swing a purchase of Eastern by himself. In 1980, Ueberroth had made about $10 million when he sold a string of travel agencies that he'd built into the second-largest in the country, but that wasn't enough even to put him in the ballpark. Pritzker, however, had the funds; if he and Ueberroth hit it off, maybe they could do something together.

As the buyers plotted throughout February, the machinists and Eastern went through the motions of negotiating a new contract. But after more than two years of fighting, neither had any intention of yielding ground. Instead, the action moved to Washington, where the politicking reached a fever pitch.

Not long after the countdown began, Wallace formally told the White House that he might ask for an emergency board. He suggested that Samuel R. Pierce, Jr., Secretary of Housing and Urban Development under Reagan, chair the board. Wallace had known Pierce for 40 years, since they were at Cornell University law school together. They had served together at the Department of Labor in the Eisenhower administration.

In mid-February, White House counsel Boyden Gray convened a group of officials to consider what to recommend to President Bush. Jerry G. Thorn, a labor department official, and Margaret Gilligan, the acting chief of staff of the FAA's administrative office, attended. The Department of Transportation sent someone, as did the Office of Management and Budget, the Office of Policy Development, and the Department of Defense, which is advised on all major actions involving commercial airlines.

The unions started lobbying for an emergency board immediately. With the support of Senator Edward Kennedy, the head of the Senate Labor Committee, they went after senators and representatives from New York and New Jersey—the states that would be hardest hit by commuter shutdowns. The AFL-CIO's executive council issued a call for an emergency board. Union officials privately expressed hope that they could win over Labor Secretary Elizabeth Dole, who was a friend of AFL-CIO president Lane Kirkland, even though her husband Robert, the Senate minority leader, had pushed Wallace to let Lorenzo have his way.

Texas Air in turn went after the new transportation secretary, Samuel K. Skinner. Union officials charged that Lorenzo was getting help from inside the White House, too, where Fred McClure, the former Texas Air vice president, had direct influence on the matter as legislative affairs advisor.

Days before the March 4 strike date, Wallace sent the president a formal request for an emergency board.

But Lorenzo had struck gold. The White House not only favored Texas Air to begin with, presidential strategists also saw a chance for Bush to come out a hero. After all, Ronald Reagan had dealt a devastating blow to labor by firing the striking air traffic controllers, and had emerged as the victorious tough guy, the toast of corporate America and the scourge of the greedy labor unions. Here was a chance for Bush to imitate his mentor. If he rejected an emergency board and a strike threw the East Coast transportation systems into chaos, hundreds of thousands of commuters would be mad as hornets. Bush could then blame labor for dragging the whole world into its private battles and making everyday Americans suffer. He even could use the outcry to push a bill through Congress outlawing secondary strikes—an idea that Labor Secretary Dole had wanted, and had even prepared legislation for, when she was Reagan's transportation secretary. Bush, like Reagan, would be standing tall.

Of course, if the pilots mounted secondary boycotts and grounded other airlines, millions of people would be up in arms. In that situation, Bush might not be so eager to take the blame. Still, that possibility was unlikely. Days before the strike date, Lorenzo assured Skinner that the pilots would never leave their cockpits. The White House assumed it would face only rail disruptions. Anyway, Bush always had a backup: if labor somehow turned the tables on him and public opinion swung against Lorenzo, he could call for an emergency board a few days after a strike got under way.

The White House plan was set. Wallace soon got word that Bush wanted to wait and see if the unions really shut down the rails or the airlines. On Friday, March 3, with the strike due at midnight, Bush met with his advisors for half an hour in the Oval Office and confirmed the decision. The White House was not going to intervene.

Now, all Lorenzo had to do was strike a deal with the pilots. As the first nonpilot at Eastern's helm since the 1930s, he couldn't, as Borman had done, draw on their sense of camaraderie in the final moment of truth. Eastern's pilots thought of Lorenzo as a financial wheeler-dealer—but he knew that, despite the tensions, rank-and-file pilots had little desire to strike. No matter what some of their leaders felt, he believed that most of them still hated the machinists and Bryan too much to be swayed by all this talk of a test for organized labor.

Just before the strike, Farrell Kupersmith, the Touche Ross accountant hired by the unions, had lunch with Phil Bakes. Eastern's president asked Kupersmith, whose word had become extremely influential with many pilots, what he intended to recommend to them. "I have no choice but to tell them to strike," responded Kupersmith. "You haven't given them an alternative."

Bakes laughed. "You're going to have footprints all over your back from pilots crossing the picket line," he replied.

Bakes and Lorenzo were right about one thing: Texas Air had the perfect opportunity to bring the pilots to its side and break the machinists once and for all. As Don Skiados, the pilot union's chief national spokesman in Washington, explained, "A lot of our guys hate Charlie. They've never forgiven him for not taking wage cuts all those years. And they still think that this whole mess with Lorenzo is all his fault anyway. Many of them would love to see him stuck with his own problem. But it goes a lot deeper than that. So many pilots have left Eastern in the last two years that the pilot group is now very fragmented. A lot of them are very young. If they stay and work in a strike, they'll have a great opportunity to shoot ahead to that captain's seat.

"Then you have a lot of the guys who are within several years of retirement. They're really the deciding factors and they don't give a damn what happens in terms of their livelihood. If they never work again, big deal. They were going to retire anyway. But on the other hand, why not work for another six months or a year and collect just that much more money? Why should they give up anything for Charlie Bryan? If Frank makes them a halfway decent offer, they'll probably go for it. But if he does something to piss them off, they'll walk. They're so fed up with him that it wouldn't take much. I don't even know what that thing might be. But if he does it, then they won't work."

Lorenzo found just the thing to push pilots over the edge.

With the strike date days away, Lorenzo at last offered pilots the job guarantees he'd baited them with for two years. Bakes sent all 3,500 pilots a Western Union mailgram with the highlights of the new offer. It said that Texas Air and Eastern had given pilots what they wanted. Lorenzo signed a side-letter that gave pilots commitments in the event of a bankruptcy. A five-year labor contract would even provide pay increases. It sounded too good to be true.

Lorenzo, however, didn't trust the pilot leaders. The union's executive council was unpredictable. If the militants insisted on fighting an ideological battle, their recommendation could sway a lot of pilots. Lorenzo decided to go straight to the rank and file himself. On March 1, two days before D-day, he sent a video to each pilot's home by overnight express. The video showed Lorenzo sitting on a couch at home in Houston, being interviewed by a journalist hired for the occasion. It lasted about 15 minutes.

"We have a fence agreement proposal that provides for guarantees against international routes leaving the company, and provides for a minimum number of captain's positions," he told the pilots. "It protects the careers of Eastern's pilots. Under a fairly unusual part of the proposed agreement, Texas Air would commit that it and Eastern would not go to a judge and attempt to have the pay of Eastern's pilots cut in the unlikely event that there were a bankruptcy proceeding."

Lorenzo then signed the new pilots union agreement on camera. All union leaders had to do was sign it, too. It would become effective the moment they did.

However, the Texas Air chief neglected to tell the pilots a few pertinent facts. The protection against bankruptcy didn't apply to fleet size, total aircraft minimums, pilot furloughs, or the number of captains the company had to employ. Kupersmith and pilot lawyers pointed out that, if Eastern broke its promise and declared bankruptcy, the bankruptcy law would wipe out all prior guarantees, including the one promising not to declare bankruptcy. In addition, the entire litany of guarantees from Texas Air and Eastern didn't apply if there was a strike at Eastern—which meant that even if the pilots didn't strike but the machinists did, Eastern could invalidate its promises to the pilots.

Nor did Lorenzo mention an estimated $64 million a year in benefit cuts—from medical and dental coverage to vacation pay, uniform allowance, and training pay—that he had slipped into the contract. Since Lorenzo was asking for a five-year deal, the total came to more than $300 million.

After two years of fighting for this deal, even Bavis couldn't take the tricks. Pilot leaders called the offer a "gimmick" and Bavis officially rejected it. For the first time, he called on his members to honor a machinists picket line. Kupersmith and Jack Suchocki, who had been put on the pilots' negotiating committee, quickly filmed a rebuttal videotape with another union negotiator. Pilots got it on Friday, the day before the strike was due to start.

Lorenzo remained convinced that a sufficient number of pilots would cross the picket lines to let him fly at least enough planes to ensure Eastern's survival. Still, he tried one last maneuver with the machinists. At nine P.M. that Friday, with the walkout coming at midnight, he changed his demands for the first time since July of 1988. Tom Matthews, Eastern's labor-relations vice president, told Wallace and Bickford that Eastern was prepared to accept $125 million in concessions instead of $150 million.

The machinists negotiating committee rejected the suggestion. The negotiators didn't even bother to caucus.

Lorenzo, however, had been serious. Right after Matthews made the offer, the Texas Air chairman called Wallace, who had been present at the negotiations. Wallace went down the hall to a private phone. "What was the reaction to the new offer?" Lorenzo asked him.

"They rejected it," Wallace told him.

"How did you feel about it?"

"It was too little, too late."

"But they had agreed to $125 million with Icahn," Lorenzo complained.

"Yes, but that involved stock for the unions. Are you saying that you will give them stock?"

"Oh, no, that's not part of the offer," said Lorenzo.

At midnight, the picket lines went up at airports around the country. The next day, almost every Eastern machinist refused to go to work. Only about 200 pilots, mostly in managerial positions, crossed the picket lines. For the third time in his career, Lorenzo had grounded an airline in a bet-the-company attempt to beat organized labor.

The turnout shocked company officials, outside observers, and even the pilot leaders. "I felt strongly that if the [ma-

161

chinists] went out, we should, too," said Hank Duffy, the pilot national president. "But I wasn't sure we'd get the solidarity. I got an assessment that only a few hundred pilots would cross the line."

In the final moments, with the fate of his empire hanging in the balance, Lorenzo had found a way to anger virtually every pilots union member. It wasn't only what they saw as his deceit, but the perceived arrogance of his video. "It was like he was saying: 'Come on back to work, children. Enough of this foolishness,' " said one pilot.

The pilots' decision to strike brought the unions closer together than they ever had been. Late on the night of the strike, Bryan, Peterpaul, Barber, and a few other machinist leaders were walking back to their hotel from the union's national headquarters in Washington, where they'd all gathered for the denouement. Jack Bavis, who had just given a television interview, bumped into the group. They walked together for several blocks, and then Bavis turned off toward his own hotel. As he did, Bryan called him back. Bryan reached out and shook his hand, saying: "Thanks, Jack."

Eastern tried to talk tough the minute the strike broke out. "This company is not waiting to see who makes the first phone call. We are putting planes in the air," said Bakes at a press conference in Miami. The company, however, managed to get only 85 of its 1,040 scheduled flights in the air on Saturday, and about 125 the next day. Union officials claimed that even these figures were exaggerated.

Over the next several days, Eastern was forced to lay off 6,000 nonunion employees who continued to show up for work. There was nothing for them to do. Thousands of Eastern flights were canceled. Angry passengers were stranded in airports around the country, clutching worthless tickets.

The railroads also were quick to move. For years they had been waiting for Congress to end the right of rail workers to engage in secondary strikes—those not directed at their own employer—which are permitted under the Railway Labor Act but are illegal under the national labor law that covers most other workers. The airlines often got their unions to sign contracts preventing secondary strikes, but the railroads had never had the strength to get similar concessions. Now they saw their chance to swing public opinion to their side. They screamed that railroads were being dragged into a labor dispute that had nothing to do with them. They blamed the archaic railway act and demanded it be changed. They also ran to the courts the day the strike began, demanding that the rail unions not be allowed to engage in secondary walkouts.

Bush moved to join them. The White House had already dug out Elizabeth Dole's old bill aimed at banning secondary picketing in railroads. Bush prepared to send it to Capitol Hill a few days after the strike began. Transportation Secretary Skinner and other officials hinted that the strike might spread. McClure, Bush's legislative affairs assistant, who claimed that he had avoided the Eastern situation because of his former employment at Texas Air, sent a group of congressmen a letter explaining Bush's decision not to go along with an emergency board. Congressional Democrats prepared their own bill, which would force Bush to declare an emergency board. They blamed Bush for not intervening to settle the dispute, arguing that he was playing politics.

Eastern also rushed into court. The company claimed that the pilots were not engaged in a sympathy strike at all. Though it appeared that pilots had honored the machinists picket lines, company lawyers argued, in reality the pilots had struck because they didn't like their own contract proposal. Since that offer had been presented informally, outside the auspices of the mediation board, there had been no mediation process as called for by law. The pilots' strike, therefore, was illegal.

The unions brushed off the suit as a sign of Lorenzo's weakness. "The fact that he's going to the court is atypical," said Bruce Simon, the pilot lawyer. "He likes to win it in the street. He's desperate, like a cornered rat."

But to the surprise of some legal experts—including mediation board lawyers who had studied the issue months before—several courts issued temporary restraining orders blocking secondary walkouts by the rail unions. The judgments plucked the bullets out of the unions' biggest guns. Now they had no way to force Congress and Bush to go along with an emergency board.

The battle seesawed back and forth for a week. The machinists appealed the rail decisions, but the courts held firm. The pilots did, too, however, and Lorenzo couldn't get his airline off the ground. Eastern laid off another 2,500 nonunion workers. In Washington, the issue quickly degenerated into a partisan battle. Congress held hearings on the strike and a House subcommittee approved the bill to force an emergency board. Texas Air lobbyists tried to swing sentiment in their favor by suggesting that Eastern might have to declare bankruptcy. Skinner told congressional leaders that he would recommend a veto. Bush repeated that he wouldn't intervene. "I still feel the best answer is a head-on-head, man-to-man negotiation between the union and the airline," he said at a press conference several days after the strike began.

Labor strengthened its forces. Pilot president Duffy declared that the union would contribute its $37 million strike war chest to the battle. Pilots could collect $2,400 a month in pay from the union—a far cry from their $80,000-a-year average salary, but enough to live on. Duffy backed off from calling strikes at other airlines, fearing that he couldn't convince their pilots to walk out solely in order to get an emergency board appointed to help the machinists. Instead he called on pilots at other airlines to engage in a work-to-rule slowdown, in which they would follow every procedure in their flight manuals to slow down airline traffic without actually walking off their jobs. The Eastern unions also kept up their search for a buyer, thinking that Lorenzo would be forced to sell. They went back to all the same people, including Icahn, Imperatore, the New Jersey trucker, and Grandview (Backe's First Flight Acquisition Corp.), which still hadn't made an offer.

The AFL-CIO appointed a task force, headed by Lynn Williams, the president of the steelworkers union, to coordinate support groups around the country. A dozen unions organized members to join Eastern workers on the picket lines at major airports. The task force and Eastern union strategists began work on a plan to hit Texas Air by picketing Continental, too. They drew up leaflets to drive home the point that a ticket bought on Continental might wind up as worthless as many of those that Eastern flyers had got stuck with. It said: "Are you sure you'll get your money back?"

Lorenzo tried everything to keep Eastern going. He signed the deal to sell Eastern's Philadelphia gates and several Canadian routes to USAir for $85 million. The company began shopping around for buyers for its South American routes and for its main machine shop in Miami, which Ryder System Inc. had looked at several weeks before.

With Eastern bringing in almost no revenue, all sides prepared for collapse. Texas Air creditors, some of whom had been blind-sided by Lorenzo's Continental bankruptcy, vowed not to be caught off guard again. They began lining up their bankruptcy attorneys. So did the unions. "If it goes to bankruptcy, we'll try to drag in Continental," said machinist advisor Freeman. "He has cross-liabilities and fraudulent conveyances between the two. We'll file our own reorganization plan. Then we'll ask the court trustee to remove Lorenzo."

Looking for a way out, Lorenzo focused on the shuttle. Eastern devoted most of its tiny pool of working pilots to keeping the shuttle flying, so that Trump would have something to buy. Four days into the strike, the Transportation Department cleared the last of the regulatory hurdles to the sale. But Trump leaped at the chance to kick Lorenzo while he was down. He demanded that Texas Air cut the price of the shuttle, arguing that it was worth less now because of the damage to its market share that the strike had caused. "The two of them have been screaming at each other over the phone for days," said a Texas Air official.

It became clear that Lorenzo had badly miscalculated about the pilots. He began to consider one of the only alternatives left: bankruptcy. "We did a recalculation of whether any pilots

165

would cross," said Harvey Miller, the bankruptcy lawyer, "and saw that they wouldn't. We didn't want to file for bankruptcy with no cash, and we were down to about $200 million."

On March 7, word came down that the company would file for bankruptcy that night if it lost the suit calling the pilots' strike illegal. When the company did lose, however, Lorenzo abruptly changed course and asked the pilots for a new negotiating session. To buy time, Eastern officials said they would appeal the suit.

The following day, Lorenzo convened a meeting in Houston of his boards of directors of Texas Air, Continental, and Eastern. Later in the evening, one director said: "I just got back from the Eastern board meeting. There were no decisions made. Mostly we were brought up to speed and we reviewed all the options. Whether to sell off assets and keep going, bankruptcy, and so on. Lorenzo was there, but he didn't do much talking. The money is flowing out pretty fast. Something like $5 million a day, or close to that. It's a crazy ballgame, and someone's going to get hurt." Kay McMurray, the newly hired Eastern director who formerly held Wallace's job as mediation board chairman, said: "A decision on which option to take has to be made within days."

That night, Lorenzo flew to New York. When he arrived, he held a conference call with the board and told them that Eastern would file for bankruptcy. At 9:22 A.M. the next morning, a subsidiary of Eastern called Ionosphere Clubs Inc., the airport-lounge holding company he had spun off and incorporated in New York, filed for Chapter 11 bankruptcy in the Southern District of New York. In a somewhat dubious legal tactic, Eastern then filed for bankruptcy in the same court six minutes later, even though the company is based in Miami. The reason quickly became clear: judges in New York's bankruptcy system are known to be sympathetic to helping management reorganize, while Miami's bankruptcy courts often side with the creditors. Moreover, Harvey Miller, who practices in New York, has had a long-standing relationship with the Southern District's chief judge, Burton R. Lifland.

At the Intercontinental hotel conference room where Texas Air announced the bankruptcy, the scene was chaotic. Fearing that employees might overreact, the company hired a guard service to make sure Eastern workers couldn't get into the room. A mad crush developed as hundreds of reporters and TV camerapeople pushed and shoved to get in. Some came without press passes and stood outside at the door screaming at the beefy guards to let them in. About 10 A.M., Lorenzo and Bakes pushed their way through the crowd and up to the podium in front. Lorenzo, who looked drawn and haggard, spoke first.

"We have not given up on our goal of seeing Eastern survive. Some people say I'm the problem. I'm not going to kid you by saying some of those statements haven't hurt me and my family. They have. But the real issue isn't me, it's deregulation. We knew when we bought Eastern that it complemented our existing assets. But we also knew it wasn't a bed of roses. I'm disappointed personally that pilots didn't see reality. We anticipated that a substantial number of pilots would cross the picket lines."

Bakes looked little better. "The last five days have been the saddest days of my life. We hope for a negotiated settled agreement with [the pilots]. If we can't get it, we hope some pilots will cross the picket lines. If they don't, we'll hire new ones. You shouldn't look at this as a death warrant for Eastern. Continental and other airlines went through this. To get our customers back, we will provide good service at a hell of a good price."

Even many die-hard Lorenzo supporters thought he had gone overboard. What had started out as economics now looked like a grudge match. Lorenzo had become so obsessed with beating the unions that rational economic decisions had gone out the window. Eastern had lost about a million dollars a day for two straight years while Lorenzo waited to break the machinists. The savings Lorenzo expected from the machinists, however, came to only $150 million a year. In two years, Lorenzo had reduced Eastern from the third-largest carrier in the nation to the seventh. He had become so determined to emerge the victor that he was willing to sacrifice the very company he had intended to save.

"I've never run into the acrimony, hatred, and irrationality that I've seen at Eastern, on both sides," said one close Lorenzo confidant at the time. "Charlie Bryan is off the wall. But so is Lorenzo. I've fought a lot of labor battles. But I can't support Lorenzo's fight now. He's fighting a war of attrition, that's all. I don't know what he's fighting for and I don't know why he's fighting."

CHAPTER TEN
Savior

From the minute he dumped the company into bankruptcy, Lorenzo fought desperately to retain control over Eastern. Much had changed since Continental had filed for bankruptcy six years earlier. Congress had plugged the loopholes that had allowed him unilaterally to cancel Continental's union contracts. Now, Lorenzo had to prove to the bankruptcy court that the company could not get back on its feet without the specific new wage levels he wanted. He also had to negotiate with labor.

Texas Air faced another problem. Eastern's pension funds were owed some $750 million. If Eastern missed its pension payments, the government pension agency would have first claim on any Eastern assets. If it couldn't get the money from Eastern, the feds could go straight to Texas Air and Continental. With Continental already on the verge of collapse, Lorenzo's entire empire could be in serious jeopardy.

In addition, there were growing shortfalls of pilots and mechanics. In the 12 months before the Eastern strike, more than 10,000 new pilots—10 times the average yearly number during the previous two decades—were hired throughout the industry. Because striking Eastern workers could land other jobs, it was unlikely that they'd return to work after a few weeks on the picket line. The shortages also meant that Eastern would have difficulty finding replacement workers.

To add to the pressure, not only had the AFL-CIO thrown its weight behind the Eastern strike, persuading other unions to offer cash, political support, and pickets; but the airline unions themselves were better prepared than they had been in 1983. The Continental fiasco had jolted the pilots union into action; once little more than an adjunct to airline management, by 1989 it had forged itself into a bona fide labor union. Pilots had mounted successful strikes at other airlines, notably United in 1985. The union also had plenty of cash; it could fight back.

The main action, however, had shifted to the ornate bankruptcy court south of Wall Street in lower Manhattan. Harvey Miller's tactic of filing in New York had worked beautifully. Though bankruptcy cases are assigned to different judges by lottery, somehow Lifland, the chief judge, often got the biggest and most controversial cases. Lifland, the most promanagement judge in an already promanagement bankruptcy district, got Eastern.

Within days of the bankruptcy filing, the unions asked Lifland to appoint a trustee to take command of Eastern. This was a rash legal step. The law allows management to be kicked out only if it engages in fraudulent behavior or gross incompetence. Union lawyers argued that Lorenzo had shown the former by stripping Eastern of assets. "The point is, if Lorenzo has been milking Eastern he shouldn't be allowed to keep running it," said James Lindsey, a pilot lawyer.

Eastern promptly countered with an even more unusual request. The company suggested that the court appoint an independent examiner to determine the validity of its asset sales and transfers. This was a clever suggestion. A trustee would strip Lorenzo of his executive powers. An examiner would delve into Lorenzo's transactions and report back to the judge. The prospect wasn't pleasant, but it would give Texas Air some breathing room. In addition, the company would have a voice in choosing the examiner. Most important, with an examiner, Lorenzo would remain firmly in charge. Although the judge would have to sign off on every move, Lorenzo could continue to look for strikebreakers and sell assets to raise cash.

In mid-March, Lifland opted for an examiner, but bestowed him with broader powers than usual. The judge spelled out his priorities clearly: he wanted the examiner to get the airline flying again. Citing the damage to the public interest involved in having one of the country's major airlines sitting on the ground, Lifland said that the normal rules of bankruptcy wouldn't apply.

Meanwhile, public opinion continued to hurt Lorenzo. Labor had dealt a clean knockout to his image, and the media pilloried him. When Lorenzo boarded a Delta flight to New York from Utah, where he had been skiing with his family, the pilot initially refused to take off. After 12 minutes, he gave in. When Lorenzo arrived at Kennedy Airport, he was heckled. Later, Lorenzo himself admitted that his name had taken on a life of its own. It's "a symbol. . . . I don't own the name anymore," he said. Lorenzo's reputation soon spread so far that his name was emblazoned in red on the Berlin Wall, with a circle drawn around it and a slash slanting through. Picketers stood outside the Lorenzo home in Houston, causing one of the mothers who drove the Lorenzo children to school in a car pool to fear for the safety of her kids. Lorenzo and his wife later began an extraordinary practice to allay their children's fears: each day before school, the parents would brief the kids . on what the papers said about their father.

Meanwhile, back at Texas Air, Carl Pohlad was fed up. Having had little success with gentle persuasion, the Minnesota Twins owner now openly raised the matter of selling to Ueberroth at a Texas Air board meeting. Shortly thereafter, at the major league baseball meeting at the Bonaventure Hotel in Fort Lauderdale, Florida, Pohlad and Ueberroth discussed a purchase of Eastern.

Spivey, not surprisingly, was in town, too. He had contacted Pohlad a few days before and had been told of the meeting planned with Ueberroth. On March 8, Spivey and Jack Bavis, the pilot leader, met for a drink at the Embassy Suite hotel in Miami, where Spivey was staying. Spivey gave Bavis Ueberroth's phone number at the Bonaventure. Bavis called, and the two talked about Ueberroth's desire to buy Eastern.

The blows from all sides were too much for Lorenzo to resist. Even before the bankruptcy, he had begun to consider seriously whether to sell Eastern. The day after the strike, Lorenzo had asked Joe Adams, the Drexel banker who helped on Texas Air's day-to-day investment banking work, to go to Houston with several of his colleagues to discuss strategy. They did several days later, when they talked about the possibility of a sale of Eastern. Lorenzo authorized Drexel to draw up a selling memorandum, which the investment bank then sent out to several prospective buyers, including Ueberroth. Of course, Ueberroth had said he was interested.

Shortly after Ueberroth and Pohlad met, Lorenzo called Ueberroth directly and said he might be willing to consider a sale. Then Lorenzo called Bavis and asked him to fly to Houston. On March 11, Bavis, accompanied by Buzz Wright, the pilot officer put in charge of the union's buyout effort, and Kupersmith, the Touche Ross accountant, met for two hours with Lorenzo, Texas Air strategist Bob Ferguson, and Eastern labor-relations vice president Tom Matthews. Bavis again suggested they come to terms by merging Continental and Eastern and unionizing both. He also proposed an ironclad fence deal as an alternative, or a sale to employees.

Lorenzo turned Bavis down on the first two points. He would, however, pursue a sale, he said. He asked whether the unions had found sufficient money and management talent to put together a credible purchase. The union representatives suggested Icahn. Lorenzo refused, claiming that Icahn couldn't be trusted. Then Lorenzo said he had been working with someone else. Though he didn't actually say that he meant Ueberroth, the pilot representatives knew, since Bavis had just spoken with Ueberroth three days earlier. "He said he was examining all his options, including selling," said Bavis a few days later. "That was the first time he ever said that to me.

Frank doesn't want to sell to the unions. Or to a competitor like Icahn. He's got too big an ego."

Lorenzo now seemed to have run out of options. On March 14, he met Ueberroth, who said he wasn't going to waste his time unless Lorenzo was serious about a sale. Lorenzo said he was. Ueberroth gathered a small team of negotiators, including the New York law firm of Latham & Watkins and an obscure investment banking company called Ardshiel Inc. Ueberroth had come to know Ardshiel when it put together an employee buyout of National Car Rental, in which Ueberroth played a small role. Ueberroth also brought in a partner, J. Thomas Talbot, a California real estate developer who also had been the chairman of Jet America, a regional airline he had helped to found in 1981. The group set to work to see if they could put together an offer for Eastern.

The following Friday, March 17, Bavis, Wright, and Kupersmith flew to New York. They had a secret breakfast meeting at the Regency Hotel with Ueberroth and Talbot. Ueberroth cast himself as the employees' savior and hero. A medium-size, charismatic person with a smooth, comforting voice, Ueberroth promised to take labor-management cooperation farther than anyone had done before. Although the machinists and flight attendants were not included in the meeting, the group discussed how to put a deal together that would give the unions a large stake in the company in exchange for concessions.

The union leaders came away with mixed feelings. Bavis liked Ueberroth, and Bryan, who had been talking to Ueberroth regularly for months, had come to trust him. But Ueberroth had come to them through Spivey. When they had met Ueberroth the previous fall, he had just met with Lorenzo. Now Lorenzo was claiming that he might sell after all, but only to Ueberroth.

Whose side was Ueberroth on? Was he acting independently or was he a front for Lorenzo? Or was Lorenzo trying to use him as a stalking horse to lure the unions into a trap? The unions were all the more suspicious because Drexel was the primary investment banker. Milken, they knew, wanted the Eastern mess resolved, but he had also backed Lorenzo for years. Latham & Watkins, moreover, was one of Drexel's chief law firms, and now Ueberroth had hired it to represent him. "I think the Ueberroth deal could be a scam," said Brian Freeman. "The guy has no money, no business plan, nothing. I think Lorenzo's strategy may be to dump Eastern on the employees after bankruptcy." Randy Barber was just as wary. "This is like spy versus spy versus spy," he said. "Dealing with Lorenzo, especially in the last six months, has been like a house of mirrors. We don't know who's on whose side."

The unions were divided about Ueberroth for other reasons as well. While their solidarity on the picket line was firm, the old union divisions had opened up again behind the scenes. Now Bavis was at the controls, and he knew it. For two years, he had had to take a back seat to Bryan, because the machinists had the open contract. Now that the strike was on, it had become clear that the machinists wouldn't last a second without the pilots. If the pilots returned, Eastern would take off and Lorenzo could wash his hands of the machinists.

Bavis reveled in his new strength. He was the one sitting at the table, negotiating with Ueberroth. His position had gotten a boost from Lorenzo. Fearing that the machinist leader might prevent Ueberroth from reaching an agreement with the unions, Lorenzo had told Ueberroth to work with the pilots and keep clear of Bryan.

The strike had shifted the balance within the individual unions, too. In the pilots' union, Bavis had been on the defensive because of other ALPA leaders' suspicions about his fence deal. Now that he had lined up behind the Ueberroth sale, he had taken charge. Though both Wright and Copeland, the militant from New York, remained distrustful of Bavis, they went along with the Ueberroth negotiation because Lorenzo had put it on the front burner.

Meanwhile, Bryan had lost ground among the machinists. Peterpaul, worried that Bryan's visibility would antagonize rank-and-file pilots who still blamed him for letting Lorenzo take Eastern, told him to keep a low profile. The machinist vice president took his union's seat on the bankruptcy's creditors' committee, which gave him a direct line on anything that happened, and sent Freeman looking for other buyers. Bryan kept looking on his own as well.

The result was a contest for control. Virtually every union power center struck out in search of different buyers. The feeding frenzy that Lorenzo had complained about in November was on again with a vengeance.

Freeman kept after Carl Icahn. He'd been calling the TWA chairman almost every day since the bankruptcy. Within days of the walkout, Freeman had called Icahn and suggested that the two of them meet, along with Kupersmith. They scheduled a meeting in New York, but when Lorenzo found out about it, he called Icahn and threatened to sue if the meeting went ahead—even though Lorenzo already was talking to Ueberroth. Faced with a possible lawsuit for interfering in Eastern's labor negotiations, Icahn backed off.

Undeterred, Freeman called Arthur Imperatore, the New Jersey trucker, to see if he was still interested. Pilot leaders bad-mouthed his efforts, just as the machinists had attacked Bavis. "Freeman just wants another deal because he'll get a fee out of it," charged one pilot official. "He's trying to kill all the other ones."

Bryan continued to work with Backe, the former CBS chieftain, and Pritzker, the Hyatt hotels owner. Buzz Wright and Jack Suchocki, the pilots assigned to the buyout effort, did likewise. They told Backe not to deal with Bavis, because they didn't want him involved in the deal.

Even though he was on the outs with Backe, Bryan, and most of the union leaders, Spivey hadn't slowed down for a minute. He had kept in touch with Wright George and with Suchocki. He had also talked to Joe Adams at Drexel, who told Spivey he needed firm financing and a solid management team before he could do anything about acquiring Eastern. Spivey then began calling everyone he could think of.

He hit paydirt with two people. A representative of Kirk Kerkorian, the reclusive owner of MGM/UA who had made a bid for Pan Am in 1987, said Kerkorian might want to get involved. Adding to the spy-versus-spy atmosphere, the representative said that Kerkorian already had talked about buying Eastern with Ueberroth, who had run an association of charter airlines Kerkorian owned years ago. Marvin Davis, the billionaire who had been one of the partners in the aborted shuttle spin-off, expressed an interest, too. Spivey told Davis he would arrange a meeting with a delegation of pilot leaders. "I'm flying to Los Angeles to meet Davis on Monday," Spivey said on March 17, the same day that Ueberroth and the pilots were gathering in New York.

Even as he proceeded in negotiations with Ueberroth, Lorenzo never ceased to fight. Eastern plowed ahead with its plan to hire strikebreakers, screening candidates and setting up a training program for new pilots. To foot the bill, Texas Air initiated talks with American Airlines about selling Eastern's South American routes. Lorenzo also girded for another bout in the single-carrier case. After postponements caused by Texas Air's legal maneuvering, the mediation board was saying that its decision would be ready in a matter of weeks.

Lorenzo and Ueberroth were frequently at loggerheads. Often, Lorenzo would use a bait-and-switch tactic that kept Ueberroth off balance. Snedeker or other Texas Air officials would argue vigorously over some point and finally agree. Then Lorenzo would say that they hadn't been authorized to make that decision, and the two sides would have to argue all over again. "They came at us from all directions," said Ueberroth's partner, Tom Talbot. "You'd think you had the issue settled, then they would come back and say it's not settled over here. That must have happened several dozen times." Ueberroth grew increasingly angry with what he saw as Lorenzo's cutthroat negotiating tactics. Pohlad acted as a peacemaker between the two, but Ueberroth became suspicious of Lorenzo's intentions. "It's possible that Lorenzo is using me as a stalking horse against the unions," Ueberroth said at the time. "But if I'm ever going to get involved, I want it to be without Lorenzo. You can't do this with the current management, because of the bitterness."

Ueberroth knew that he had to make a clean break with

Lorenzo: he didn't want to buy Eastern under terms that would leave Texas Air with any control in the company. But independence came only with money. Fortunately, Kerkorian was a longtime mentor worth something on the order of $1 billion. He and Ueberroth had been close friends for many years. Ueberroth asked Kerkorian if he would help, and Kerkorian agreed. But Ueberroth knew that he would have to give Kerkorian some of his ownership in Eastern if he brought him in, so he continued to scout for money elsewhere.

Ueberroth also kept talking to Backe and Pritzker. On March 18, a day after his meeting in New York with the pilot group, he told Backe that a deal might go through. In the previous weeks, the three had agreed on a plan. Pritzker would buy Eastern. Ueberroth would be the chairman. Mort Ehrlich, the former Eastern vice president who had been nominated as Grandview's choice for manager, would be the president in charge of day-to-day operations. However, there was growing friction between Ueberroth and Backe. Ueberroth didn't keep Backe or Pritzker informed of all the progress he was making with Lorenzo. Sometimes they heard rumors—about Kerkorian's involvement, for instance. They began to suspect that Ueberroth was leaving them out in the cold.

Then Ueberroth hit the jackpot. Drexel offered financial support in an Eastern buyout. This wasn't just the hand of Mike Milken, who had become caught up in the government's crackdown on securities traders and largely had stepped out of the picture. Drexel as an institution needed to protect its franchise in the junk-bond market. In 1989, Wall Street was growing nervous about junk bonds. If the economy hit a downturn, all those companies leveraged to the hilt from junk-bond takeovers might not be able to make the payments on their loans.

In this context, Lorenzo's troubles were bad news. Drexel had peddled more than $1 billion in stocks, bonds, and equipment trust certificates for Texas Air, Continental, and Eastern. As a result, many big Drexel clients were in for a piece of Frank Lorenzo. If he went under and those clients got stuck with worthless paper, they'd point the finger at Drexel for pushing it on them in the first place. To prevent this from happening, Drexel was willing to bail Lorenzo out of his mess before he wreaked further damage on Drexel's image.

Ueberroth was home free. He didn't have to call on Kerkorian. Nor did he need Backe and Pritzker, whom he promptly stopped calling. Feeling angry and betrayed, they began to think about how to mount their own offer.

Ueberroth and Talbot holed up with Lorenzo at Texas Air's Rockefeller Center offices in New York and began negotiating virtually around the clock, shuttling back and forth between Rockefeller Center and Latham & Watkins's nearby offices in midtown Manhattan, where Bavis, Kupersmith, and several other pilot representatives were camped out. Lorenzo did everything he could to retain control, but Ueberroth had his own bankroll now and insisted that Texas Air would have no financial stake in Eastern after the sale. Finally, Lorenzo agreed. Several days into the talks, the pilot leaders, who regularly met Ueberroth's team in between the negotiation sessions with Texas Air, raised an even thornier issue: Who would run the company for the 60 or so days that it would take for the creditors and the judge to clear the sale?

"Originally, we said we'd come in as operators to ramp it up during the 60 days," Talbot said shortly thereafter. "But . . . Lorenzo said: 'I own the stock until the deal's done. When you pay me, you can run the company.' It was a tough chicken-and-egg question. He said, 'Trust me, we're in bankruptcy, we can't run away.' "

Lorenzo proposed that he run the company during the 60 days. If he then reneged and refused to sell after Eastern cleared bankruptcy, Texas Air would pay Ueberroth a $20 million fee. Ueberroth wasn't happy, and neither were the union representatives. Nevertheless, Ueberroth decided to go ahead and make a formal offer to the Texas Air directors, even though the issue wasn't completely resolved.

"We think we have a transaction that is very close," Ueberroth said March 29. "In the next hour or so, we'll have a firm offer to send to Texas Air's board, which is meeting in Houston. Lorenzo and I, we're not getting along on the question of control and other issues. We may resolve it, but the 60-day interim period is still the big question."

Throughout the talks, Lorenzo had kept scouting for a way out. He had sent Marvin Davis Eastern's financial statements overnight so Davis could make up his mind whether to make a bid. Lorenzo also had contacted Pritzker, who had decided along with Backe to go to Lorenzo with a competing bid after Ueberroth dumped them. On March 23, Lorenzo had told Pritzker that he was unhappy with Ueberroth's offer, and asked Pritzker if he wanted to make one of his own. Five days later, Lorenzo gave Pritzker permission to talk with the pilots.

Only Icahn got the cold shoulder. After his handshake deal with Lorenzo had fallen apart in February, Lorenzo had decided that he could never reach an agreement with him. Lorenzo told Drexel again that Icahn couldn't re-enter negotiations with Eastern's unions. This galled Icahn, who already was furious with Drexel for stepping in to help Ueberroth buy the company. Icahn had used Drexel's junk-bond machine repeatedly since tapping it to buy TWA in 1985 and considered himself one of Mike Milken's best customers. Now Drexel not only was helping a rival, but had turned against him and warned him to keep out of the picture. Even though Icahn was good friends with Leon Black, the head of mergers and acquisitions at Drexel, and played poker with him every week, not long thereafter, Icahn took some of his investment banking business away from Drexel and gave it to Merrill Lynch.

The union leaders too had kept looking for alternatives during the Lorenzo-Ueberroth negotiations. The machinists, in particular, were worried about getting railroaded into a pilot-driven deal. The machinists had heard rumors that the Ueberroth sale would never come off because Bryan would never accept steep concessions. This fanned the flames of Bryan's suspicions about Bavis. "It was an uncomfortable catch-22, I can tell you," said Bryan. "They set it up so that I was going to kill the deal unless the [machinists union] took a real devastating hit. If it didn't, I'd get the blame once again. That was Lorenzo's idea, and Bavis went along happily." To counteract this, Bryan urged Ueberroth to get back together with

Pritzker. Ueberroth, who kept taking Bryan's calls throughout this period, didn't do so.

The rivalries amongst the pilots worked against Pritzker. Even before Lorenzo gave him and Backe the okay to talk to them, Backe had been dealing with Wright and Suchocki, who were handling the buyout effort, not Bavis. Now Bavis was pushing Ueberroth and did his best to shut out Pritzker and Backe. "We couldn't make anything stick with the pilots because we were in with Bavis's rivals, Buzz Wright and the rest of them," said Gelman, whose consulting firm did most of the analytic work for the Pritzker-Backe effort. "They thought they had the power to do a deal, but they didn't."

The same day he said a deal was close, Ueberroth sent a preliminary offer to the Texas Air board, which had convened in Houston. The next day, March 30, the board formally debated its merits. (As they did so, Marvin Davis saw a fatter target and pulled out to make a run at Northwest Airlines.)

Pritzker also sent in a last-minute bid for Eastern. Though he didn't offer as much cash as Ueberroth—he was interested primarily in the tax advantage that would come from doing sale-leasebacks of Eastern's planes—his overall bid topped Ueberroth's by some $90 million, depending on how it was valued. Lorenzo wasn't concerned that Pritzker's deal was shakier than Ueberroth's, which already had firm financing from Drexel—he wanted to use the new offer to whipsaw the baseball commissioner.

On Friday, March 31, Pohlad called Ueberroth, who was in Nashville, Tennessee, to tell him that Texas Air's directors had approved the sale but that he had been outbid by $90 million. In a flurry of phone calls, Pohlad and Joe Adams, the Drexel banker, informed Ueberroth that he could have Eastern, but only if he split the difference between his bid and the higher offer by kicking in another $40 million.

It was Ueberroth's last day in office as baseball commissioner. Furious, he withdrew his offer for Eastern, chartered a plane, and flew home to California, where he and Talbot headed out to the desert to play golf.

"Frank couldn't leave it alone," said one of Lorenzo's advisors. "He told Ueberroth to pay $40 million more and to take it or leave it. Peter said no, and then he disappeared. Everyone said: 'You're kidding, he can't do this.' When it became clear that he really had gone, Lorenzo said: 'Holy shit.' "

When Pritzker heard what was going on, he too got mad and rescinded his bid. "You don't shop someone's offer around like that," said a Pritzker advisor at the time. "You don't do that in honorable negotiations. It's just not done."

Texas Air officials frantically began calling Ueberroth's lawyers, trying to locate him and Talbot. Finally, Pohlad tracked them down. He convinced Ueberroth to return to the table. Talbot flew to New York, while Ueberroth waited a day longer. "There was a lot of fighting over whether to sell at first," said one Eastern director. "But then everyone went along."

On Monday, April 3, Talbot began negotiating with Texas Air while Ueberroth headed back to New York to join him. The unions had told Ueberroth informally that they would give him the same deal they had worked up for Grandview: some $200 million in concessions in return for about 30 percent of Eastern's stock. But they were still extremely concerned about the 60-day interim period. If Lorenzo reneged afterward, Ueberroth would collect a cool $20 million for his pains and they would be stuck working for Lorenzo all over again. "All Lorenzo had to do was write a $20 million check and Ueberroth was gone," said Bruce Simon, the pilot lawyer. To be sure, the unions could strike again, but the rank and file might feel so bamboozled that another walkout would never get off the ground. Lorenzo would win.

Talbot suggested that the unions sign interim labor agreements with Ueberroth. The pacts would expire the day Eastern emerged from bankruptcy. If Lorenzo reneged, new contracts would kick in that would restore the unions to their pre-strike pay scales and even provide raises in future years. That way, Lorenzo would have to pay an impossible price to keep control. For added security, Lorenzo had to agree not to sell assets or change routes during the 60 days.

That Monday and Tuesday, Texas Air officials and Ueberroth's team shuttled back and forth between Lorenzo's offices and Latham & Watkins. By the end of the day Tuesday, the deal looked set. Ueberroth's team wanted a press conference for 10 A.M. Wednesday, April 5. The media was alerted and a hotel conference room was reserved in midtown Manhattan. The pilots in Miami were beside themselves with joy. They had won. They celebrated until three in the morning. But when Texas Air and Ueberroth's team met at 7:30 A.M. Wednesday, Lorenzo put seven more items on the table. The haggling began again. The press briefing was canceled.

Lifland, the bankruptcy judge, fumed with impatience. Two weeks earlier, he had ordered a court officer to appoint an examiner, a move that he had been putting off because of the impending sale to Ueberroth. On Tuesday, Eastern had asked for a further delay, fearing that an examiner with strong powers might impede the talks and perhaps cut into the price Texas Air would get—but Lifland put his foot down. He appointed David I. Shapiro, a Washington lawyer who had helped to engineer a solution to the Agent Orange case.

The judge gave Shapiro broad powers to get Eastern out of bankruptcy quickly. "I want a process that will eliminate the hidden agendas," Lifland said in court. "This grounded airline is a wasting national asset. Planes are not flying, and nobody has suggested why it's in the public interest why this court should stay its hand. I want planes flying again."

But Ueberroth was furious with Lorenzo's last-minute changes. At first, he said he wouldn't negotiate anymore. Then he demanded $1 million for each of the seven changes Lorenzo had asked for. That got Lorenzo's back up, and the entire deal looked ready to collapse. Then Pohlad and Joe Adams of Drexel intervened. They convinced Lorenzo and Ueberroth to talk it over with each other. Adams arranged for the two men to meet alone at the Boardroom, a private lunch club on Park Avenue. After 90 minutes, they finally made a deal. In the end, Ueberroth agreed to five of Lorenzo's last-minute modifications, and Lorenzo agreed to cut the price by $5 million.

"This happened all the way through," said Talbot, Ueberroth's partner, shortly thereafter. "Every time they came back to us for more, we asked for something from them. It was like

sitting in a bazaar in Iran, dealing rugs. It was just unbelievable. Lorenzo would put the bait out there, then you'd look
and, where did it go? It gets yanked back, then Lorenzo puts
it out again. I can understand why the unions are so angry
with him.

"Finally, I saw a change in Lorenzo's attitude. He began to
realize that he would really have to let go. When we came
back on Monday, we put in the agreements that they couldn't
sell assets or change routes. It seemed to me that there was a
release at that point. That's when mentally they sold the company."

On Thursday, April 6, Ueberroth and Lorenzo held a joint
press conference in Manhattan to announce their agreement.
Ueberroth stated that labor would own 30 percent of the new
company, which would be called Eastern Airlines Employees
and Service Co. "It will be a new concept in aviation," he
said. "We look at labor as our partners."

Once again, Lorenzo had made out like a bandit. He had
purchased Eastern for next to nothing and then walked off
with hundreds of millions in assets. Now he was selling the
dregs for $464 million. Though only $200 million was in hard
cash, he was getting $79 million in Eastern assets, including
some of its airport gates and slots. In addition, Ueberroth
would waive $185 million that Texas Air owed Eastern for
some of the previous assets it had taken. Still, Lorenzo was
unhappy. "It's a day of very mixed feelings," he said. "We
didn't buy Eastern to sell Eastern. It was not our preferred
course. But we've been in a very tough situation."

Ueberroth came out even better. He and his partners, including Talbot, would get 30 percent of Eastern's stock. The
unions would get another 30 percent. Drexel would sell the
rest to outside investors. From its own coffers, Drexel was
putting in $200 million—the only cash involved in the whole
deal. Essentially, Drexel was purchasing a bankrupt airline
from one of its clients and then handing it over to another
one. Texas Air even agreed to pick up a $5 million tab for
Ueberroth's legal and investment banking fees.

Ueberroth's agreement with Texas Air gave him a deadline

of midnight Tuesday—a mere five days—to strike a deal with the unions. Immediately after the news conference, Ueberroth met with union officials. That night, he flew to Washington to start negotiating the concession package. Over a two-hour dinner at Gary's, a favorite watering hole of machinist leaders, Ueberroth and Talbot sketched out the deal he had just signed with Texas Air.

On Friday, April 7, talks began in earnest. About 30 union leaders and their financial advisors began meetings at the machinists headquarters in downtown Washington. Talbot spoke for Ueberroth, who headed off to Los Angeles to address Drexel Burnham's annual junk-bond conference. Joe Adams represented Drexel. Shapiro, the newly appointed bankruptcy examiner, took charge, assisted by Harry Jones, the U.S. trustee, whose job as an officer of the bankruptcy court was to run the daily mechanics of the Eastern case.

From the beginning, the going was rough. Ueberroth's team decided that it actually needed $210 million in concessions. The extra $10 million wasn't a problem; the way the overall amount should be split was. Bryan thought that the machinists' share of the total should come in at about $125 million. The pilots figured that Bryan should take much more. This brought to a head all the history of antagonisms between the two unions. It also confirmed Bryan's fears that Bavis had been setting him up when the pilot leader had jumped at Ueberroth's proposal over those of other potential buyers. Under the pilots' interpretation of the unions' 1986 cooperation agreement, the pilots would contribute about $30 million, and the flight attendants under $20 million. Since the pilots intended to tap one of their two pension funds for their share, Bryan's members would be the ones taking the real pay cut. He complained but, under Shapiro's heavy hand, finally agreed to take $166 million.

Ueberroth's purchase proposal was an even bigger problem. The unions were concerned that Ueberroth had given away the store and left Eastern with insufficient cash. They also worried about management. Ueberroth himself knew little about the day-to-day running of an airline, and Talbot's experience hadn't involved a major carrier. In addition, Ueberroth had no corporate planners like Icahn, no team of consultants like Backe. Nor did he have a detailed business plan that specified which routes Eastern would fly, which planes it would use, or what prices it would charge. The union leaders and their lawyers and financial advisors all felt that Ueberroth might be in over his head.

Moreover, the machinist advisor, Freeman, and Kupersmith, the accountant hired by the pilots, argued that if the shuttle deal with Trump ever was approved, Eastern would have a hard time getting off the ground. This worried Ueberroth, who lacked the staff and expertise to analyze Eastern's operations and finances, and had relied primarily on Drexel and Lorenzo for such information.

The union leaders also disliked Talbot's new compromise on interim control. They didn't like the idea of working for Lorenzo during the 60-day period, no matter how many guarantees Texas Air gave. Bryan, who was especially concerned, would raise cain about this all weekend.

Shapiro didn't want to hear it. A gruff, tough-talking bear of a man, Shapiro cursed and screamed and pounded his fist until the papers jumped off the table. They had a deadline to meet and he wasn't going to take no for an answer.

On Friday, while the negotiations were going on in Washington, Lifland held a session in New York. Saying that he had seen no response to his "request that these birds start to fly immediately," he added his own deadline of Wednesday for the unions and Ueberroth to come to terms.

Shapiro slapped everyone with a gag order from the bankruptcy court so that a deal could be reached without posturing for the media. Then he kept the parties negotiating Friday and all day Saturday. Finally, on Saturday afternoon, he announced that he had come up with a way to get around the problem of the unions going back to work under Lorenzo. He said he'd get Lifland to appoint a trustee to run the carrier during the crucial 60-day period. Shapiro called the judge, who, according to Shapiro, indicated that he might go along with a trustee. In a dramatic statement that Saturday, Shapiro said: "Lorenzo is off the table."

Ueberroth returned from California that night in time to pick up the tab at Gary's, where the entire group went for dinner again. When they gathered at 7:30 A.M. Sunday in Shapiro's law offices in downtown Washington, Shapiro locked them in. To enforce the gag order, he banned phone calls unless a secretary listened in, and ordered takeout for all meals. He was determined to keep the pressure on until they'd finished. Later in the day, he kicked Freeman out of the meetings because he felt that the financial fears he raised about Eastern were beginning to worry Ueberroth. "I told Brian I'd kill him if he didn't get out of there," said Shapiro.

At two A.M. the 15 members of the pilots executive council were roused from their hotel rooms to vote on the deal. Finally, as the sky began to lighten, the package was completed and approved. "Shapiro was like Captain Bligh," said an exhausted Randy Barber that Monday, April 10.

The unions weren't entirely pleased with the result. But after years of Lorenzo, it was no time for cold feet. Ueberroth told them more about the management team he was trying to line up. Already Martin R. Shugrue, Jr., whom Lorenzo had fired recently as Continental's president, had agreed to serve as chief executive officer.

Drexel also had given more assurances. Over the weekend, Joe Adams promised that Drexel would contribute another $100 million to help Eastern get off the ground during the initial ramp-up period. He also suggested that Drexel could raise another $600 million or so, mostly in added debt. The $365 million from the shuttle sale to Trump could be used as collateral for another loan, and Eastern also could sell some of its planes and then lease them back. "Mike Milken kept telling me that money wasn't the issue," said Adams a short while later. "The question was, would the unions go along? So we just said we thought the deal was doable and that we'd do what we could to finance it."

On Sunday, Shapiro also had nailed down his new scheme

on the control issue. The unions would get a lifetime ban on Lorenzo's ever owning stock in Eastern. The unions then sat down with Jones, the U.S. trustee, to hammer out the legal paperwork necessary for Lifland to appoint a trustee for the 60 days. Shapiro asked former Secretary of State George Shultz to be the trustee, but Shultz, a director of Boeing, one of Eastern's creditors, begged off. Former Defense Secretary Frank C. Carlucci, however, agreed to take the post. Then Shapiro called Eastern president Phil Bakes with the news. Bakes, Shapiro said, was strongly opposed to a trustee. Shapiro had several phone discussions with Bakes.

Monday morning, everyone headed back to their hotels for a quick shower before they were due to return to New York. When Ueberroth got to his room, he received a call from Lorenzo, who, presumably having heard from Bakes about the trustee, asked how it was going. Ueberroth refused to talk to him. "I'm under a gag order from Shapiro," he said, and hung up the phone.

Bleary-eyed but filled with a sense of accomplishment, the union leaders, Shapiro, Ueberroth, and Carlucci headed to Washington's National Airport for the 9:30 A.M. Pan Am shuttle to New York. When they arrived at La Guardia Airport, they were met by an anxious delegation of lawyers sent out by Harvey Miller, Lorenzo's bankruptcy lawyer. Shapiro brushed by, telling them he was appointing a trustee. The group arrived at the bankruptcy court and went straight to Lifland's chambers, where Shapiro reported that they had beaten his deadline by a full two days. After the meeting, the group, punchy from lack of sleep, went around the corner to a small restaurant for lunch.

By now, much of the deal was out. The papers ran front-page stories trumpeting Ueberroth as the next Lee Iacocca. Many back-room players emerged, thankful that the ordeal was over and ready to take a bit of credit for helping the savior of Eastern Airlines. Pohlad spoke about his role for the first time, saying how he told Lorenzo in 1988: "Either we work it out with the unions, or maybe we'd better sell it."

Even Mike Milken, who had been indicted on securities

charges less than two weeks earlier, told of his involvement. "Nearly a year ago I told Frank Lorenzo there were big problems and that Peter Ueberroth was the right guy for the job and that this was the right time. Frank made a lot of constructive suggestions. But there were problems. You had a situation in which people weren't communicating with each other. Even Frank Borman, an American hero and astronaut, couldn't get the unions and management to work together. I don't think one side was completely at fault. Frank had a strong vision for the airline, that's tough to give up. But I don't believe there was any choice. My view was that it would be better for Texas Air and Continental in the long run if Eastern employees were given the opportunity to build their own company. You've got to treat people as equals, and make them feel like it's their company. I don't know if I had any impact or helped persuade Frank. But, I can tell you, there were many discussions on the subject."

Spivey was in a triumphant mood, too. "I've made 5,000 phone calls and had 300 plane flights trying to save this airline," he said. "I went through the entire Fortune 500 one by one, calling everyone who was reasonable. Where else would you start if you'd never done something like this before?" Then, for the first time, he delivered the kicker. "We get 5 percent of the deal for bringing in the buyer, which is about $23 million. That will be an equity stake or cash, it's not clear yet." Just an hour before, he had sent letters laying out his claim to everyone involved, including the judge, Ueberroth, the examiner, and the counsel for the unions. "But don't mention this now. It would be very distasteful to bring money into it. Sure, it's nice to make money, but I have my heart in it."

In Judge Lifland's chambers, however, Eastern's fate was rolling around once again. Although Shapiro had promised everyone in Washington that the judge was behind him, now it seemed that Lifland had cooled toward the idea of replacing Lorenzo with a trustee. Lawyers and others involved claim that, after Shapiro called Bakes on Sunday, Bakes called

Harvey Miller, and Miller phoned Lifland and read him the riot act.

Miller denies this, pointing out that such private communications with a judge would be in violation of bankruptcy rules. He claims that while he did talk to Bakes on Sunday, Bakes only said that Shapiro was discussing the merits of a trustee. According to Miller, Eastern's president didn't understand that Shapiro actually would request a trustee. It's difficult to believe that Bakes, a lawyer himself, would not have understood and emphasized the seriousness of a trustee, particularly when, according to Shapiro, he had reacted heatedly to Shapiro's statement about it. It's even harder to believe that Miller, the country's top bankruptcy lawyer, wouldn't have recognized the import of the idea, however casually mentioned.

Whether or not Miller leaned on the judge in private, Miller made no bones about his position on Monday. Lorenzo, he threatened, would resist a trustee. Miller pointed out that Lifland could be setting a dangerous precedent by replacing Lorenzo without even a hearing. The implication was clear: Lifland, a judge who had presided over many high-profile bankruptcies, could be jeopardizing his reputation if he acted rashly. And Miller's own reputation carried a lot of clout. He had been heavily involved in writing the country's new bankruptcy laws from 1973 to 1978.

When Ueberroth and his crew returned from lunch, the cheery scene had changed. Lifland told Ueberroth and the unions to work it out with Texas Air and avoid a trustee. Everyone gathered at the Vista International Hotel a few blocks from the courthouse. Shapiro put them in separate rooms, and a round of shuttle diplomacy ensued.

The effort continued on Tuesday. Lorenzo showed up at the Vista, accompanied by Bakes. The proposals flew thick and fast in an effort to overcome the trustee issue. Lorenzo proposed that Ueberroth and his associates be put in command of Eastern during the interim period, but that Texas Air remain the technical owner; in exchange, Lorenzo insisted that Ueberroth agree to lock up his purchase of the carrier after the 60-day period was over. The original agreement between Texas Air and Ueberroth had allowed both sides to back out at any time before the deal closed. Lorenzo didn't want to turn over the management of Eastern only to have the former baseball commissioner walk away if he had trouble getting the airline back on its feet.

Ueberroth refused to lock himself in to the purchase before he had done his "due diligence"—before his lawyers and accountants ensured that all the assets Eastern said it had were really there. After all, throughout the negotiations Ueberroth's team had gone only on the word of Texas Air and Drexel officials.

Then Texas Air suggested the airline sit on the ground during the interim 60 days. That way, the unions wouldn't have to work for Lorenzo, because the airline wouldn't be flying, and Texas Air would have its money before anyone else took over. Then Lorenzo reversed himself and suggested 30 days. Kupersmith, the accountant, added another suggestion: a clause that would call for the sale price to be adjusted if the due diligence process found some assets to be worth less than Texas Air had claimed. Ueberroth didn't like these ideas, either. If Eastern didn't fly for another 30 days, it could lose so many more passengers to American or Delta that he might never make a go of it. He'd still be left with a mess on his hands.

After the discussion, Lorenzo left the room and Harvey Miller went to tell Shapiro what had happened. The examiner said he thought the problem really was a matter of price. He asked Miller if Lorenzo would cut the purchase price by $90 million to induce Ueberroth to lock up the deal. That, he suggested, would cover Ueberroth for any unanticipated problems Eastern might encounter as he tried to get the airline flying again during the interim period. Miller said he didn't have the authority to speak for Lorenzo in his absence, so Shapiro said he'd suggest it himself. He asked Miller to accompany him, and the two went back down to Ueberroth's suite.

When Shapiro outlined his idea to Ueberroth and Talbot,

Ueberroth turned him down. After all the times Texas Air officials had changed positions, Ueberroth had no intention of bargaining with anyone but Lorenzo himself. And he certainly wasn't going to deal with Shapiro, who in Ueberroth's view had reneged on the trustee appointment. Ueberroth looked Shapiro straight in the eye and said: "I don't deal with emissaries."

"I am an officer of the court designated to do this," Shapiro responded.

"I'm not dealing with you," Ueberroth shot back.

Then Miller interjected, "I don't have to deal with you either," he barked, and stalked out.

Minutes after Miller and Shapiro left, Lorenzo called Ueberroth and said that he refused to cut the price.

Shapiro decided that they were getting nowhere. At three P.M., he returned to Lifland and, through a court officer, formally requested a trustee. Tempers flared as Miller fought back. At one point, Lifland could be heard behind closed doors shouting at Miller: "Dammit, Harvey, if you want the planes in the air, all you have to do is sign the paper." Moments later, Miller emerged into the hallway. Shapiro, who was standing nearby, tried to get his attention. "Harv," he shouted. Miller turned to look at him and said, "Shove it," and stormed off down the corridor.

Like a Greek chorus, the creditors now chimed in with their own ominous warning. They'd been left out of the proceedings and knew virtually nothing of the Ueberroth deal. To them, everything was happening too quickly. The creditors' committee issued a statement that expressed "its serious concern about certain significant aspects of the Texas Air–Ueberroth transaction." Ironically, the creditors had the same concerns as the unions about the viability of Ueberroth's business plan. Unaware of Drexel's offer to help raise additional financing, they worried that Lorenzo was making off with so much that Eastern would be left permanently crippled.

In the courthouse, Lifland tried unsuccessfully to lighten the mood by making popcorn for everyone. Shortly after seven P.M. Tuesday, Lorenzo showed up at the courthouse in re-

sponse to a summons by Miller. With him were Bakes and
Chuck Goolsbee, Texas Air's general counsel. The judge called
Lorenzo, Bakes, Ueberroth, and Talbot into his chambers to
hash the matter out. Lifland tried to persuade Ueberroth to
go along with the 30-day idea. The judge left, and the four
men argued for another hour and a half. When they emerged,
they told Lifland that they couldn't agree.

Later that night, the lawyers from all sides gathered in the
court for a conference. Shapiro gave a status report. While he
was recounting the events of the day, Robert J. Rosenberg, one
of Ueberroth's lawyers, spoke up. All he got out of his mouth
were the words "Harvey said." Miller, apparently frightened
that Rosenberg was going to mention the proposal that Lorenzo cut the price by $90 million, and concerned that it would
appear as if he had gone along with the idea without Lorenzo's
permission, exploded. A large, sometimes arrogant man,
known for his aggressive approach and occasionally volatile
temper, he grew purple with rage. In the presence of Judge
Lifland, Miller grabbed the smaller Rosenberg by the necktie
and literally lifted him off his feet. "You little twerp," he
screamed, "don't you ever say Harvey Miller said anything
again."

The debate resumed Wednesday morning, but no one could
put the deal together again. Ueberroth and Bakes called a press
conference for late in the afternoon. Lifland, looking foolish
with a former defense secretary hanging about his court and
a former baseball commissioner furious at him, at first objected to the press conference. He then asked Ueberroth and
Bakes to read a statement saying they still were negotiating
at his request. Both refused. Haggard and nearly incoherent
from lack of sleep, Ueberroth told reporters: "We are deeply
disappointed that this transaction lapsed. Our agreement with
Texas Air is finished, terminated, and is over." He refused to
lay blame on anyone. "I'm not going to participate in throwing
stones."

But the recriminations shot in all directions. In the media,
the blame fell to the unions, who were seen as stiff-necked
and unrealistic in their demand for a trustee. Few people knew

that Bruce Simon, the pilot lawyer, had told Shapiro that the unions would let Ueberroth run Eastern while it was technically still owned by Lorenzo. The union leaders themselves didn't know what the $90 million offer to Ueberroth had been all about. Not aware that an alternative had been possible, the unions were mad at the judge for not appointing a trustee.

Ueberroth blamed Lifland, too. Although Texas Air had agreed, after an argument, to pay him $3 million of the $5 million it had promised to pay him for legal and banking fees, he was angry. Later that evening, back in his lawyers' offices, he spoke about how he felt. "The judge said he would appoint a trustee, but he didn't. That killed the deal more than Frank did. Six days ago, when we entered this process, we thought the biggest hurdle was labor. We achieved that overnight without sleeping. But we couldn't get through the other hurdle. It was difficult, and damn disappointing, but that's that." Talbot was even more bitter. "We have nine agreements with the unions. Lorenzo couldn't even get one agreement in three years. I call that incompetence. That alone should be enough for a trustee."

Shapiro pinned everything on Ueberroth. "Ueberroth wanted control so he could fly the airline and see if he could ramp it up," he said later. "Then if he had trouble, he wanted to walk away from the whole deal. Freeman scared Ueberroth by saying Eastern couldn't fly without the shuttle. Ueberroth came in not knowing his right toe from his left, and Freeman terrified him. So he refused to get locked up. I said to him: 'I've got 28,000 people to give $1 billion in concessions over five years and you're telling me you refuse because you're afraid for your reputation?' His answer: 'I'm not going to be locked up.' So the judge wasn't about to appoint a trustee. Lorenzo said he was prepared to do it without a trustee if Ueberroth would take control in 30 days. But Ueberroth wouldn't go for it, even for a lower price. I don't blame the unions, because they said they were willing to go along without a trustee."

A few days later, after Ueberroth had returned home to California, Shapiro tried one last time. He called Ueberroth and suggested that he would try to get Lorenzo to lower the price by $200 million. Shapiro hadn't discussed this with Lorenzo, who probably wouldn't have gone along, since he already had rejected the $90 million reduction. After all, it would have meant that Ueberroth would get Eastern basically for nothing, since Drexel was only putting up $200 million in real money in the first place. Ueberroth called back and said no.

Harvey Miller basically agreed with Shapiro, except that he didn't think Shapiro should have suggested a trustee in the first place. "Shapiro said, 'Let's have a trustee,'" said Miller. "But you can't do that without a hearing. Due process is at stake. Ueberroth and Texas Air fought over the trustee issue and agreed Lorenzo would stay in. You don't convict people without a trial. Who sells something and transfers the title before he gets paid? Also, the creditors could alter the asset transfers" in the Ueberroth deal. "That's why Lorenzo didn't go along."

A week or two later, Lorenzo held a small press briefing in Texas Air's Rockefeller Center offices. He spoke about the 60-day period and why the issue of interim management had been such a stumbling block. "Pete and I spent most of our time on that. You never turn over property until you get paid for it. That's basic. But you also try to give protection to the buyer once he puts his dollars on the line. As a result, we decided that Ueberroth would have approval over all sales and route changes. Pete would be co-chairman. Legal management wouldn't change and Bakes would stay on. But three of Peter's people would be added to the board and several of his associates would get titles as officers of the company and go to all meetings." But if a trustee had taken over, Lorenzo said, "the plain fact is that we couldn't be sure the deal would close, or what the price would be."

Lorenzo had a valid point about getting his money before he let go. He knew that once he was out of the picture, the creditors almost certainly would lean on a trustee to change the terms of the deal and give Lorenzo less. But it was debatable whether he really owned anything at this point anyway.

Texas Air owned Eastern's stock, but the company had essentially surrendered many of the rights of ownership when it had put Eastern into bankruptcy. Eastern's stock probably wasn't worth much of anything under the circumstances. Even if it was, the issue for Lorenzo seemed more a matter of pride than of money. After all, $90 million in assets wouldn't make or break Continental or Texas Air at this point.

Who was to blame for the collapse of the Ueberroth deal? The public put the blame squarely on the unions, whose apparent refusal to compromise torpedoed the best chance they ever had to rid Eastern of Lorenzo. But they were willing to give ground, as Shapiro readily admitted. Shapiro may have been right in thinking that Ueberroth was in a bit over his head and grew reluctant to buy the airline when he realized the extent of Eastern's mess. Ueberroth's high-handed treatment of Shapiro seemed to confirm this view.

But in fact, the real blame lies not with the unions or Ueberroth, but with Lorenzo. Ueberroth told Shapiro that he wouldn't discuss locking in his purchase in exchange for a lower price not so much because he feared for his reputation, but because he had lost all trust in Lorenzo. If such a deal was going to be made, Ueberroth knew it had to be made personally with Lorenzo. If he tried to arrange something with Shapiro or Miller, or any intermediary, Lorenzo would pull one of his usual tricks.

Shapiro's suggestion was a good one. But it was Lorenzo, not Ueberroth, who refused even to consider the idea. Shapiro blamed Ueberroth because he wasn't told about the phone call Lorenzo made to the commissioner minutes after Shapiro and Miller walked out of his hotel room. "I never knew that," he said when he was told of the call a year after it happened.

Lorenzo was responsible for the agreement's failure in another way as well. Even if he had agreed to accept $90 million less, there was still the matter of the due diligence. If it turned out that anything he had said to Ueberroth about Eastern wasn't true, the price would have had to be adjusted again. But such an adjustment would have had to occur after the sale had gone through. This meant that Ueberroth would have had to trust Lorenzo to follow through on a price-adjustment procedure. But Lorenzo's bargaining style—his demands to change terms in a deal even after he had agreed to it, as he had done with Icahn and repeatedly with Ueberroth—had destroyed any faith Ueberroth might have had in anything Lorenzo said.

"This would have opened the door to disputes down the line," said Talbot. "Who would adjudicate if, for example, the Miami-to-London route's operating certificate didn't allow us to operate between certain hours? We would go back to Texas Air and say that reduces the price. They suggested someone like Shapiro as the arbitrator. But after having been in his hands and the hands of the bankruptcy court and seeing them go 180 degrees on a flat-out promise to put in a trustee, I was not willing to place arbitration back in their hands."

"We had experience with Frank before," Ueberroth added, "and once burned, twice shy. With anybody saying, 'Don't worry, we'll work out the price after you've owned it for six months,' well, we didn't take it seriously."

The unions felt angry and defeated as they debated their next move. Meanwhile, Lorenzo spelled out what Texas Air intended to do. It would rebuild a smaller airline using employees who had crossed the picket lines, plus any it could lure back and any it could hire. "Eventually, we can serve 60 to 80 cities, which is 50 percent of the pre-strike airline," said Bakes. Once again, Lorenzo set the course on his usual route. He was going to tough it out.

CHAPTER ELEVEN
Lorenzo's Pyrrhic Victory

As the smoke cleared, the hopelessness of Texas Air's predicament sank in. When Ueberroth left for California, he took with him the best shot Lorenzo had to extract himself gracefully from the Eastern imbroglio. Now Texas Air faced an embarrassed and irate judge who seemed determined to force a sale. The dashed hopes of thousands of union members only reinforced their determination never to return to work for Lorenzo. If a sale didn't come off, the creditors would opt for full-scale liquidation, which could drag Texas Air and Continental into the fray as well.

Lorenzo moved quickly. Shortly after Ueberroth left town, Texas Air set out to sell nearly half of what remained of Eastern. Lorenzo claimed that his goal was to repay debtors and get a smaller airline flying again—but in reality, it was just an extreme version of his usual strategy to keep his options open at all costs. It was a dramatic way of seizing the initiative in an effort to keep control of the company away from the unions, the court, and creditors. "We are long-term players in the industry," Lorenzo said at a press briefing not long after the Ueberroth deal collapsed. "We're not just crazy and emotional. We try to be logical business managers."

Texas Air, however, had surrendered considerable power when Eastern declared bankruptcy. Although Lorenzo remained in nominal control, the real power lay with the court. In addition, the interests of the creditors had become legally paramount. With Eastern in bankruptcy, they had become in effect Eastern's owners.

In a normal Chapter 11 bankruptcy, the point of the law is to get the company up and running again. Usually management proposes a reorganization plan. The creditors appoint a committee to represent their interests, and often other groups, such as the public stockholders, do the same. These committees sit in court and tell the judge whether they like the company's plan. At the end of the process, the debt holders vote on whether to accept the company's reorganization plan. Then, no matter how they vote, the judge decides whether the plan will go through.

At Eastern, the main creditors' committee was somewhat unusual. The unions, which still owned stock in the company, also were debtholders, because Eastern owed them pension money and other benefits. As a result, they got four of the sixteen seats on the creditors' committee. This gave them access to all the inside information that the company had to show its creditors. Since the unions wanted Eastern to be sold, they were in a good position to sway the other creditors. It quickly became clear, however, that these other creditors were divided—some were willing to consider a sale, others wanted to liquidate.

Lorenzo's new plan for a smaller airline was designed to cut a path through these conflicting interests. It allowed him to offset the momentum for a sale by offering the creditors an alternative. He stated that he would raise $1.8 billion by selling off about 40 percent of what was left of Eastern. Some proceeds would go toward rebuilding the airline, the rest would go toward repaying his creditors.

Texas Air played its hand well. While the company denied that selling almost half of Eastern was a move toward liquidation, it also assured creditors that if the plan didn't work, the smaller airline could be liquidated. "We'd oppose full liquidation," Bakes said when he announced the plan at a press conference. "But if creditors want it, we'd say that our plan is not incompatible with that idea."

A phased liquidation, which would avoid triggering the bankruptcy laws that would require Eastern to pay off its nearly $1 billion in pension liabilities, also was the best way to protect Texas Air. This was Lorenzo's Achilles' heel. If the creditors moved for immediate liquidation and all of Eastern's pieces didn't bring enough to pay off the pension funds and the creditors, Texas Air and even Continental could be liable.

The battle was touch-and-go for months. For the first few weeks, it looked as if the judge's attitude would help the unions. Lifland's primary goal was to get the airline flying again. As he saw it, the public's concern was to keep one of the country's airlines flying. This isn't normally what motivates bankruptcy judges. Indeed, it may be a dubious legal goal; at the least it was an unorthodox interpretation of Chapter 11, which is generally used to help get a company back on its feet while ensuring that its creditors are satisfied. Though almost every interested party complained about the judge's approach at one stage or another, there was little anyone could do about it. Lifland ran the show until Eastern emerged from bankruptcy. At that point, each party could appeal. In this case, however, a sale or a liquidation or a new labor agreement probably would render any appeal a moot issue.

Lifland's concern to get Eastern flying was the main reason he had jumped at the Ueberroth sale, at least initially. It had seemed like a perfect out, and he had instructed Shapiro, the examiner, to get it done, no matter what. When Lorenzo and Harvey Miller faced him down, Lifland moved quickly to cover his embarrassment. He and Shapiro told union leaders that if they could come up with a viable deal that would satisfy creditors, the court would make sure Lorenzo sold to them, even if it meant appointing a trustee.

Within days of Ueberroth's failure, Lifland's court was filled with people who wanted to buy Eastern. A Hasidic diamond dealer from Antwerp showed up with three children in tow, saying he had access to $250 million in cash. An English insurance firm connected to a group of Algerians offered to help buy the company by giving it 30 months' worth of free jet fuel, which could have been worth hundreds of millions of dollars. Freeman convinced both Pritzker and Icahn to reenter the bidding process. A multimillionaire Chicago commodities dealer named Joseph J. Ritchie hired Shearson Lehman to help him formulate a bid. Another banking house, Prudential-Bache Capital Funding, began to organize a bid with William R. Howard, a highly regarded airline manager who had been a vice president at Eastern for years and became the president of Piedmont Airlines in 1983.

Ueberroth, too, quietly waited for events to swing back in his favor. Pohlad continued to push Lorenzo to sell out. Ueberroth told union leaders that if Lorenzo called him back in, he would come. But this time, he and Pohlad hoped to get Lorenzo to surrender control over all of Texas Air, Continental and Eastern included.

Lorenzo, whose pride had been stung enough, put his foot down. On April 17, Texas Air announced that Eastern was no longer for sale. This was yet another slap in the face to Lifland, who had just said in court that he wanted to continue the process of finding a buyer. Lorenzo didn't care. At the press briefing he had called several days earlier to explain the failure of the Ueberroth deal, he had taken great pains to say that he had decided to sell Eastern of his own accord. "I had been meeting with Ueberroth for well over two years," said Lorenzo in response to a question concerning Pohlad's responsibility for putting the deal together. When asked privately why he was so angry about the reports concerning Pohlad's involvement, he replied, "It makes me furious. It's not true and I don't want other papers to print things that aren't true." What, he was asked, about Milken saying he had urged Lorenzo to sell to Ueberroth? "Did he say that?" Lorenzo demanded. "Well, he's just a financier," he snapped angrily. "He has nothing to do with our company."

Meanwhile, Lifland did everything he could to keep the crisis atmosphere going. He instructed Shapiro to sift out any viable offers, and, still only days after Ueberroth had left, told him to report back in less than a week, when the judge said he would decide whether Eastern should be sold. This launched the unions into another series of frenetic meetings.

The unions now had what Bavis called their "suitcase" deal, which offered the $210 million a year in concessions they had agreed to for Ueberroth. The pilots, who still had the upper hand among the unions, handled the majority of the buyers. The influx of people became so heavy that Bavis set up a screening committee. Jack Suchocki, a supporter of Copeland, the militant, handled the initial contact with any interested parties. If he decided that a proposal warranted further hearing, he passed the prospective buyers on to Buzz Wright and Bavis, who began serious negotiations. They worked with Shapiro, who did his own interviews with bidders to see if any were serious.

On April 24, all the parties assembled in Lifland's court for the deadline he had set. Shapiro spoke to a standing-room-only audience packed with several hundred journalists, potential buyers, and lawyers and bankers for the unions, Eastern, and the creditors. He said he had identified four or five potential buyers and planned to set a deadline of one week for all bids to be submitted. He added that he planned to investigate the unions' request for a trustee, and that he would examine all Lorenzo's asset sales. Since Lorenzo insisted that he wanted to keep selling assets to get money for a smaller airline, Shapiro also said the court would listen to any Texas Air plan.

This set off a mad tug-of-war. The unions did everything they could to muster a buyer, while Lorenzo did everything he could to block them. Eastern dragged its feet about letting the buyers see its books. The courts insisted that the company open them up. But the airline continued to delay, knowing that the longer Eastern didn't fly, the less likely it was that any buyer could get it going again.

The creditors were trapped. Companies such as Boeing, General Electric, and Airbus Industries stood a chance of repossessing their planes—but like the banks and other creditors, what they really wanted was their money. Usually, creditors to a bankrupt company forgive some debt because they know that, if the crippled business can be made profitable again, payments on the remaining debt can be resumed. The only other choice in most cases is to liquidate, which often leaves them trying to sell used equipment to buyers who know they are desperate to sell. In the case of Eastern, there was a third possible choice—if the unions could arrange a sale of the company.

The unions did their bit by opposing Lorenzo's moves to sell more assets. Their first battle was to block the sale of the shuttle to Trump, which still hadn't closed. The union leaders also waltzed around with all the buyers. After nearly two months of one deadline after another from Lifland, Pritzker and Backe made a tentative bid and then dropped out, as did Icahn, Spivey, and most of the others. By the end of May, the field had been narrowed to the Prudential-Bache–Howard team and Ritchie, the Chicago options trader. Union leaders decided they had to choose one group and get behind it, to present the court with the best deal possible.

Shapiro tried to help the process along, but he set impossibly high standards. He told the unions that any buyer had to make an offer to Texas Air that was so good that it would be patently unreasonable for Lorenzo to refuse. He said such an offer would have to give Texas Air about the same price that Ueberroth did. Insiders said that Shapiro expected the creditors to chop the price down once the deal got under way. But by setting a price similar to the one Lorenzo had accepted from Ueberroth, Shapiro said the judge would have safe ground for imposing a trustee if Lorenzo refused to accept it again.

Shapiro, who still felt burned by Ueberroth's refusal to agree to lock up his deal, added another item to his criteria. He insisted that any buyer had to put at least $100 million in cash, up front, into Eastern to be used to start the airline up. This was an extreme demand. Shapiro was demanding that someone commit $100 million to Eastern before they even bought it. Whoever did so might get their money back if Eastern failed again, but only in the unlikely event that all the existing creditors got theirs back first.

Lorenzo played the situation to full advantage. Though Lifland had weekly hearings to put pressure on all sides to reach an agreement, Lorenzo did all he could to stall. As he did so, Eastern's value fell. By mid-May, when Howard and Ritchie were ready with offers, it would have been ludicrous for anyone to pay as much as Ueberroth had agreed to. Lorenzo also continued to push to sell off more of Eastern. In an emotionally charged hearing, the judge agreed to let the shuttle be sold to Trump. This swung the momentum decidedly in Lorenzo's favor. Lifland continued to approve asset sales after that, even though each sale further damaged the chance that any buyer could make a go of what remained of Eastern.

As May drew to a close, the unions finally settled on Ritchie as the buyer they wanted to go with. The 42-year-old maverick in the Chicago commodities market was the head of Commodities Research and Trading Group, which stressed equality and teamwork among its employees. Ritchie also had money. He was willing to risk some $25 million out of his own pocket toward the $100 million Shapiro had demanded up front.

Howard and Prudential-Bache thought this made no sense. "That was an irrational and foolish test Shapiro set," said Lew Kaden, the Davis Polk lawyer who had represented the outside directors when Eastern was sold to Lorenzo, and who now had been brought in to represent Pru-Bache. "No one is asking Lorenzo to put up money for his plan to restart the airline. I can understand employees doing that, but investors would be crazy to do it. This has never been done in the history of bankruptcy as far as we know."

But Ritchie, it turned out, couldn't deliver. His partners, who promised to put up the rest of the $100 million in risk capital, got cold feet. Neither he nor Shearson, his investment banker, was able to persuade anyone else to invest.

The unions finally decided to take the matter into their own hands. If no one would invest in Eastern, they would buy it themselves and use Ritchie as a front to get Lorenzo to sell. They were determined to meet any test, even one as ludicrous as Shapiro's $100 million in risk money. They went to the AFL-CIO for help. Recognizing the importance of Eastern to the labor movement, the other unions offered unprecedented assistance. More than a dozen of them agreed to put in $5 million each from their unions' pension funds to invest in an Eastern buyout. This raised nearly $70 million in commitments, which came close to topping off what Ritchie had promised.

It quickly became clear that commitments like this wouldn't satisfy Shapiro. The union pension funds couldn't actually requisition any money until they had the terms of a deal in their hands. Shapiro wanted the money before it got to that stage. AFL-CIO officials soon found a way out. Over Memorial Day weekend, AFL-CIO secretary-treasurer Thomas R. Donahue negotiated with several banks to loan them the money. Each union agreed to co-sign a loan for $5 million. "Then after a few months, the idea was to convert the loans to pension-fund investments," said Donahue shortly thereafter.

Shapiro still wasn't satisfied. He wanted cash on the table, not loan agreements. In desperation, the unions dug into their own pockets and came up with $50 million in new wage cuts, on top of the $210 million in concessions they already had committed to. Half of this would come from the machinists and half from the pilots. In addition, the pilots agreed to add in $25 million from one of their two pension plans.

Finally, Lifland called another hearing for Thursday, June 1. This, he said, would really be the last time he would hear buyout proposals.

Ritchie and the unions continued to negotiate. On the night before the hearing, Ritchie's bankers from Shearson showed up at Shapiro's room at the Drake Hotel in Manhattan and laid out a business plan for a revived Eastern, including a general outline of how many planes it would fly and when it would begin to make money. Shapiro was unimpressed. Ritchie and Shearson hadn't done a full-blown plan with details of routes and prices. The examiner didn't put much stock in their profit projections for a new Eastern, either.

At one A.M. after the Shearson reps left, the union leaders appeared at Shapiro's hotel door, accompanied by their advisors and Ritchie himself. They presented him with a new idea concocted largely by Farrell Kupersmith, the accountant, and finalized while the Shearson bankers were talking to Shapiro. It was the most desperate suggestion labor had ever made in all the years of battle at Eastern.

Essentially, the unions said that they would match the performance Lorenzo was promising in his plan. Even though Lorenzo's plan clearly was designed to give creditors a liquidation as a backup alternative, and thus was unrealistic in many regards, Kupersmith saw that the unions had to come up with a better proposal. He suggested that if Ritchie bought the airline, the unions would commit themselves to make up the difference on a month-by-month basis for any losses Eastern might incur that were greater than those projected in Lorenzo's plan.

Initially, the money would come from the 30-percent stock ownership labor was to receive. If that wasn't enough, labor would make added concessions on top of the $210 million. This would include the $50 million in new wage cuts, and, if necessary, up to 35 percent in yet another round of cuts in pay and benefits. Finally, if the losses continued, the unions would sell assets in order to pay Eastern's creditors. "We're putting our bodies between Eastern's assets and the creditors and indemnifying them against any possible loss," said Randy Barber.

The idea was virtual economic suicide. It meant that union members could wind up working for half the pay they had received before the strike. Union officials were so desperate not to let Lorenzo win that they were willing to ask their members to work for pay levels the airline industry hadn't seen in years.

This got Shapiro's attention. He told the unions to talk to the creditors and to make an offer to Lorenzo. On Friday, June 2, Ritchie and the labor representatives met with Joel Zweibel of Kramer Levin Nessen Kamin & Frankel, the chief lawyer for the creditors. They presented the latest proposal to him and to Goldman, Sachs and Earnst & Whinney Inc., whom the creditors' committee had hired as technical advisors. The meeting lasted until five minutes before the next hearing was due to begin at Lifland's court. The creditors said they were quite interested in the new idea. As the unions departed for the court, Kupersmith accidentally left behind the notes that he had used to make his presentation. In them he had scrawled "A-bomb safety net," to describe the unions' plan. The point was clear: the unions were willing to A-bomb themselves if necessary to give creditors an option other than Lorenzo.

The atmosphere in the court was charged. Shapiro recounted his adventures of the previous night. He asked Lifland to make one last extension, until Monday, to give Ritchie time to make an offer to Lorenzo and to let Zweibel inform his committee of the latest offer. Lorenzo's lawyer, Harvey Miller, protested, saying no one had yet talked to Texas Air about how much it would offer, and that with no viable offers out there, Texas Air still didn't want to sell. "All this is doing is extending the strike," he told Lifland. "These are just labor politics going on here."

Lifland granted the extension anyway. The following day, June 3, Ritchie and an assistant flew to Houston to make a proposal to Texas Air. Lorenzo refused to see them, and instead passed them off on Ferguson, Texas Air's corporate strategist. The three met for four hours. Ritchie made an initial offer of $200 million in preferred stock plus $259 million that would come from Eastern forgiving debts owed it by Texas Air and Continental. It wasn't what Ueberroth had offered, but it was in the ballpark. Ritchie expected to bargain up from there.

Ferguson responded by saying that Lorenzo thought Eastern was actually worth more than it had been when Ueberroth was around. He said that it would probably take something like $500 million to convince Lorenzo to sell. Ritchie "didn't even know what was in the Ueberroth offer," said Miller. "I told him it was about $500 million in value, so if you're serious in this game, that is where you're starting from. I told Shapiro this many times."

Ritchie returned to New York with the news: Lorenzo wasn't budging. In fact, he wasn't even being anywhere near reasonable. It was absurd to say that an airline that had barely flown for months was worth more than when it had been essentially grounded for a few weeks.

Now the only way to do the deal was for the judge to appoint a trustee. Union leaders thought that they had reached the moment of truth. Lorenzo had overplayed his hand by actually upping the price. If that didn't anger Lifland, nothing would.

On Monday, June 5, the parties gathered in court. Zweibel, the creditors' lawyer, told the assembled crowd that the creditors had looked at the latest proposal over the weekend and "determined that it was an interesting one. But it is not feasible absent consent from the debtor and equity holder." This was what the unions wanted. The creditors, who had the vote over any reorganization plan, had agreed to at least consider the unions' proposal. Zweibel had gone on to point out the obvious: nothing could be done on a voluntary basis without agreement from the debtholder, Eastern, and from Texas Air, which owned all of Eastern's common stock. It was up to the judge to force the plan through, by a trustee if necessary.

Then Shapiro spoke. "Several weeks ago, I advised the unions, Ritchie, and Howard that the notion of putting in an offer and getting the consent of the creditors, and then asking for a trustee wouldn't work. I said that they had to put an offer on the table that in my judgment Texas Air couldn't reasonably refuse. It had to at least be equal to Ueberroth's offer of cash. Failing that, I don't have the tools to work with. But that offer wasn't made during Ritchie's visit to Texas. Had it been, it might have been a different situation. So I come to the following conclusion, that [Texas Air and the creditors] should be devoting their energies to Eastern's plan or a liquidation."

Shapiro baffled nearly everyone. Eastern hadn't flown more than 10 percent of its flights since March 3. Other airlines had moved into many of its markets, picking up passengers and keeping them with frequent-flyer programs. It wasn't difficult to see that the company wasn't worth anything near what Ueberroth had offered. Union leaders couldn't understand what had happened. "When you figure out Shapiro, let me know," complained Peterpaul the next day. "Every time we

207

talk, we start arguing and he cusses. He has a foul mouth. I do, too, but I think I've met my match."

It soon became clear what lay behind Shapiro's statement. Shapiro, explained a representative of the creditors, "made the mistake early on during the Ueberroth negotiations of thinking that he could have a trustee appointed and that that would effectuate a sale over the debtor's objection. He made that promise to the unions. After a while, he began to realize that this would create a great deal of litigation. When I saw the unions' modified plan last Thursday, it was of general interest to the creditors, though it still needed work. But Shapiro had already decided to bury it. His charge was to get the airline flying. He would have looked like a hero if he got a buyer. But with the debtor objecting, he decided the only way to get flying is to support Lorenzo's plan. Liquidation will be over his dead body. His view was that if he was enthusiastic about Lorenzo's plan in court, that it would break the strike by getting pilots to go back to work."

When Shapiro heard that people were saying he wanted to break the strike, he got on the phone in a panic. At first, he denied that anything of the kind was going on. Then he opened up. "Let's put it this way. It's not correct that I'm trying to break the strike. But it's not 100-percent wrong. There's no question that the airline is worth at least $100 million less than when Ueberroth made his offer. But that's not the point. If they go in and offer a sweetheart deal like that, and Lorenzo turns it down, then I have something to do. His conduct would be irrational. But they refused to make the goddamn offer. So the judge says he wants Lorenzo's plan to go forward because it is the only thing I have in front of me."

The court's fear of Lorenzo had caused Shapiro to set impossibly high hurdles for the unions. He wanted them to find a buyer willing to commit to an unreasonable price on the assumption that it might be knocked down later. This had forced labor to agree to work for half pay so Lorenzo could make out like a bandit all over again. Once again, the court had been faced down. After pushing for a sale for some two months, the court flipflopped and decided that it would help

Lorenzo try to break the strike. Lifland still wanted to get Eastern flying at any cost. If he couldn't break Lorenzo, he'd try to break the unions.

The unions had little hope left at this point. Though they continued to work with Ritchie, the pilots felt they had no choice but to talk to Lorenzo again. "Our problem is if pilots buckle and go back to work," said Bavis. "If large cracks appear in the line, I'd bring them back to work. I have a contract, and I'm not going to let Lorenzo replace us like at Continental. This would be difficult for me politically. After Lorenzo said he would sell to Ueberroth, I made a lot of statements about how bad Lorenzo is. So my members may blame me if we have to return to work. But I'll do it if I have to. I won't sacrifice jobs for my ego."

Bavis was as good as his word. Under the auspices of the mediation board, the pilots began negotiations again with Eastern. The machinists were livid. They knew that if the pilots went back to work, they'd be out of their jobs permanently.

The machinists didn't have to worry much about the pilots caving in, however: Lorenzo took care of that. Out of the 3,500 pilots who went on strike, he offered to let 950 return to work. That was unacceptable to the pilots. Lorenzo then applied to Lifland for permission to end the union's contract with Eastern— the same trick he had pulled at Continental. Because Congress had changed the law, Lorenzo stood little chance of repeating the move—but he had another plan up his sleeve. He wanted to force the pilots to negotiate on his terms. When Congress changed the bankruptcy law, it specified that a company can't abrogate a labor contract without first negotiating with the union. It added, however, that the union must negotiate with the company. If the pilots didn't make a serious attempt to talk about going back to work, Lorenzo would have grounds for convincing Lifland to end their contract.

The pilots returned to the bargaining table. By mid-July, Lorenzo had raised the number of jobs he was willing to offer to about 1,200. By this time, about 300 more union pilots had crossed the picket line, and Eastern had managed to hire about

700 more nonunion pilots who currently were being trained. Lorenzo calculated that he needed a total of 2,300 pilots to fulfill his plan, restoring Eastern to a little more than half its pre-strike size.

The offer split the pilots down the middle. It was a lousy deal for the 2,000 or so union members who would never work at Eastern again. Bavis didn't think that they had much choice, though. If they didn't take it, they'd be left with nothing at all, just like at Continental. Skip Copeland and the other militants thought that Bavis once again was trying to sell out to Lorenzo. On July 17 and 18, the pilots' executive council rejected Lorenzo's offer.

Several days later, Lorenzo delivered a new punch. On July 21, he filed a formal reorganization plan with the bankruptcy court. It promised to repay creditors in full. This was the first formal pledge to creditors Lorenzo had made—but the creditors were still suspicious. After all, Eastern wasn't even making the limited flight schedules it had promised earlier would be part of the plan. The carrier was so desperate for business that at one point it began offering a 50-percent discount for corpses shipped aboard its planes before August 31. Eastern went so far as to offer bonus frequent-flyer miles to funeral directors based on the volume of business they brought to the company.

Nevertheless, with Lifland still against liquidation and no union buyout in sight, it looked increasingly like the creditors would have little choice but to go along. Then Lorenzo pulled a rabbit out of his hat. To meet its promised flight schedule, Eastern announced that it would soon begin leasing planes, complete with crews, from Continental.

Using Continental to break the strike at Eastern seemed a clear indication that Texas Air was operating both airlines as a single carrier. Lorenzo, however, correctly assumed that Lifland wouldn't care. The single-carrier case was hung up at the mediation board, which was waiting for the Senate to confirm two board members; in any event, the board's lawyers were reluctant for the board to deliver an opinion while Eastern remained in bankruptcy court. The board thought that Texas

Air would prevail on Lifland to put the decision aside, arguing that bankruptcy law took precedence over labor law. Although this was a questionable legal proposition, Lorenzo was counting on Lifland's ego and the judge's desire to honor his pledge to get Eastern flying again. True to form, Lifland did allow Eastern to lease Continental planes.

In late July and August, as Eastern began to increase its flights, it began to look more likely that the creditors would approve Lorenzo's plan and let the carrier emerge from bankruptcy. Lifland did everything he could to help Lorenzo. Though Shapiro believed, and had even made a statement to the effect, that Lorenzo had a prima facie conflict of interest running Eastern, Lifland kept postponing the hearing he had scheduled on the union's petition to have Lorenzo kicked out of Eastern and replaced by a trustee. On August 1, Lifland postponed the hearing again until October.

Bavis was getting desperate. The pilots' executive council met to consider what to do. Bavis brought Shapiro in to speak to the council, and the examiner made an impassioned speech, arguing that the pilots should jump at the chance to go back to work and lock up any jobs they could. He suggested that they could go to court over the 700 jobs that Lorenzo wanted to give to new trainees, and perhaps win them back as well. Bavis agreed, arguing that if they missed this opportunity, none of them would ever work at Eastern again. At a stormy five-day session called shortly thereafter, Henry Duffy, the national pilot president, also concurred, and made a similar speech to the Eastern pilot group. Ten of the seventeen members left on the executive council at this point agreed—but they decided to go back to the members first.

When they did, Copeland, the militant, campaigned hard against returning to Eastern under Lorenzo. His attack swung the union against Bavis, who again was portrayed as too willing to cave in to Lorenzo. In the end, 80 percent of the executive council voted to continue striking. "Bavis wanted to get his foot back in the door," said Ron Cole, the pilot spokesman who sided with Copeland. "But the rank and file revolted." Says Duffy: "It was a risk for Jack. I think he was right to take it, but it was a misreading of the group and he lost."

Although Bavis failed, his call for a return to work panicked some of his members. Over the next couple of weeks, as more than 200 strikers returned to work, the strike almost collapsed. By the end of August, Eastern began hitting its targeted flight schedules.

Toward the end of the month, the issue of the strike came to a head in the national union. Eastern's pilots, led by Copeland, argued to change the union's rules so that any Eastern pilot who went to work at another airline would keep his seniority. Copeland also asked for a national work stoppage by all members in support of their strike. The national leadership, however, was ready to throw in the towel. Duffy and other officials didn't think that the strike could be won from the streets. On August 20, the governing council of the national union in Washington voted against both requests.

In early September, Eastern's pilots took their revenge. They kicked Bavis out of his job as head of the executive council and replaced him with Copeland.

There was little Copeland could do, however. Lifland continued to do all he could to help Lorenzo, approving virtually every substantive company request and opposing almost all the union ones. By allowing Lorenzo to sell assets, Lifland essentially permitted him to restructure Eastern even before the company presented a formal reorganization plan that the creditors could have voted down.

With the deck loaded against labor, the pilots held another nationwide vote on whether to continue the $2,400-a-month strike payments that the union had been paying each Eastern pilot. The measure passed, but by a razor-thin margin. In fact, if Eastern pilots hadn't been allowed to vote, the measure might have failed. The message was clear: pilots union members at other airlines were ready to give up on Eastern.

In October, Copeland and other newly elected members of the executive council tried one last strategy. Throughout the summer, Eastern's unions had been lobbying Congress to pass

212

a law that would force President Bush to appoint an emergency board. When it became clear that the administration wouldn't budge, the unions came up with what they thought would be a compromise. They suggested that Congress pass a bill to set up a bipartisan commission to recommend a settlement at Eastern. It would fall short of a full emergency board, but could set the stage for further Congressional intervention. The measure passed the House by a voice vote, and the Senate by 65 to 35.

The pilot leaders decided to hold off on a return to work until they saw whether Bush would accept the compromise. Because the bill held out some hope of a resolution, it would give the union a face-saving way to tell its members to return to what few jobs were left at Eastern. On November 21, however, Bush vetoed the bill, saying it would "hinder saving Eastern Airlines and the jobs of its employees." Lorenzo sent the president a message thanking him for having "the courage and a clear vision of the need to keep the airline industry competitive."

Two days later, Buzz Wright, who had remained on the Eastern executive council, called for a vote to end the union's sympathy strike. With Copeland refusing to participate, the vote passed—but the decision meant little in practical terms. Lorenzo had cut Eastern down so much that it no longer needed any union pilots to return to work. Eastern now had about 1,800 pilots, about half the number it had when the strike began. Of these, 800 or so were union members who had crossed the line since March. The remaining 1,000 were newly hired pilots. Concluding the strike didn't earn the union any jobs, but it did give the union the right to sue Eastern for the 1,000 jobs it had lost to nonunion workers.

The day after the pilots' decision, the flight attendants agreed to end their strike. Only Charlie Bryan refused to give in. "We're not going to go back or go away, that's for sure," he said shortly thereafter.

The unions knew they had been beaten. Many machinists, especially the thousands who worked in Miami, remained without work. Hundreds still were going to soup kitchens for food. They faced a stark choice: move from their homes and try to start over, or accept non-mechanic jobs at much lower pay. The pilots, too, were suffering. Many of the older ones never would work again. Others might get a job with other carriers, but only at the bottom of the ladder.

But no one seemed to have any regrets. After Buzz Wright persuaded his colleagues to end their strike, he resigned from the pilots executive council, and sent out applications to all the major airlines. "I never heard from anyone but little Midway Airlines. I'm literally starting over at the bottom there. I'm still in training, and making $3.35 an hour, the minimum wage. I'll start at $23.70 an hour here for the first 12 months. At Frank's airline, I was making $68 an hour. Here, a 12-year captain gets $80, but that will take 12 years. However, they don't kick people around like Frank does."

"Lorenzo still has to deal with the animosity of the scabs who crossed the picket line," said a former Eastern flight attendant. "They are not gung-ho Eastern employees. They did it out of desperation. They're not a dedicated work force. Without that, I don't see how Eastern can survive when American and United are making money because the people who work for them respect them."

"We may lose our jobs, but Lorenzo doesn't have an airline," said William Sutton, a chief steward in Eastern's avionics shop in Miami. "No one wants to work for him anymore. I'll go get another job, but I'll bet he doesn't go get another airline after destroying this one."

"What does Frank have now?" asked Bavis, the former pilots leader. "In the long term, neither Eastern nor Continental are competitive. You can't run an airline in a service industry if labor and management are totally antagonistic with each other. Even though Lorenzo won, he lost. And even though we lost, we won in the long run, because the airline isn't going to make it. That doesn't get our jobs back, but it proves us right. There's some bitter satisfaction in that."

"You have not one but two losers here," agreed Kupersmith, the accountant hired by the pilots. "I don't think Lorenzo has won a viable airline in the end. He may last for awhile, even for years, but Eastern will be on the brink all the time. Lorenzo can keep selling assets to keep alive, but I don't call that viable. Lorenzo is operating a high-wire act. Continental is just as bad. Texas Air won't join the ranks of the five successful carriers that dominate the industry."

CHAPTER TWELVE
The Last Deal

By December of 1990, with the unions largely out of the picture, the focus of the battle narrowed to the negotiations between Texas Air and Eastern's creditors. Lorenzo continued to promise the creditors that they would be repaid 100 cents on the dollar under his plan to bring Eastern out of bankruptcy. But as airline industry traffic softened, Eastern began losing more passengers. Toward the end of the month, the carrier was filling less than 50 percent of its seats. In desperation, Eastern slashed ticket prices. This brought the airline more passengers, but at prices that wouldn't even cover Eastern's costs.

Finally, in mid-January, Lorenzo dropped all pretenses. Texas Air proposed a reorganization that called for paying creditors only 50 cents on the dollar. In other words, they would get about half of the $1 billion they were owed. The creditors reacted bitterly. After all, Lorenzo's repeated promises to repay them in full were part of the reason that they hadn't fought harder when Lifland had insisted that liquidation was out of the question. But the creditors soon realized that they had waited too long to resist. Goldman, Sachs, the investment banking house the creditors had hired to analyze

Eastern, said that the industry downturn had changed the picture. Breaking up Eastern, Goldman advised, would bring creditors only 20 cents to 40 cents on the dollar. In that context, even Lorenzo's 50 cents looked better.

In mid-February, after more sparring, the creditors finally agreed to swallow the losses Lorenzo had forced upon them. Over the objections of the unions, the creditors' committee accepted a plan of reorganization from Texas Air. It called for them to be paid $490 million. Only $300 million would be hard cash, and that would come not from Texas Air but from Eastern itself. The money would be raised by the anticipated sale of the South American routes to American Airlines. But Texas Air didn't get off the hook entirely. The remaining $190 million would come from two notes, one issued by Eastern but guaranteed by Continental and the other issued by Continental itself. In other words, if Eastern failed again after it emerged from bankruptcy and had to be liquidated, Continental would be at least partially responsible for backing up Eastern's remaining debt.

The creditors weren't happy with the deal. Two of them, GE and Rolls-Royce, both of which were owed money for airplane engines, abstained from voting on the proposed plan. And Goldman, Sachs advised the creditors' committee that Lorenzo's proposal had many strings attached to it, which he could use to lower the promised $490 million even further if Eastern continued to do badly in the marketplace. But with liquidation an even worse option, the creditors went along with Lorenzo anyway.

Shortly after the agreement was reached, Shapiro added the last piece to the puzzle. All along, he had been negotiating separately with Texas Air about Lorenzo's asset-stripping. On March 1, Lorenzo agreed to pay $280 million to settle the charges out of court.

Shapiro's findings were a major moral victory for the unions. In his report, Shapiro said that he had investigated 15 transactions Texas Air had made with Eastern, starting with the purchase of the company itself. He concluded that evidence of possible improper action existed in 12 of them. In total, the report said, Texas Air may have deprived Eastern of $280 million to $400 million. This vindicated everything the unions had been saying for years: that Texas Air had been "cherry-picking" Eastern for its assets to the point where the airline had been pushed toward bankruptcy. The report said, for instance, that the System One reservations system that Lorenzo had taken away for a $100 million note was really worth $250 million to $300 million.

Despite the tough language, however, Shapiro's settlement let Lorenzo off the hook. All along, he had said that he would consider replacing Lorenzo with a trustee if sufficient evidence existed of a possible conflict of interest. But as part of the settlement, Shapiro rejected the trustee idea, saying specifically that he was interested primarily in trying to remake Eastern into a viable airline again. Both he and Lifland had decided that the only way to do so was to let Lorenzo run the show. "It's as if the court had found Texas Air guilty of child abuse and then awarded the parent custody of the child," said Randy Barber.

Shapiro also agreed to make the $280 million penalty as easy as possible on Texas Air. Of the total, only $133 million would be actual cash put up by Texas Air. The rest consisted of a host of dubious changes in Eastern's relationship with its parent that would do nothing to help Eastern if it couldn't survive as a smaller airline. For instance, the settlement called for Texas Air to reduce, but not eliminate, the $500,000-a-month management fee it charged Eastern for financial and legal assistance. The arrangement also gave Eastern options on 40 new planes that Continental had ordered.

Lorenzo's salvation, however, was tempered by the industry-wide slump that had begun in the fall of 1989. To fill Eastern's half-empty seats, Lorenzo slashed prices. In early January, Eastern announced new "Anywhere" fares. Though the airline's bookings shot up from a low of 200,000 a week in mid-December to more than 1 million by mid-January, the fares did little to help the company's financial situation. Lorenzo's plan was to give away seats to leisure passengers in the hope that their presence would bolster the confidence of the all-important business flyer. Lorenzo also started a new first-class fare aimed at the business flyer, which allowed passengers to upgrade for only $10 more than the price of a full coach seat. Neither plan worked: the business community didn't want to take a chance on Eastern.

On March 22, Eastern and Texas Air officials told the leaders of the creditors' committee that the hard-fought February agreement was off. They also estimated that Eastern's 1990 losses would be more than double the $145 million loss the company had projected just weeks earlier. In fact, Eastern needed $80 million just to keep operating—money that Lorenzo insisted be taken from the escrow account the court had established for the $1.8 billion in asset sales that Eastern had initiated when the bankruptcy began.

On March 27, when Eastern made its formal proposal to the full committee, the creditors lost all patience. For a year, they had gone along with Lorenzo, allowing him to break the unions' strikes, to sell assets, and to use $320 million from the escrow account to run Eastern. When he had cut his repayment from 100 cents to 50 cents on the dollar, they had still gone along with him. But this was too much. The money being frittered away was their own, not Lorenzo's. Even Texas Air admitted that its Eastern stock was worthless.

The creditors' response was quick: Texas Air had to stick with the 50-cent repayment deal. The committee warned that it would fight the company's effort to withdraw more money from the escrow account. From now on, it said, Texas Air would have to fund any Eastern losses. The committee also passed a resolution saying that should Lorenzo refuse, they would ask Judge Lifland to appoint a trustee to liquidate what remained of the carrier.

Six days later, on April 2, Texas Air told the creditors that it wouldn't go along with their demands. Instead, the company proposed a new reorganization plan that would pay creditors about $250 million: a mere 25 cents on the dollar, with only 5 cents of it in cash. The rest would be in notes from Continental and Eastern.

On April 10, the furious creditors filed a formal motion with Lifland asking for a trustee. "Eastern has now been operating under the protection of the Bankruptcy Code for more than one year," they wrote. "During that period of time, Eastern has experienced constant, ever-increasing, and seemingly never-ending losses of staggering proportions. . . . There should be no mistake that it is the unsecured creditors of this estate who are being asked to fund the continuing fantasies of Eastern and Texas Air. Texas Air has admitted to this Court . . . that the value of its common stock has been wiped out. . . . Thus, it is the creditors who are the only economic interest remaining in this case. . . . Those creditors have now said, 'No more!' . . . The Committee will no longer tolerate Eastern's and Texas Air's inability to adhere to an agreement once reached. The history of this case convinces the Committee that even if a new plan was negotiated, Texas Air and Eastern would again find a basis to renege.

"Texas Air and Eastern have regularly blamed others for their missed projections, dismal performance, and regular reneging. First it was the unions; next the activities of the Examiner; . . . and now, this Committee. This finger pointing is truly a pathetic effort to hide the real culprits, who can be found in the executive offices in Miami and Houston."

Lifland, who had put off the unions' demand for a trustee hearing in October, and who had seemingly ignored Shapiro's stinging report on Lorenzo's asset-stripping, finally acted. He set a hearing for three days later, on Friday, April 13.

The creditors strengthened their position by dropping their March 27 request for liquidation, and instead called for a trustee who would pursue a sale or take action to "enhance the value of the estate."

This was a smart move. Lifland always had made it clear that he wanted to save Eastern. It now was obvious that his strategy had been a failure. The creditors, aware that Lifland didn't want to admit that his tactics had backfired, gave the judge a way out. By retracting their March 27 call to liquidate, they asked only that Lorenzo be removed.

The creditors had other reasons, too. Eastern still had its

South American routes, which Lorenzo had agreed to sell to American Airlines for about $350 million. But in the summer of 1989, Lorenzo had broken the deal because of a Continental lawsuit alleging that American's computer reservations service was biased against Continental's listings. When American had agreed to buy Eastern's South American routes, the carrier had insisted that Continental drop the lawsuit. Lorenzo had refused, even though it was a clear conflict of interest for him to kill the sale simply to benefit Continental.

In the fall of 1989, when the industry went into a downturn and Eastern's losses grew, the creditors contacted American themselves, and pushed Eastern to sell the routes. Finally, in mid-December, Lorenzo and American again agreed to the sale.

By April, however, the deal still hadn't received government approval. Thus, on March 27, when the creditors had called for a trustee to liquidate Eastern, Texas Air was quick to point out that a liquidation might cause the government to kill the sale. If this happened, the routes would revert to the government, and Eastern would be out $350 million. When Shapiro told the creditors that he agreed with Texas Air's assessment, the creditors quickly put an end to all talk of liquidation.

The maneuvering over liquidation set the stage for the court battle that began on Friday, April 13. From the beginning, Texas Air tried to argue that the demise of Eastern was the real issue. "The creditors say that management is not capable of managing," Bruce R. Zirinsky, a lawyer from Harvey Miller's bankruptcy law firm, told Lifland. "But you will hear that management has done an admirable job of running the company. What you're hearing from the creditors' committee is frustration." In reality, Zirinsky said, "the committee is seeking liquidation."

Though the chances of Eastern's surviving at this point were exceedingly slim, no matter who was in charge, Lifland made it clear that he wanted to hear nothing about liquidation. "It's not a question of good faith," he said in response to Zirinsky, "it's a question of the horrendous losses." In his view, Lifland said, the hearing was in many respects akin to an indemnification hearing, a procedure that had been done away with when the bankruptcy laws had been changed years before. What he meant was that the losses at Eastern had grown so large that if Lorenzo wanted to continue to run the company, he would have to pay for any future losses. Lifland was holding Lorenzo's feet to the fire, threatening him with a trustee to make Texas Air kick in money to Eastern.

All day Friday, and again on Monday and Tuesday, Texas Air's lawyers tried to show that Eastern's management had done as good a job as was possible under the circumstances. A trustee, they argued, would lead to liquidation.

Meanwhile, negotiations between the creditors and Texas Air continued behind the scenes. As Lifland's hostility toward Texas Air's argument became increasingly obvious, Lorenzo started to move. In secret discussions on Friday, Texas Air offered to pay the creditors 27.5 cents. They said no. Then on Monday, Lorenzo raised the offer again—this time to 30 cents—and also agreed to split some future losses at Eastern with the creditors. He said that Texas Air would pay up to half of the $80 million that Eastern had said it needed from the escrow account to keep operating. That went at least part way toward meeting the judge's demand for indemnification.

The creditors refused. Lorenzo had added a host of protective conditions. For instance, his offer was conditioned on Lifland's approving Shapiro's asset-stripping settlement by June 30. If Lifland didn't act by that date, Texas Air could walk away from paying the 30 cents, leaving the creditors with only the $133 million from the Shapiro settlement, and no chance to recover more. Lorenzo added that the $40 million that Texas Air would put in an escrow account to help pay Eastern's losses would revert back to Texas Air if Lifland didn't make the June 30 deadline. Once again, the creditors would be stuck funding Eastern's losses.

On Wednesday, April 18, with only two witnesses remaining in the trustee hearing—Bakes and Lorenzo—time was running out. Lorenzo could retain control of Eastern and block a trustee if he put in enough money from Texas Air to satisfy the creditors. Lifland made it clear that this would do the trick. The creditors, however, were demanding 50 cents on the dollar, which amounted to about $500 million.

Lorenzo also had to worry about the $1 billion in pension liabilities that Eastern still owed. As Eastern began negotiating to pay the creditors more money, the Pension Benefit Guaranty Corporation, the federal pension agency that oversees private pension plans, had begun to assert itself. The agency had the right to collect the $1 billion from Eastern, just as the creditors had the right to collect their $1 billion. But if Eastern was unable to make good on its pension obligations, federal law allowed the agency, unlike the creditors, to go to Texas Air and Continental for the rest of the money. And the agency didn't have to settle for 50 cents on the dollar, or any amount under the full $1 billion. Moreover, if agency officials felt the company could no longer meet the payments, the law allowed it to terminate Eastern's pension plans. This would make Eastern and Texas Air immediately liable for the full $1 billion. Since Eastern couldn't possibly pay it all, Texas Air would have to pay the rest. Such a demand could plunge floundering Continental and Texas Air into bankruptcy.

Lorenzo was in a bind. Indeed, just days before the trustee hearing began, the agency had threatened to terminate Eastern's pension plans unless Texas Air promised that a trustee wouldn't eliminate Texas Air's responsibility for the pension debt. Lorenzo had had no choice but to agree. The pension agency warned Texas Air that if it paid too much to Eastern's creditors, the agency would terminate the plans anyway. "We didn't give Frank a specific dollar amount on how much he had to keep in Texas Air," said Diane E. Burkley, the pension agency official who headed the negotiations. If Texas Air paid creditors 45 cents on the dollar, she said, the company "would have a legitimate concern that we would raise a stink and terminate the pension plans. At 35 cents, it was a more marginal question."

Wednesday morning, Phil Bakes went on the witness stand. All week, the courtroom had been packed with reporters, union representatives, and Eastern officials. Now most of Eastern's top officials had arrived.

223

Bakes gave a summary of the major management decisions he had made since the strike. He argued that while mistakes had been made, no one else could have done much better. He made clear that he had discussed every major step with the creditors, and received their approval. At about 10:30 A.M., Lifland, who had a previous engagement, recessed the hearing until 3 P.M.

Shortly after the recess began, the creditors' negotiating sub-committee met at the nearby offices of Goldman, Sachs, the committee's investment banking advisors. They discussed the Monday offer from Lorenzo, and formally rejected it. Then Texas Air's lawyers came over for about an hour, to make one last-ditch effort to strike a deal.

As the discussions progressed, the creditors gave ground in an effort to avert a trustee. They dropped their 50-cent demand and offered to settle if Texas Air would increase its offer to 37.5 cents. Knowing the bind Lorenzo was in with the pension agency, they tried to make the deal as easy on Texas Air as possible.

First, they wanted the company to make the 30 cents it had offered a real 30 cents. The original offer on Monday had consisted of a mere $49 million in cash. Given the dubious financial state of Eastern and Continental, the carriers' notes that made up the rest of the payment were nothing more than junk bonds. As a result, although Texas Air said its offer was worth $300 million, the creditors figured that it might really be worth somewhere around $250 million, or 25 cents. Now the creditors wanted Texas Air to improve the terms and conditions of the notes to bring their value closer to 30 cents.

"We just said it has to be a real 30 cents," said one creditors' negotiator who was present at the meeting at Goldman's office. "We didn't say how, we agreed to work that out later."

The creditors then asked for 8 percent of Texas Air's common stock, worth about $25 million, or 2.5 cents, and 19 percent of Eastern's own stock. Both of these demands were tailored so that Lorenzo could avoid trouble with the federal pension agency. Though the Texas Air stock would dilute the net worth of the parent company, the fact that it wasn't a cash payment meant that it probably wouldn't worry the pension people. The creditors kept their demand for Eastern stock at 19 percent, since if Texas Air gave away 20 percent or more of Eastern, then it no longer would be legally obligated to repay Eastern's pension funds.

The creditors' main concern wasn't money. It was to pin Lorenzo down to a commitment he would live up to. "We weren't that far apart on economics," said a creditors' representative. "But we were miles apart on who would bear the risk of implementation of the deal. Lorenzo wanted to keep his loopholes, so he could push off until December whether he would fulfill his proposal, after he could see if Eastern improved."

Texas Air refused the creditors' offer.

When court proceedings resumed at three o'clock, no details of the backroom negotiations had leaked out. Lorenzo, who hadn't been in court since Friday, reappeared. As he was entering the courthouse, a reporter from the *Los Angeles Times* corralled him in the hall. According to the reporter, Lorenzo told him that Texas Air had made its final offer on Monday, and that there was nothing new: "They can take it or leave it," the reporter quoted Lorenzo as saying. When word of Lorenzo's statement spread, several reporters ran to the phones and fired off stories with the news.

As the hearing resumed, Bakes took the stand again. He continued to defend his record at Eastern. Asked what impact a trustee would have on Eastern, he said: "I believe that there will be a much heightened risk of a liquidation of the company, whether intended or not."

When Bakes had finished, Lifland called a short recess. Lorenzo walked to the front of the courtroom where the press sat, and confronted the *Los Angeles Times* reporter he had spoken with earlier. "I never said 'They can take it or leave it,' " Lorenzo said, glaring. "I said we have no plan to make a new offer. That was all." The reporter protested, but Lorenzo continued to insist that the reporter had got it wrong.

Shortly after six P.M., the hearings resumed and Lorenzo took the witness stand. Not long into his testimony, he began

225

to give a summary of the entire negotiations between him and the creditors. None of this had been made public. In fact, the creditors and Texas Air had said throughout the negotiations that the talks would be confidential. Joel Zweibel, the creditors' lawyer, objected to Lorenzo's making the talks public, but Lifland let him go ahead. Lorenzo recounted how Texas Air had made an offer on Friday, then increased it to 30 cents on Monday. Lorenzo described the various conditions and clauses that Texas Air had made as part of its offer.

Lorenzo then launched into one of the most astonishing performances of his life. Sitting on the witness stand with the fate of his airlines hanging in the balance, he began to negotiate the terms of his offer. He negotiated not just with Zweibel, who was cross-examining him, but with Lifland. It was obvious now why he had been so worried about the "Take it or leave it" statement. At the last minute, he had realized that he had run out of time. For years, his standard bargaining tactic had been to negotiate a deal as ferociously as possible, haggling over every point in an attempt to wear down his adversary. Then when the other side thought they had an agreement, he would return the next day and say he had forgotten several points. Lorenzo did this with Ueberroth, with Icahn, and almost continually with the unions. Now he laid out the whole negotiations in open court. After he had finished, Texas Air's lawyer asked Lorenzo: "Lastly, Mr. Lorenzo, this offer is right now on the table, is that not true?"

"Yes," Lorenzo replied.

A few minutes later, as Zweibel challenged Lorenzo's interpretation of some of the loopholes, Lorenzo said: "I should point out to you that Texas Air stands quite prepared to discuss if there are problems in a mechanism. We don't think we have all the answers, we are quite prepared to talk about that."

Texas Air's lawyer then asked: "Would it be fair to say, Mr. Lorenzo, that with respect to everything that's in this proposal that Texas Air has put on the table, except for the question of consideration, that Texas Air is willing to discuss with the committee and to negotiate and try to resolve any problems they may have with respect to anything else?"

"That's correct," Lorenzo replied. "But even with regard to the subject of consideration, if the committee would like to restructure and rearrange the debt shares, we are prepared to do that. We are not prepared to change the overall economic value."

Lorenzo, however, had played his deal-making game once too often. Lifland several times challenged him on the terms of his offer, catching him in blanket statements about Texas Air's guarantees that were undermined by the loopholes the judge spotted in the offer.

When Lorenzo left the witness stand, he seemed to realize that his brinksmanship had put him over the edge. As Lifland called a short recess, Lorenzo rushed out of the courtroom, looking drawn and worried. Bob Ferguson, Texas Air's corporate strategist, followed him outside into the hall and suggested that Lorenzo go into a side room where the company's officials had been holding their conferences. Lorenzo brushed him off and walked out of the court, past the television cameras, and into a waiting limo. Back inside, Bakes tried to explain to several reporters why one of the loopholes Zweibel had attacked Lorenzo about was no big deal. "That was put in to address the demands of one creditor," he said. "It can be fixed."

When asked why Zweibel had sounded so angry, Bakes responded: "Come on. Zweibel was just negotiating in there. You're older than that."

Five steps away, Zweibel was leaning against the wall, chatting with Bruce Simon, the pilots lawyer. Zweibel said that he couldn't believe what had happened in the courtroom with Lorenzo. "He was up there negotiating on the witness stand, desperate. That's just like Lorenzo. He will negotiate until the guillotine hits something solid."

When the hearing resumed at 7:20 P.M., Shapiro rose to give his summary of the case. ". . . In my view the issue on this motion is not Eastern's hands-on management . . . [it] is $1.2 billion in losses. . . . When has a debtor ever been allowed to continue running a company in the face of such losses when it has also lost, and lost totally, the confidence of the creditors' committee?

227

"The issue in reality, and I say this more in sadness than in anything else, is really Mr. Lorenzo. Can anyone blame the creditors for being outraged? . . . I think this Court knows from what it's seen, and I know from what I have seen, that Mr. Lorenzo only starts negotiating at the very last minute . . . and once he makes a deal, Mr. Lorenzo can't sleep on it, unfortunately, he tries to renegotiate it, and that's likewise his style . . . he is just a tough guy to make a deal with."

Shortly thereafter, at about 8:30, Lifland called another recess, saying he would have a decision within an hour.

As everyone filed out of the courtroom, the Eastern and Texas Air lawyers and officials went into a back room. Zweibel and some of the other creditors' representatives went across the street to a restaurant, as did Shapiro and a half dozen lawyers and representatives of the unions. They all spoke about Lorenzo's attempt to bargain on the witness stand and whether Lifland would listen. Everyone was convinced that the judge would install a trustee. Several people also said that Harry Jones, the court officer whose job it would be to suggest a candidate, already had come up with someone.

Still, there was always the chance that Lifland wouldn't go through with it. After all, he had promised a trustee a year ago, when Ueberroth was around, only to back off at the last second. And Lorenzo couldn't have been clearer in his appeal to the judge to let him bargain a little more. Maybe Lifland would put off a decision until the next day, which might give Lorenzo a chance to wriggle free again.

At about 10 o'clock, Lifland entered the courtroom. As he began to read, it was clear that he had written much of his decision days before. It was filled with dozens of citations of previous trustee cases, complete with the reference numbers, which he couldn't possibly have researched in an hour and a half.

Lifland was harsh in his judgment of Lorenzo: "The unsecured creditors cannot be forced to subsidize a debtor-in-possession forever. In this instance, with Mr. Lorenzo at the throttle, or hovering over the throttle of Eastern, [it] has used $1.2 billion to fuel this reorganization trip. The time has come to replace the pilot to captain Eastern's crew.

". . . Eastern's owner/manager as personified by the chairman of the board of both the parent and the debtor is not competent to reorganize this estate.

"The debtors also argue that the committee's motion is actually a disguised attempt to have the Eastern estate liquidated. . . . However, the motivation of the committee . . . is not relevant. . . .

"Furthermore, as has been reiterated several times throughout this hearing, this Court has always considered that a trustee, if appointed, would be empowered, indeed mandated, to operate and manage this airline as a going concern. . . .

"In conclusion, this Court finds that evidence, clear and convincing, has been presented which mandates the appointment of a trustee. . . ."

The words had barely left the judge's mouth when several wire-service reporters burst out of the room and ran down the hall to put out the news: Lorenzo was being run out of Eastern.

Lifland continued for several more minutes, ruling that the trustee could withdraw the $80 million from the escrow account to run the airline. When the judge finished, Harry Jones, the court officer, got up and announced that he had selected a candidate for trustee: Martin Shugrue, the Continental president whom Lorenzo had fired in early 1989, and who also had been Ueberroth's choice to run Eastern.

Zirinsky, Eastern's lawyer, jumped to his feet. He demanded that Lifland wait to approve Shugrue until Texas Air could review the issue. He pointed out that there is a requirement that a trustee be a disinterested person.

Lifland said he didn't want to wait until tomorrow. His last words were: "I do so order Mr. Shugrue's appointment."

Two days later, Shugrue had his first meeting with Phil Bakes, who promptly resigned as Eastern's president.

Despite Lorenzo's departure, Eastern will probably be liquidated. After Shugrue's appointment, the creditors said that they had talked with several large airlines interested in buying what remained of Eastern. With Lorenzo gone, such a sale is a possibility. It's even conceivable that business flyers will fly Eastern again. However, both possibilities are long shots.

Whatever happens, Lorenzo's legacy is the destruction of an airline. When he came to Eastern in 1986, it was the country's third-largest airline. At the end of March 1990, it had sunk to number nine, making it the smallest major carrier. In fact, Eastern was closer in size to the airlines called nationals than it was to the majors. For the first three months of 1990, Eastern had 4.7 percent of the national airline market. American and United had about 18 percent each. America West and Southwest, the two nationals directly below Eastern, had about 2.5 percent each.

A week after Lifland removed Lorenzo, the government approved the sale of the South American routes. As soon as they are sold, Eastern will be little more than the regional airline it was fifty years ago.

"Lorenzo killed an airline," said John Backe, the former CBS president. "If he did it just to kill a union, that's unthinkable. And I think he did. It's hard for me to fathom."

One of Icahn's associates said that the TWA owner likened the story of Lorenzo's fight at Eastern to *Moby Dick*. "Frank was like Captain Ahab," Icahn reportedly said. "He was obsessed with beating Charlie Bryan and the unions."

Lorenzo did win the battle against Eastern's unions, putting out of work a majority of the 42,000 people who were employed at the company when he bought it. This Pyrrhic victory, however, left him too weak to continue his attacks on labor costs. Consequently, members of both the pilots union and the mechanics union throughout the industry are rid of their biggest foe. "Lorenzo is not in a position to set wage patterns in the industry anymore," said Bruce Simon, the pilots lawyer. "And no other buccaneer will be able to do it now, either. That's just as important as getting rid of Frank, the individual. There has been a mood in this country over the past decade that you can beat up on unions and get away with it. The message here is that maybe you still can, but not in the airline industry. That is a major victory."

Nor is Lorenzo in a position to continue his war against labor at Continental. In August 1989, he had said that the battle at Eastern hurt traffic on Continental and that a change in ownership might be beneficial. That August, Lorenzo called Donald Trump three times to urge him to buy Continental. Trump officials say that Lorenzo told Trump that his negative image had become a liability. "Frank wanted about $400 million to $500 million," said a Trump official at the time. "But Continental is a mess. It needs rationalizing, its infrastructure has been destroyed, and Lorenzo fired all the managers and never hired new ones."

Trump asked for advice from Bruce Nobles, the former Pan Am shuttle president whom Lorenzo had lured away to take over Eastern's shuttle and who stayed on when it was sold to Trump. "I recommended that he not buy it," said Nobles. "It's too highly leveraged. The question about Continental is simple: Do you want to bet the farm or not by buying it?"

Lorenzo's future in the airline industry isn't rosy. When he took Continental into bankruptcy in 1983, he claimed that the new demands of the marketplace compelled him to slash labor costs. Deregulation, not demonism, was at work, he argued. There's at least some truth to this; in retrospect, however, it's clear that his approach was ineffective. Only a flooded employment marketplace allowed him to get rid of so many Continental employees so painlessly.

By 1986, when he acquired Eastern, the labor market had changed. The major airlines had expanded as deregulation nearly doubled the number of passengers, from 240 million in 1978 to more than 450 million a decade later. Early in the 1980s, the large carriers were hiring about 1,500 new pilots every year. By 1988, that number had jumped to 10,000. Industry analysts predict that hiring will continue through the mid-1990s at a pace of 4,000 to 6,000 new pilots a year.

It's unlikely that Lorenzo can transform Continental into an airline where employees don't hate their jobs so much that passengers hate to fly with them. Today, Continental is a patchwork monster that few business people have the patience to fly, no matter what the price. In January 1990, Total Research Corporation, a Princeton, New Jersey, market research firm, published a study of how consumers feel about 91 major brands, from candy bars to credit cards. Continental had the worst overall standing of the entire group based on the four measures of consumer perception the study used. Worst of all, Lorenzo's carrier was rock-bottom with regard to repeat customers' perceptions of quality.

The financial picture is just as grim. In some respects, Lorenzo may have been glad to let go of Eastern, because he no longer has to worry about sinking Texas Air money into what had become a bottomless pit. However, there's not enough left of Eastern to satisfy the debts owed to the creditors and to the federal pension agency. The agency is likely to go after Texas Air for money. Moreover, Lorenzo's removal from Eastern voided the settlement that Shapiro had worked out on the asset-stripping charges. The creditors are now free to pursue the charges in court.

Lorenzo's record is a dismal one. The combined performance of Eastern, Continental, and Texas Air has been the biggest business failure in the history of the airline industry. Texas Air set an industry record in 1988 when it lost $718 million. In 1989, it topped that figure by losing $885 million. In early 1990, *Fortune* magazine's survey of the companies most admired by corporate executives showed Texas Air at 301 on a list of 305.

The failure of Lorenzo's approach is particularly clear when compared with the way the other major carriers pulled through deregulation. To counter the frenzied competition of the early 1980s, they installed sophisticated computerized reservations systems to allow them to determine who flies when. The big carriers also developed hub-and-spoke systems, in which each airline set up hubs through which it funnels most of its passengers. Although this left many smaller cities with less service than before deregulation, it turned out to be much more efficient than just flying anybody anywhere.

By the late 1980s, while Continental was still mired in endless employee disputes, chaotic service, and heavy losses, United, American, and Delta were all enjoying record profits. The stronger carriers achieved this success without dramatically lowering employee expenses. Indeed, by 1990 only a handful of troubled carriers, most notably Pan Am and TWA, continued to ask employees for help.

Lorenzo did some good for the flying public. His low fares gave many middle-class people unprecedented access to the airways. What's more, the failure of his methods and the success of other major carriers today is hardly unalloyed good news for leisure travelers. As the strongest and biggest carriers consolidated their hold on the skies, fares started going up again. In 1988, ticket prices jumped about 8 percent—the first time since deregulation that they had topped inflation.

It's also true that some airline employees are probably overpaid. That can't be said about flight attendants, however, who start off at about $11,000 a year and rarely make more than $30,000; and airline mechanics, though they are at the top of the U.S. working class, don't earn more than their counterparts in the auto industry or in aerospace. The only real argument comes over pilots, who, with an average pay of nearly $100,000 a year in 1990, have an income nearly four times larger than the median household income.

Lorenzo never really believed in low fares as a end in themselves. Though his statements about the changing marketplace brought him tremendous support from politicians and editorial writers around the country, they didn't represent his full view.

Only in the fall of 1988 did his true thoughts surface. Lorenzo had just forged an alliance between Continental and Scandinavian Air Systems. SAS had bought 10 percent of Continental's stock; in return, it offered to put Continental employees through its famous training school. SAS also agreed to form marketing links between its flights from Europe and Continental's routes inside the U.S. The move took the industry by surprise. Here was Continental, the low-cost airline, linking up with one of the world's classiest carriers. The reason, Lorenzo explained, was that Continental's image needed changing. The years of poor service had hurt.

When it was reported that Lorenzo was abandoning his high-volume, low-budget concept, the Texas Air boss tried to set the record straight. "That was never my concept," he argued.

"I'm very capable of high fares, too. Look, we raised the [Eastern] shuttle fares by 25 percent since we bought it. We never had a dream for a low-fare, high-volume carrier. We're building a quality airline, not a volume one. I don't know if Don Burr's dream would have worked [at People Express], but that was completely different. He had 180 seats on his planes. We have marketing costs like the best carriers. Burr didn't even deal with travel agents. We have hot meals. We're refitting People Express planes with hot ovens because that's what passengers want. If we were trying to make a budget airline, we wouldn't do all this.

"You're associating low costs with low fares. The two are not related. We need to have competitive labor costs because when we look at the rest of the equation, in some areas we have higher costs, and our competitors have vastly better advantages, for example in marketing. We don't have low fares at Continental except when we think it's the best way to maximize revenue. You got to distinguish a dream from where a guy's going. We had to sell at low prices after bankruptcy because that was the only way to get passengers to fly again."

In other words, for Lorenzo, low fares were an expedient, not a philosophy. In a matter of years, he had catapulted himself from a small-time financial consultant with $1,000 in his pocket to someone who controlled the country's biggest airline companies. He had gotten there by taking advantage of an opportunity, a surplus of labor in the marketplace, to make employees pay his way. Now, if he could charge high fares and make them stick, he'd do it without thinking twice.

Would Eastern's fate have been any different if Lorenzo had taken a softer approach? It's true that Eastern had serious, perhaps even insurmountable, problems—but when Lorenzo showed up, labor was not foremost among them. The pilots and flight attendants had just cut Eastern's labor costs to reasonable levels by industry standards. For equity's sake, perhaps the machinists should have kicked in, too; but their cuts were not sufficient to make or break the company, which actually managed to make a modest profit until Lorenzo started cutting it to pieces. "I still don't understand why Lorenzo had a big fight with the unions," said a Lorenzo advisor. When he bought Eastern, "its financials were getting better and it had the 20-percent cuts from pilots and flight attendants."

Lorenzo was so obsessed with beating labor over the head that he never faced Eastern's real dilemmas: Rickenbacker's inherently unstable route structure and Borman's high debt load. Instead of devising practical solutions, such as merging with a carrier that flew complementary routes, Lorenzo stripped Eastern and made off with net proceeds of up to $750 million in assets.

Reducing labor costs could have been one way of dealing with the routes and debt. But doing this in an adversarial fashion made no sense. Eastern's fractious unions were difficult to get along with, and, like most airline employees, they tended to blame the difficulties of deregulation on management. But even conservative, instinctively probusiness outsiders like Walter Wallace thought Lorenzo's tough-guy approach was all wrong. Some months after the strike started, the mediation board chairman explained why he thought Lorenzo's approach had failed.

"When a carrier makes a case for extreme concessions, there are certain conditions that must exist. One, you have to make a case and be absolutely persuasive with the unions that you have a need. Also, there can never be anything that smacks of antiunion or union-busting behavior. And your credibility has to be beyond reproach.

"Lorenzo missed out on all three points. And if you can't get all three points, then you have to do real collective bargaining. You can't just go to the courts or the board for help. You have to take a position that is understandable and justifiable. If he had asked for, say, half the $150 million he wanted from the [machinists], it gives me the wherewithal to beat the union over the head. If he had, I could have and would have. He started with 2,000 items on the bargaining table. And he wanted to do it in a month. His demands were unrelated to his demands for [an impasse]. We did resolve all 2,000 in the first six months. There were substantial savings on the table for Eastern by then. Then he asked for $150 million and called it his final offer. Never departed from it until three hours from when the clock ran out. In my book, that's not collective bargaining."

Lorenzo, however, didn't want to play by the rules. He knew what he wanted and he stuck to it, even though his demands were not based on careful financial calculations. As a result, he won the battle, but lost the war.

It's possible that even the most cooperative of managers might not have been able to bring Eastern's divided unions together. Still, the company's employees had shown a willingness to do almost anything to keep their jobs and their company going, provided they were included in the process.

Lorenzo never saw that. Like many American managers, all he knew was force. To be sure, Lorenzo was an extreme example, but he shares with other managers the attitude that employees, union or nonunion, will resist unless beaten into submission.

Perhaps employees will submit, if given no other choice. But as other companies are coming to realize, confrontation is not the path to success. If Lorenzo had come into Eastern making the kinds of proposals Ueberroth and other potential saviors did, a strong and viable airline might still be flying. Instead, little remains but ashes.

NOTES

Most of the interviews for this book stem from reporting I did as *Business Week*'s labor editor. Since I began that job in March 1985, I conducted some 600 to 700 interviews with roughly 200 different people involved in the ongoing strife at Eastern Airlines. These include employees and officials at Eastern, Texas Air, and Continental, as well as those at rival airlines; local and national union leaders; friends and acquaintances of Frank Lorenzo; Wall Street bankers and lawyers; industry consultants and analysts; and other observers of airlines. Beginning in 1988, I had 7 or 8 interviews with Lorenzo, varying from brief conversations to discussions lasting up to two hours. I also took part in another half dozen news conferences or small sessions for reporters that Lorenzo gave at various points.

Other participants in Eastern's struggles were equally generous with their time (although Lorenzo later became angry with me and declined to be interviewed specifically for this book). Peter Ueberroth spoke with me 9 or 10 times, both in the midst of his involvement and afterward. Frank Borman shared his thoughts with me in five or six conversations, some of them quite extensive.

Many other players took even more time and trouble to share their side of Eastern's drama with me. Union leaders and their advisors spoke with me at all hours of the day and night, from their homes, from hotels, from portable phones, and from planes. Over the years, some of them talked with me dozens and dozens of times, including John Peterpaul and Charlie Bryan of the machinists; Randy Barber and Brian Freeman, financial advisors to the union; Jack Bavis, the pilot leader; Bruce Simon, the pilots' outside lawyer; and about a dozen other officials, lawyers, and advisors at Eastern's three unions. Several advisors of Lorenzo and top Texas Air officials spent many hours speaking on a confidential basis with me throughout 1988 and 1989, both from the office and from home, usually at considerable risk of incurring their employer's wrath.

Because of the sensitive and highly public nature of the conflicts at Eastern, many of the interviews were given to me in the heat of the battle on an off-the-record basis. Most of the people involved subsequently agreed to be quoted by name for this book, for which I thank them gratefully. A handful of others, primarily those who still have connections with Lorenzo, chose to remain anonymous. Quotes taken from newspapers, magazines, and other printed sources are cited in the notes. Quotes that were printed in *Business Week* also are listed in the notes.

I am grateful for the assistance I received from a number of other people. Mort Janklow and Anne Sibbald listened to my ideas from the very beginning and encouraged me to pursue them. They made this book possible.

I want to thank my editors at Simon and Schuster, Alice Mayhew and David Shipley. They devoted many hours to poring over my writing, and helped to shape it into its present form. Eric Rayman, Simon and Schuster's legal counsel, also gave freely of his time.

Many of my colleagues at *Business Week* contributed to this book. Pete Engardio, our former bureau chief in Miami, spent more than four years reporting and writing stories with me about Eastern, starting from before Lorenzo came onto the scene. Pete also took the time to read my manuscript and give me advice on it. Bob Arnold, my editor during much of this period, put in many hours helping me to analyze the events that took place at Eastern. And I am grateful to Steve Shepard, Sally Powell, and Mark Morrison, who supported me during this venture.

Several other people helped me as well. Robert Coram gave generously of his time and knowledge. Brandon Lawrence gave me his views on what I wrote. And Jay Gissen gave me the original idea to write a book on Frank Lorenzo and Eastern.

Harry and Joanne Bernstein, who have been observing the labor movement for more than thirty years, gave me their insights into most of what occurred in this book and read the manuscript closely. And Margaret Monahan, who sat beside me writing her own project as I wrote mine, gave me constant motivation throughout the past year.

Chapter One

19 *". . . Continental-bashing"*
    The Wall Street Journal, May 15, 1987, p. 5.

Chapter Two

30 *"Frank Borman's integrity . . ."*
    U.S. Dept. of Labor, *Labor-Management Cooperation at Eastern Air Lines* (1988), p. 16.

Chapter Three

37 *". . . prepared to take steps"*
    The Wall Street Journal, Jan. 20, 1986, p. 4.
37 *"No bank wants . . ."*
    The Wall Street Journal, Jan. 24, 1986, p. 16.
42 *"We were interested only . . ."*
    Business Week, Mar. 10, 1986, p. 105.
53 *"I think Mr. Lorenzo . . ."*
    Business Week, Mar. 10, 1986, p. 107.

Chapter Four

54 *"You don't get sentimental . . ."*
    Business Week, Mar. 10, 1986, p. 104.
56 *"We've given the [machinists] . . ."*
    Miami Herald, May 1, 1986, p. 5.
57 *"That fucking contract . . ."*
    Eastern Air Lines Inc. v. *Air Line Pilots Assn.*, Civil Action No. 88-1246-CIV, U.S. District Court, Southern District of Florida, vol. 2, p. 9.
63 *"The program has apparently . . ."*
    U.S. Dept. of Transportation, *Report to the Secretary, Preliminary Investigation of Texas Air Corporation and Its Subsidiaries*, vol. 1, (May 25, 1988), p. 172.
70 *"This is the kind . . ."*
    Business Week, Feb. 8, 1988, p. 21.

Notes

Chapter Five

77 *"the unions uncovered ..."*
In Re: Eastern Air Lines Inc., Debtor, Exhibits to Declaration of Farrell P. Kupersmith, U.S. Bankruptcy Court, Southern District of New York, Exhibit 56.

93 *"The record shows ..."*
Air Line Pilots Assn. v. Eastern Air Lines Inc., 703 F. Suppl. 962 (D.D.C. 1988), U.S. District Court, District of Columbia, Aug. 30, 1988.

Chapter Six

100 The Spivey Assignment ...
Robert Rosenberg, *The Spivey Assignment: A Double Agent's Infiltration of the Drug Smuggling Conspiracy,* New York: Holt, Rinehart, and Winston, 1979.

Chapter Seven

126 *"We have, in fact ..."*
Associated Press, May 17, 1989.

126 *"Nothing. The problem ..."*
USA Today, May 23, 1989, p. 4.

129 *"I don't want ..."*
The Wall Street Journal, June 9, 1989, p. 1.

130 *"Who do you know ..."*
Business Week, Mar. 10, 1986, p. 107.

Chapter Ten

171 *"... a symbol. I don't own ..."*
Vanity Fair, Dec. 1989, p. 240.

183 *"It will be a new concept ..."*
New York Times, Apr. 7, 1989, p. A-1.

183 *"It's a day of very mixed ..."*
New York Times, Apr. 7, 1989, p. D-5.

187 *"Either we work ..."*
Business Week, Apr. 24, 1989, p. 26.

Index

A-300 jets, *see* Airbus A-300s
absenteeism, at Eastern, 63–64,
  121, 122
Adams, Joe, 172, 175, 180, 182,
  184, 186
Adams, John B., 57, 60, 61, 64, 134
advertisements, Borman in, 21
AFL-CIO, 124, 151, 152–53, 157
  buyout aided by, 203–4
  strike supported by, 164, 170
Airbus A-300s, 22, 76–77, 78, 147
Airbus Industries, 201
air-conditioning packs, safety and,
  122–23
Air Line Employees Association, 12
airline industry, airlines:
  competition in, 13–14, 16, 23,
    32, 121, 232
  deregulation of, 13, 15, 23, 91,
    121
  Eastern battle and, 120–21
  government regulation of, 13,
    62–63
  nonunion, 13–14, 27, 84
  public opinion and, 121
Air Line Pilots Association (ALPA),
  15–18, 36, 39–40, 174

Master Executive Council of,
  39–40, 45, 48
Touche Ross & Co. hired by, 74,
  75
Airport Ground Services Corporation, 75, 78
air shuttle, Eastern, 77–78, 81–83,
  152
  Trump and, 111–12, 114, 137,
    154, 165, 185, 186, 202, 203
air shuttle, Pan Am, 82
air traffic controllers, Reagan's firing of, 7, 152, 157
American Airlines, 13, 22, 38, 91,
  176, 217, 221, 232
American Express, 69
Amtrak, 135
Anderson, William E., 148, 149
Ardshiel Inc., 173
Art of War, The (Sun-tzu), 26
asset-stripping, 58–59, 71–78, 81–
  85, 91–92, 111, 128
  DOT report and, 128
  gate sales and, 76, 147, 165
  Shapiro's investigation of, 217–
    218, 220, 222, 232
  and union request for trustee, 170

241

Index

242

Index

Index

Index

Index

Index

Index

Index

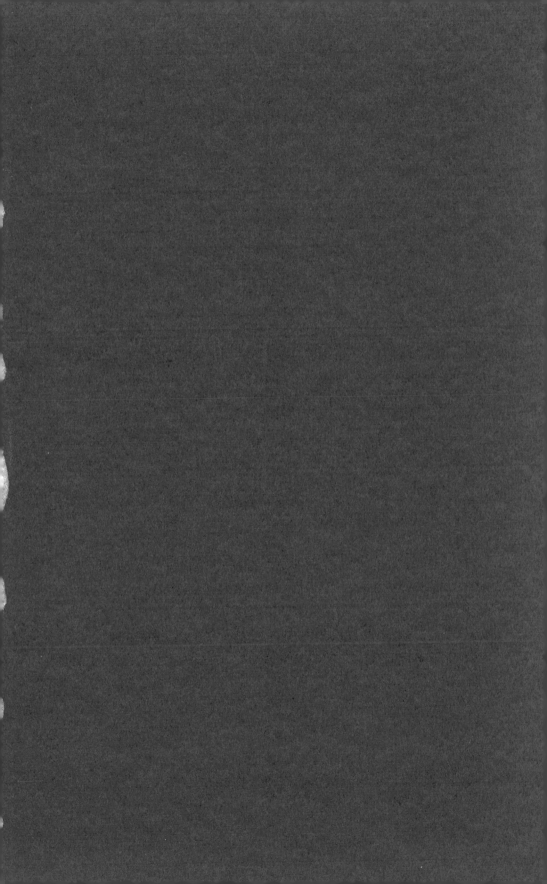